Optimizing Data and New Methods for Efficient Knowledge Discovery and Information Resources Management:

Emerging Research and Opportunities

Susan Swayze
The George Washington University, USA

A volume in the Advances in
Knowledge Acquisition, Transfer,
and Management (AKATM) Book
Series

Published in the United States of America by
   IGI Global
   Information Science Reference (an imprint of IGI Global)
   701 E. Chocolate Avenue
   Hershey PA, USA 17033
   Tel: 717-533-8845
   Fax: 717-533-8661
   E-mail: cust@igi-global.com
   Web site: http://www.igi-global.com

Library of Congress Cataloging-in-Publication Data

Names: Swayze, Susan, 1968- editor.
Title: Optimizing data and new methods for efficient knowledge discovery
   and information resources management: emerging research and opportunities
   / Susan Swayze, editor.
Description: Hershey, PA : Information Science Reference, [2020] | Includes
   bibliographical references and index. | Summary: "This book provides
   insight into the theory, practice, and policy related to data, knowledge
   discovery, and information resources management"-- Provided by
   publisher.
Identifiers: LCCN 2019037708 (print) | LCCN 2019037709 (ebook) | ISBN
   9781799822356 (hardcover) | ISBN 9781799822363 (paperback) | ISBN
   9781799822370 (ebook)
Subjects: LCSH: Information resources management. | Information retrieval.
   | Big data.
Classification: LCC ZA3085.5 .O68 2020 (print) | LCC ZA3085.5 (ebook) |
   DDC 025.04--dc23
LC record available at https://lccn.loc.gov/2019037708
LC ebook record available at https://lccn.loc.gov/2019037709

This book is published in the IGI Global book series Advances in Knowledge Acquisition, Transfer, and Management (AKATM) (ISSN: 2326-7607; eISSN: 2326-7615)

British Cataloguing in Publication Data
A Cataloguing in Publication record for this book is available from the British Library.

For electronic access to this publication, please contact: eresources@igi-global.com.

Advances in Knowledge Acquisition, Transfer, and Management (AKATM) Book Series

ISSN:2326-7607
EISSN:2326-7615

Editor-in-Chief: *Murray E. Jennex* San Diego State University, USA

MISSION

Organizations and businesses continue to utilize knowledge management practices in order to streamline processes and procedures. The emergence of web technologies has provided new methods of information usage and knowledge sharing.

The **Advances in Knowledge Acquisition, Transfer, and Management (AKATM) Book Series** brings together research on emerging technologies and their effect on information systems as well as the knowledge society. **AKATM** will provide researchers, students, practitioners, and industry leaders with research highlights surrounding the knowledge management discipline, including technology support issues and knowledge representation.

COVERAGE

- Cognitive Theories
- Cultural Impacts
- Information and Communication Systems
- Knowledge Acquisition and Transfer Processes
- Knowledge Management Strategy
- Knowledge Sharing
- Organizational Learning
- Organizational Memory
- Small and Medium Enterprises
- Virtual Communities

IGI Global is currently accepting manuscripts for publication within this series. To submit a proposal for a volume in this series, please contact our Acquisition Editors at Acquisitions@igi-global.com or visit: http://www.igi-global.com/publish/.

Titles in this Series

701 East Chocolate Avenue, Hershey, PA 17033, USA
Tel: 717-533-8845 x100 • Fax: 717-533-8661
E-Mail: cust@igi-global.com • www.igi-global.com

Table of Contents

Preface

Over the past decade the use of data has moved to the forefront of technology and business. Massive amounts of data are collected and used for numerous and varied reasons. Data is used to aid in decision-making, for learning/training of human capital and machines (machine learning), and for the accumulation of knowledge toward future goals and advancements in business and new or expanded technologies.

The chapters in this book explore aspects of data modeling, knowledge and information management, learning and training of human capital, and the experiences of information technology workers. The growing use of data for modeling, whether it is behavior, risk, or income, is a key component of modern business. Through technological advances, organizations continue to grow and expand the solutions and services offered to customers—this impacts internal staff (human capital) as it relates to how work is conducted (and the challenges that result from a technology-infused work environment). Organizations, both academic and corporate, must also grapple with how best learning will be created and provisioned for human capital as well as how internal human capital training (delivery and timing) impacts the ability to support customers and new technologies.

Data, learning, and information and resource management are part of every component of life. There are many points of data used by individuals, every day. The data is based on gained knowledge from experience, research, structured (informed, planned) and unstructured (learned by doing) training and usage of tools (i.e., products, solutions, observations, etc.). Data usage, knowledge, and information management affects individuals in one way or another and in all walks of life.

WHO SHOULD READ THIS BOOK?

The topics included in this book may be useful for individuals, businesses, and technical enterprises focused on the use of data to extend and support current and future human capital, business practices, and technological advances. This book is intended for academics, practitioners, business and IT thought leaders, business and

IT professionals, and anyone who is interested in examining knowledge discovery and management, big data usage and modeling, as well as resource training and management.

ORGANIZATION OF THE BOOK

The chapters in this book explore who is doing the work and the challenges that workers encounter, how work is accomplished, the ways in which human and information resources are managed, and data optimization case studies that represent how data may be modeled and resourced for solution expansion and decision-making:

- **Knowledge/Information Technology Workers:** The experiences of knowledge/information technology workers, whether individually or in teams, shape the technology work itself through workplace culture and practices;
- **Knowledge Discovery and Information Resources Management:** The development and application of decision support models, communication to enable successful organizational change, and best practices and advances in technology-enabled learning are challenges faced by many of today's organizations;
- **Optimizing Data:** The use of large volumes of data to model current and future capabilities, institute new methods of information and data handling, and support decision science for decision-making can provide a critical advantage for corporations seeking to leverage data for competitive advantage.

Chapter 1: Grief and the Psychological Transition Process Among Information Technology Team Members (Letitia Larry)

Change is a constant in most organizations. Organizations implement change for various reasons – to improve, react, or reinvent either their product or the way that business is conducted. Information technology is often critical to the dynamic change process that includes working with people, processes, and systems. The focus of the interview-based study of health information technology/information technology workers represented in this chapter is to describe the transition process inherent to organizational change events as it relates to the experiences of individuals within information technology teams responsible for implementing the change.

In this chapter, the author explores the premise that the psychological transition process of information technology team members is key to achieving successful change. Specifically, the success of technology changes in organizations depends on how information technology teams tasked with implementing the change appreciate the value proposition posed by the change and subsequently respond to it. The author concludes the chapter with multiple recommendations to support the transition of information technology teams during and after a change effort.

Chapter 2: Re-Defining Work-Life Boundaries – Individual, Organizational, and National Policy Implications (Donna Weaver McCloskey)

The increase in mobile computing has shaped the work and private lives of knowledge workers due to the erosion of temporal and physical boundaries between work and personal time and space. Prior research categorized the work-life boundary in terms of segmentation and integration but the author suggests that with the rise of mobile technology, the work-life boundary is comprised of three dimensions—schedule flexibility, home boundary permeability, and work boundary permeability.

In this literature-based chapter, the author highlights relevant research studies as a foundation for addressing work-life boundaries from individual, organizational, and national policy perspectives. Even though several countries have made work-life balance issues part of their legislative agendas, the author advocates for formal and informal cultural changes to transform work-life conflict into work-life harmony.

Chapter 3: User-Created Online Learning Videos – Collaborative Knowledge Construction Through Participatory Design (Adesola Olulayo Ogundimu)

Learning has been defined as the transfer of information for the creation and/or extension of knowledge. Learning was viewed as a distinct form – one in which knowledge was accessed through mediums, artifacts, repositories, and knowledge infrastructures that were bound by space and location. Technological advances have increased opportunities through which knowledge is discovered, created, and transferred.

In this chapter, the author builds upon relevant literature to expand methods for knowledge transfer that once focused on individual processes toward more collaborative, collectively-constructed learning environments. The author advances participatory design, a humanistic approach to learning that is focused on learning or user-focused design and the co-creation of the learning environment itself. Further, the author suggests that participatory design facilitates the application of best practices in the creation of online learning videos.

Chapter 4: A Composite Risk Model for Optimizing Information System Security (Yahel Giat and Michael Dreyfuss)

The task of strengthening information security poses a serious dilemma for organizations. In order to determine the optimal investment scheme while avoiding an overreaching security system, it is important for security staff to identify the riskiest elements of their information system and determine the best tools to improve the security of these elements. In response to these challenges, the author presents a two-step information technology risk-management decision support model that emphasizes breaches and risks and applies the decision support model to illustrate its effectiveness.

In this chapter, the authors present a dynamic model—they first quantify the risk of each component in the information technology security system and then seek to optimize different security tools and approaches to address the risks. The authors then apply the model to the information system at a large college in Israel as a case study. The application of the model resulted in the identification of risky subsystems that required greater investment to improve the college's information technology security.

Chapter 5: Communication Matrices for Managing Dialogue Change to Teamwork Transformation (James Calvin)

The digital revolution has introduced new technology platforms that have an impact on how organizations adapt to meet technology and people orientation challenges. The role of developing and implementing change management practices to achieve human-centered goals often requires methods and tools, such as appreciative inquiry, to promote and sustain conversations among team members in order to enhance and strengthen team/teamwork practices. The premise is that, through crucial conversations, new organizational capacity can enable better team management by establishing more effective communication matrices as new technology is introduced.

In this chapter, the author presents a four-sequence process focused on communication as a conduit for organizational change. The change management process was implemented with the human resources unit within a U.S.-based business organization that was working toward competence in conducting crucial conversations to advance organizational change. The author conducted a narrative-based inquiry to examine the effectiveness of the process both from the perspective of HR team members (within the organization) and from the author that implemented the change process (external view).

Chapter 6: Using Big Data to Understand Chinese Users' Intentions to Tap Through Mobile Advertisements (Jing Quan)

The development of mobile technology makes it possible for mobile advertisers to use various applications to push advertisements to electronic devices. Mobile advertisers can analyze user behavior and preferences and achieve more accurate advertising content. In this chapter, the author presents a data optimization study regarding mobile advertising as an emerging field. The presentation and response to marketing previously relegated to other devices or marketing modes is discussed in comparison to how to present and what may be presented in the mobile device community.

The author exemplifies aspects of big data analytics by extracting a large amount of back-end data from a mobile advertising company located in China and creating both explanatory and predictive models to aid in decision-making. The specific application of these techniques resulted in two empirical, testable models predicting effectiveness of mobile advertising. One model resulting from the logistic regression analysis predicted the likelihood that a user would tap through a particular advertisement based on a set of environmental factors whereas the second, more nuanced, model, based on a Bayesian network analysis utilizes conditional probabilities to predict the probability of subsequent behavior (tap through) based on data representing users' past behavior accessing advertisements. Both models create the opportunity for data-driven decision-making in the mobile advertising industry.

Chapter 7: Big Data Adoption – A Comparative Study of the Indian Manufacturing and Services Sectors (Hemlata Gangwar)

Big data has changed how organizations work. If data is knowledge, then big data is exponential knowledge. Big data contributes to advances in the business, scientific, and technical fields by introducing extended analytics gained from amalgamated data sets. The author presents a study focused on the factors associated with the adoption of big data and its relative advantage to organizations. The study highlights the importance of systematically evaluating the factors associated with big data adoption at the industry level.

Utilizing survey data from 478 firms in India (210 manufacturing firms, 268 service firms), the author constructed a structural equation model based on the Technology Organization Environment (TOE) framework in which 10 hypotheses related to big data adoption were empirically tested. This study quantitatively analyzed the applicability of each of the three contexts—technological, organizational, and environmental—to provide a more holistic assessment of the factors related to big data adoption. Additionally, the study results contribute to the extant literature regarding big data adoption, namely that differences were detected within the data based on type of firm as well as the exploration of data privacy and organizational data environment as determinants of big data adoption. This chapter provides an empirical examination of big data adoption in one country; however the quantitative results coupled with a relatively large sample size provides a strong degree of generalizability regarding the technology, organizational, environmental, and security challenges that impact big data adoption.

CONCLUSION

This book examines the who (individuals and teams), the how (best practices, models, processes), and the what (data optimization) of knowledge discovery. Information management influences the individual, teams and the enterprise, as does the reverse – in a cyclical relationship. The chapters provide various perspectives and cases focused on knowledge workers, knowledge discovery, and data optimization. Taken individually, each chapter presents an in-depth examination of a topic associated with knowledge discovery. Taken collectively, these seven chapters provide a breadth of understanding of the knowledge discovery spectrum. The topics covered in the book are not only important, but timely. As I write this preface, teachers, professors, parents, as well as K-12 and college students, are utilizing technology for teaching and learning. Workers of all types are meeting remotely and accessing data stored in the cloud to carry out daily organizational functions. Knowledge workers are utilizing supercomputers and big data to address today's most complex problems—specifically creating epidemiological models based on prior data and predictions of human behavior. Truthfully, there cannot be enough written about data, technology, knowledge discovery, and the people who implement or interact with it. The more we know, the more able we are to plan, and in many cases, react to today's unpredictable world.

Susan Swayze
The George Washington University, USA

Letitia Larry
LCDC, LLC, USA

Acknowledgment

The editor would like to thank each of the chapter authors who contributed their time and expertise to this book. I would like to recognize the reviewers who contributed to the quality, coherence, and enhancement of chapters. I would also like to acknowledge the valuable contributions of the editorial advisory board members who, in addition to reviewing chapter submissions, uniquely contributed to the completion of this volume. And finally, I wish to thank the staff at IGI Global for their unwavering commitment during this unprecedented time.

Susan Swayze
The George Washington University, USA

Chapter 1
Grief and the Psychological Transition Process Among Information Technology Team Members

Letitia Larry
LCDC, LLC, USA

ABSTRACT

Information technology (IT) employees are responsible for planning, implementing, and supporting new solutions and services in support of enterprise shifts to accommodate new methods and modes of doing business and/or providing products, solutions, and services to internal users, external customers, and partners. But IT workers do not always have a say or input into the choices made by leadership and business managers as it applies to new technologies. This can lead to rework and failure upon initial deployment. In addition, change without inclusion of those responsible may have a negative impact on IT staff and the outcome of the overall change effort. In this chapter, the author explores the experience of personal transition and the impact of organizational change on those responsible, IT workers.

INTRODUCTION

Because organizations are continuously evolving, adjustments must regularly be made to the infrastructure, systems, and roles and responsibilities of those organizations. In turn, with new systems come new modes of doing business and changes to operations (Goodman & Loh, 2011) that impact both internal and external stakeholders. It is

DOI: 10.4018/978-1-7998-2235-6.ch001

expected that certain Information Technology (IT) disciplines (such as solutions architecture, development/engineering, data management, verification/testing, and technical and customer support) within an enterprise will continuously go through, promote, and support change (McDonagh & Coghlan, 2006), especially in the area of information technology driven business innovation. Change is not necessarily a negative process but it may be deemed negative based on the individual experience and how change is handled. Although justifiable, changes of any sort succeed or fail based on whether the people affected are willing to do things differently and, in today's business environment, understand the primary drivers of these changes (Bridges, 2010; Goodman & Loh, 2011). On this point, and according to Bridges (2010), the psychological transition process is the most important factor in achieving successful change for the organization and its workforce.

BACKGROUND

The success or failure of technology changes in businesses and other types of organizations depends on how information technology teams handle the change and appreciate the value proposition to both the business and the individual/team. Knowledge of planned change may act as a positive influence on change agents. It is essential to emphasize that *transition* and *change* are not identical concepts. One is a precursor to the other; in other words, change encourages or causes transition of some sort, with transition being understood as a psychological concept and change understood as a kind of event. According to Bridges (2010), "Change is situational: the move to a new site, the retirement of the founder, reorganization of the roles on a team…Transitioning, on the other hand, is psychological; it is a three-phased process that people go through as they internalize and come to terms with the details of the new situation that the change brings about" (p. 4).

In a prior publication, the author examined the human component of change, emphasizing the dynamics of the transition process on eight selected subjects working within an information technology environment (Larry, 2017). The qualitative study was used to provide insights and understandings to the following research question: *How are the phases of transition experienced by individuals within information technology teams during a major change effort?* The researcher used the Kübler-Ross grief construct (denial and isolation, anger, bargaining, depression, and acceptance) as the theoretical lens through which to investigate the transition process in action; and Bridges' three-phased transition theory (ending, losing, letting go; the neutral zone; the new beginning) to delve deeper into the individual experience of IT employees during change.

PURPOSE

The purpose of the research was to further understanding of the transition process— inherent to change events—as it related to the experiences of individuals within IT teams under study, taking into account the dynamics of change efforts (implementation and support activities) which included working with people, processes, and systems. The point is that change events occurring within technology-driven organizations position IT workers at the nexus of dealing with both people and systems in order to facilitate the mandated change and move the organization forward. Thus, handling multiple areas of technological concern and interacting with a variety of people intensifies the demands with which members of IT teams are faced when implementing and supporting change. It was the aim of this study to provide an opening into the lived experiences of IT team members who spoke to their encounters with change, the psychological transition processes, and their understandings of these dynamics in their professional lives. The team dynamic provided context to the individual experiences of transition as it related to the higher-level psychological process as posited by Bridges, and the individual feelings associated with transition as put forward by Kübler-Ross.

Kübler-Ross Grief Construct

A grief construct is simply defined as "a normative means of grieving" (Kearney & Hyle, 2003). The term grieving is now applied to many types of loss, such as the death of a loved one, the loss of a job or income, major rejection, the end of a relationship or divorce, drug addiction, incarceration, the onset of a disease or chronic illness, an infertility diagnosis, and even minor losses, but was originally applied specifically to the experience of death by Dr. Elisabeth Kübler-Ross at the University of Chicago medical school. Kübler-Ross began using the term "transition" to express the movement from one stage (life) to another (death) and the term has been used to describe and express the psychological process experienced as caused by a change event. The use of the term "transition" to express the psychological process aided in expanding the use of the grief construct beyond death and dying. The five stages of grief, as conceived by Kübler-Ross (1969), are: (a) denial and isolation, (b) anger, (c) bargaining, (d) depression, and (e) acceptance. Following are definitions of each stage:

1. Denial is defined as "refusal to accept the diagnosis or change event" (Kearney & Hyle, 2004, p. 114; Kübler-Ross, 1969, p. 52);
2. Anger is defined as "feelings of anger, rage, envy, and resentment associated with the impending death or change event" (Kearney & Hyle, 2004, p. 114; Kübler-Ross, 1969, p. 64);
3. Bargaining is defined as "attempts to trade one action for avoidance of death or loss" (Kearney & Hyle, 2004, p. 114; Kübler-Ross, 1969, p. 94);
4. Depression is defined as "the replacement of anger with a sense of loss" (Kearney & Hyle, 2004, p. 114-115);
5. Acceptance is defined as the final stage in which "anger and depression about death or loss has dissipated; an emotionless state". (2004). (p. 115). Kearney & Hyle.

The stages, or phases, as referenced in the grief construct, are not linear and may be replaced, repeated, or occur simultaneously. Repetition of different phases of grief extends the transition process that may add additional time to the change effort. This may have a profound impact on the overall timeline/schedule. Understanding how IT teams process transition, the purpose of this study, provided data regarding how change is best handled as it applies to the overall transition process experienced by those who are responsible for implementing and supporting change efforts.

Bridges' Transition Model

Bridges (2004, 2010, 2013) defined transition as a psychological part of change experienced by human beings, and that change happens continuously. Like Kübler-Ross, the term "transition" is used to express a psychological process as experienced due to a change event. Bridges process is a higher-level process that is used to express the overall phases of transition and provide context to the criteria established in the Kübler-Ross grief construct as the IT team provides overall context for the shared experience of individual team members that informed this research study. Bridges (2004, 2010, 2013) proposed three phases of transition that occur, over time and at different speeds, based on where change is initiated:

1. Letting go of the old ways;
2. Going through an in-between time when the old is gone, but the new isn't fully operational; and
3. Coming out of the transition and making a new beginning.

Bridges (2013) observed that those who initiate the need for change acclimate to change most quickly. Those who have change handed down to them, without explanation and support, experience change and the associated phases of transition most reluctantly.

METHODOLOGY

The author interviewed the IT workers regarding their individual experiences of transition due to a change effort. Each semi-structured interview ranged between 60 and 90 minutes. Interview questions queried participants on: (a) their roles and responsibilities prior to, during and after the revolutionary change event, (b) how the change event was introduced, (c) what support was provided for the change event and associated transition process, (d) feelings and reactions experienced during different phases of the change event/transition process, (e) the outcome of the change event with associated feelings, (f) a reflection of the change event and transition process, and (g) whether or not other change events and transition processes may have affected the most recent transition process for the individual.

Participants

Health information technology (HIT) is a subset of IT. The focus of health information technology is the support of health systems and the associated data prescribed by the system (Brailer & Thompson, 2004), whereas information technology focuses on the systems themselves (Oxford University, 2015). There were eight research participants with varying degrees of experience at different levels within the HIT firm or IT agency. A brief description of each participant provides context to how each participant responded and his or her overall demeanor. Descriptions also provide context into the accumulated data as years of experience, work culture, and cultural background may shape user responses, including the linearity of feelings and responses or lack thereof. Note that pseudonyms have been used to protect individual participants.

Angela is from the United States and possesses more than 20 years of overall experience as an in-house employee in HIT, and approximately six years in the current role as Testing Team Lead and Tier 2 Support. As a Testing Team Lead, Angela is responsible for: (a) writing test plans to verify solutions, (b) authoring test scenarios to simulate customer use, (c) assigning testing activities to junior, mid-level and senior testing staff, (d) working with the business analyst to verify requirements are verified, (e) tracking testing issues and providing metrics on issue reports, (f) mentoring testing staff, and (g) working with other technical disciplines and providing troubleshooting of issues and issue resolution for end users and customers.

Deepak is from India and has more than 10 years of experience as both an employee and contractor in IT, and has participated in more than one revolutionary change initiative. Deepak is a contractor acting as a Senior Software Engineer and Systems Architect often times leading major change efforts as a supervisor and/or as a hands-on participant. As a Systems Architect, Deepak: (a) researches, designs and develops software solutions, (b) instructs and mentors other staff on design and development best practices, (c) works with third-party vendors to complete systems architecture design and development, and (d) provides Tier 3 technical support to resolve solutions issues found by vendors and customers.

Cara is from Africa and has more than 10 years of experience—initially as a contractor then as an internal employee for an HIT firm—and has participated in at least two revolutionary changes within the HIT firm (one as a contractor and the other as an employee). Cara serves as an IT Configuration Manager, leading infrastructure, systems environment and solutions integration and implementation efforts for external consumers while providing support to internal customers. Cara is responsible for: (a) infrastructure management of servers and databases in support of corporate solutions and services and internal development and testing, (b) environment builds, (c) solution releases and release management, and (d) vendor coordination for upgrades and external tools.

Donna is from the United States and has more than 20 years of experience within an HIT enterprise. Donna was a Lead Software Tester and Tier 2 Support, and participated in two major change events during the course of employment with the company. Donna retired during the course of the data gathering process for this research study. Donna was responsible for: (a) writing test cases and scenarios in support of solutions development and release, (b) reporting issues found during testing, and (c) troubleshooting assigned customer issues for submission to solution development staff for correction.

Priya is from India and has approximately four years of experience in IT as a contractor. Priya served as a Senior Quality Assurance Analyst, Reports Engineer and Customer Support. Priya is responsible for writing test scenarios and test cases, data entry, solutions testing and verification, and customer support during user acceptance verification.

Lei is from China and has more than 20 years of experience in IT as both an in house employee and contractor. Lei is a contractor acting as an Enterprise Architect and has served as a chief information officer and chief technology officer. Lei is a leader and manager, often times initiating revolutionary change events acting as the expert for new technology. Lei is responsible for: (a) research and development of systems to support enterprises, (b) design and development of solutions, (c) hiring and mentoring of technical staff, and (d) management of human resources.

Gina is from the United States and has more than 20 years of experience as an in house employee in IT and HIT companies, or agencies, and as a contractor for IT enterprises. Gina is a Senior Test Analyst and Tier 2 Support, currently an employee acting in a Testing Team Lead role at the HIT firm. Gina: (a) provides mentoring to managers, directors and senior directors in the organization and coaches peers, (b) writes test plans and test scenarios for solutions verification, (c) leads new initiatives for electronic systems, (d) reports on and manages metrics, and (e) supports the oversight committee and customers during user acceptance verification and audit.

Vishal is from India and has a decade of experience as a contractor within IT consulting firms. Vishal is a Senior Functional Tester and Test Lead, both hands on and a supervisor responsible for leading testing efforts. Vishal has participated in at least two major/revolutionary change efforts for government agencies. Vishal is responsible for: (a) authoring test plans, (b) creating test cases and test scenarios, (c) assigning test cases for execution to testing team members, (d) recording and managing issues found during testing, and (e) providing support to customers during verification.

Analysis

Categories are clusters of codes that form a pattern, with similarity and regularity (Saldaña, 2013). Categories in this research study were related to the feelings and behaviors observed in data. Categories and themes aligned with the phases of loss in the Kübler-Ross grief construct.

With the Kübler-Ross stages of loss and the Bridges phases of transition serving as the organizing frameworks, Figure 1 displays the codes, categories, and themes that emerged. One theme, The Change Link: Outcome/Successful is a descriptive emergent code. The Change Link shows the change process and how it impacts effectiveness of team members along with the end state of the change event. Data analysis from this research study showed that the end state of a change directive was always successful regardless of the feelings experienced throughout the transition process. Success was a consistent theme in the study and was experienced by all participants.

Figure 1. Participants' perceptions in relation to the Kübler-Ross stages of loss and the Bridges phases of transition (Larry, 2017, p. 94)

Codes	Category *Kübler-Ross and Bridges*	Themes
Denial, disbelief, isolation, limited or no support, no training, no help, limited resources, one-to-many	Denial and Isolation	Isolation from others; unique role
Upset, mad, angry, rage, envy, resentment	Anger	Anger due to lack of communication, direction and support
Bargaining, deal making, schedule slippage, no end date, ongoing, trade, avoidance, handling expectations, go back, negotiation	Bargaining	Constant negotiation due to unreasonable demands and schedules
Overwhelmed, helpless, tired, loss, low, depression	Depression	Loss of direction and little to no support; helplessness
Emotionless, acceptance	Acceptance	Required acceptance of the change initiative and the associated outcome
Disbelief, surprise, terror, horror, disgust, anger, frustrated, stressed, dissatisfaction, insecurity, worry, anxiety	Ending, Losing, Letting Go	Frustration at not being heard, communicated to or supported; anxiety due to not being able to meet leadership's demands; stress as a physical and emotional response
Uncertain, mood swings, doubt, emotionless, disbelief/could not believe it, acceptance, overwhelmed, vulnerable	The Neutral Zone/The In-Between	Required acceptance of the change initiative and the associated outcome
Confident, assurance, excited, happy, anticipation	The New Beginning	Confidence that anything is possible once the change initiative is complete; excitement prior to change initiation
Successful, completion, unsuccessful, ongoing	Change Link: Outcome/Successful	Success as an expectation; no room for failure

THEMES

The perceptions of research participants group into themes across the stages of loss and transition (the categories) as posited by Kübler-Ross and Bridges, respectively. The first theme is mapped to the first research category and stage of the Kübler-Ross grief construct (Denial and Isolation) and points to those who participated in new roles and/or roles that were unique to the group or enterprise; the only person in the role experienced a sense of isolation as there was limited to no direction on how to convey or proceed in the role from predecessors or management/leadership thus moving the individual to proceed as she/he deemed appropriate. The second theme as mapped to the second research category/stage of Kübler-Ross grief construct and the first phase of Bridges transition process (Anger) was experienced by research participants in reaction to lack of communication about the change initiative, lack of response to reported issues and concerns by management/leadership, and lack of support, via training, to aid in processing and supporting the change event. The third theme as mapped to third research category/stage of the grief construct (Bargaining) was experienced by study participants who constantly had to negotiate responsibilities and completion of tasks associated with meeting unreasonable schedule demands. This theme was ongoing throughout the completion of the change initiative for those participants who experienced it. The fourth theme as mapped to the fourth research category/stage of the grief construct (Depression) was experienced in combination with isolation when there was little to no direction from or support by supervisory staff, or leadership and the individual participant did not know what to do; she (Angela) felt helpless. Theme five, *required acceptance of/acclimation to the change event*, was universal for all participants in the study but one participant did not recognize it as such as she still suffered through ongoing cycles of transition although team members had moved on. Acceptance did not mean that each individual was ready for work or to move on; some were and some were not.

All study participants expressed feelings related to theme six of the research as mapped to the first phase of Bridges' transition – Ending, Losing, Letting Go. Research participants consistently listed frustration at not being recognized or heard when expressing concerns or issues with the change initiative, and stress as a physical and emotional response while trying to accomplish tasks with limited to no training and few resources. Additionally, there was "anxiety" about what was to come, how new things would be accomplished or received (or not); and meeting overall demands of the position and responsibilities associated with her or his role. Theme seven, *required acceptance*, was related to those last disparate emotions experienced prior to determining that there was nothing else to do but accept what was occurring. Although acceptance was indicated, Frustration and Anger were still apparent in lingering feelings that overlapped with the associated phase of transition. Theme eight, *confidence*, that something was accomplished and anything could be accomplished, was one of the last themes expressed in data. Other feelings associated with the category pointing to the theme: happiness, excitement and anticipation—were experienced by some study participants at the onset of the change initiative not at the end of, or after, the change initiative. The final theme, *success*, was expressed and experienced by all study participants. Success was aligned with completion of the change initiative regardless of whether the initiative/project went well or not. Success was not an indication of the goodness or positive experience associated with the change event. Failure was not an option and the change initiative was a requirement for the individual and all (the IT team) involved.

Anger appeared as the most frequently identified feeling/behavior. Bargaining and Acceptance tied for the second most expressed stage of loss by participants, while Denial and Isolation and Depression tied for the third most experienced stages of loss—thus accounting for all five most frequently coded responses that the researcher subsequently identified as the key categories of this study. There were 34 occurrences of Anger in interviews, 27 occurrences of both Bargaining and Acceptance in interviews, and 18 occurrences of both Denial and Isolation and Depression represented in the data collected from eight interviews.

The author discovered that research participants experienced all phases of the Kübler-Ross stages of loss, although not necessarily in the order originally presented by Kübler-Ross. As stated by Kübler-Ross, feelings and responses to change may not occur in order and may occur cyclically and simultaneously. The feelings associated with Bridges' phases of transition (Ending, Losing, Letting Go; The Neutral Zone/ The In Between; and The New Beginning) also emerged, but participants did not always experience these feelings in the order outlined in Bridges transition model. Three study participants expressed that they experienced Excitement and Happiness, phase 3 of the Bridges transition model (The New Beginning), prior to the initiation of the change event.

Lastly, outcomes, as expressions or manifestations of the later stages/feelings associated with transition, were identified and coded by the researcher as "Successful". For example, study participants widely identified or used the term "Successful" during the Kübler-Ross Acceptance phase. In effect, participants appeared to use this code in association with completion of the project or change event with which he or she had been involved. Regardless of the emotions experienced or the difficulty of the project, and even if the project was (or is) ongoing, the change initiative was considered a success if some component of the overall change event was completed. Success, as described by participants, was more situated toward "surrender" or "resignation" rather than a successfully completed task or project. An example of a component of a change event/initiative is when a phased approach to deliver different parts of the overall initiative was put in place once it was discovered that all could not be accomplished on time, on budget, with existing resources and/or within schedule. All that needed to be accomplished included changes to systems and solutions infrastructure, systems and solutions architecture, business processes and procedures, practice, policy and the associated documentation and knowledgebase of information. In addition, internal resources, external oversight groups and end users may have required training on new methods of doing business or requesting and receiving customer and technical support.

The experiences of study participants are displayed in Figures 2 and 3. Some feelings, such as Anger, overlapped with other responses to change using the Kübler-Ross grief construct in Figure 2. For each study participant, the box in the column for a specific category is marked with an "X" if it was experienced by the research participant. The grey space between each stage of loss represent the gap in time between movement from one stage of loss to another; a period of fuzziness where feelings or responses may not have been fully defined or realized and/or a true transition to the next stage was not complete. Note that the prevalence of each participant's experience of a stage of loss is not represented, only that the participant experienced the specific stage at some point in the transition process.

Figure 2. The Kübler-Ross stages experienced by participants (Larry, 2017, p. 100)

Participant	Denial and Isolation	Anger	Bargaining	Depression	Acceptance
Angela	X	X		X	
Deepak		X			X
Cara	X	X	X		X
Donna		X	X		X
Priya		X	X		X
Lei				X	X
Gina		X			X
Vishal			X		X

Happiness and/or Excitement occurred for three study participants prior to or at the beginning of the change initiative instead of during the last stage of transition (The New Beginning) as expressed in the Bridges transition model in Figure 3. This expression of the data leads to expansion of the Bridges transition model to a phase that occurs while waiting for change to begin. Although Acceptance is also a response to transition represented in the Bridges transition model in phase 2, The Neutral Zone, it does not have the same meaning as that represented by Kübler-Ross where Acceptance is the personal resignation to the change or loss and readiness to move on. Acceptance as represented by Bridges is described as creating a new way of thinking and working. Per the data, research participants did not experience feelings associated with phase 2 of the Bridges transition model and only one experienced phase 3, The New Beginning.

Figure 3. The Bridges phases experienced by participants (Larry, 2017, pp. 101-102)

Participant	Pre-Change (Excitement, Happiness)	Ending, Losing, Letting Go (Anxiety, Frustration, Stress)	The Neutral Zone	The New Beginning (Confidence)
Angela		X		
Deepak		X	X	
Cara	X	X		
Donna	X	X		X
Priya		X		
Lei		X		
Gina	X	X		
Vishal	X	X		X

FINDINGS

The researcher presents an analysis of (study) findings based on eight categories—Anger, Bargaining, Acceptance, Denial and Isolation, and Depression; and Ending, Losing, Letting Go, The Neutral Zone and New Beginnings—that emerged from the qualitative data analysis. Excerpts of interview responses from study participants are also included in support of findings.

Study Finding 1: Anger / Kübler-Ross Stage 2: Anger

The researcher identified Anger as the most frequent category found in the data analysis process. As described by Kearney and Hyle (2003), anger signifies "feelings of anger, rage, envy, and resentment associated with the change event" (p. 114). For the purpose of this study, Anger represents the second stage of the Kübler-Ross grief construct. This category incorporated several codes (descriptors of feelings) across the interviews, including anger, rage, envy, and resentment. However, only anger was consistently expressed across interviews. For example, participants expressed that they typically experienced anger as a response to company leaders' lack of support; that is, limited or no information, no training, no individual support, limited communication, or lack of inclusion in planning of the change event – thus leading to the theme associated with the category (Anger).

Angela expressed anger over not being given information about the reason for the change initiative and how it would impact her role. There was no direction provided on how the Test Team Lead role should be carried out going forward, nor any information provided about whether current responsibilities, assigned to the Team Lead role, should be completed as before or would change. There was a lack of clarity, no understanding of how the Test Team Lead fit into a new organization structure that split the team into two groups, one for projects and one for enterprise solution releases. As the change directive was handed down without direction or support from the supervisor, it left Angela with open questions and concerns and no feedback or understanding about how to proceed regardless of how many times additional information was requested. Angela was angry and overwhelmed. In Angela's words:

Anger that the whole project will go forward, and it wasn't clearly defined to everyone. Even isolation, because I felt like there was a lot on me that I was supposed to get done because it wasn't clearly communicated. That is where the anger and isolation came from. (Larry, 2017, p. 114)

Cara was brought into the organization as a contractor to assist with solution build management and environment engineering. Soon after being brought in, a major change initiative to automate solution provisioning was initiated. Cara was asked if there was interest in assisting with this new direction and the response was yes. Then Cara was thrust into being the change agent not just within the enterprise but with known and unknown vendors, an external oversight committee and for internal teams and customers, without assistance from other staff. Responsibilities included infrastructure management (servers, computers, development tools, databases) and customer relationship management for internal company users of the infrastructure and external customers. Cara had to: (a) work in several roles, and (b) work across disciplines within the organization while being new to the organization, new to the role and not having resources or historic corporate knowledge in support of the "as is" state of the infrastructure and environments. The interviewer had to perform interviews with staff across disciplines and explain why the change project was necessary and how it benefited the individuals interviewed when asked "what's in it for me?" There were a lot of people who were against the initiative and Cara had to persuade staff and customers of the positive reason for the change, while learning about the internal culture, infrastructure systems and developing a new method of operations. As Cara stated, "I felt anger. I felt isolated, like there's a new kid on the block, being thrown in. I felt all of the resentment having to prove myself while I need something" (Larry, 2017, p. 115).

Gina was assigned to a corporate change initiative as a member of a cross disciplinary team to allow for speedier delivery of solutions, using Agile methods with four-week Sprint development and verification cycles. Per Gina, although a specific methodology was to be used and one training class was provided, there was no means to resolve inconsistent practices to deliver software on an accelerated cycle. New enhancements and requests for changes were constantly being requested which required longer development and delivery cycles thus destroying the reason for the change initiative – to deliver solutions changes rapidly. Gina continued to bring issues to the committee established to assist with practice and process issues within the Sprint team and to senior management, but senior management was hands off and the committee often times did not know how to resolve issues. Gina stated:

It's just sometimes in my frustration levels, just puts me to the point of anger because I feel like people are not listening. Because you're trying to do as much as you can on a shoestring budget instead of having brought in additional resources. That's not being done, and I don't get to see the budget. I have no idea what the funds look like, but I just feel like they're trying to deliver things on a shoestring budget. But, of course, it could be possible, but in the end you're burning out your resources. I think what's happening right now is that people are starting to get burned out. (Larry, 2017, p. 116)

When a change event was thrust upon the individual, or when the change event was initiated by the company or agency with little to limited input from the individual IT employee, anger was a common response as evidenced from feedback from Angela. Two consistently cited reasons for experiencing the feeling of anger related to (a) lack of communication in terms of instructing or directing the individual regarding the need for the change event and (b) lack of guidance relative to how to best implement the change event. Gina noted that anger was the response she experienced during that transition process. This code (and category) of Anger was present in most participants' interview responses—regardless of their levels of experience, whether she or he was an internal employee or contractor, or whether she or he was a member of the Health Information Technology (HIT) or Information Technology (IT) group of participants.

The data also showed that some participants experienced feelings—anger, frustration, and stress—associated with the first phase of the Bridges transition model: Ending, Losing, Letting Go. As previously defined, Anger is typically associated with feelings of rage and envy. Frustration is defined as "the feeling of being upset or annoyed as a result of being unable to change or achieve something" (Oxford Press Dictionary, n.d.) or "the prevention of the progress, success, or fulfillment of something" (Oxford Press Dictionary, n.d.). Stress is defined as "a state of mental or emotional strain or tension resulting from adverse or demanding circumstances (Oxford Press Dictionary, n.d.).

As an example of workplace frustration and stress, Gina pointed out that although the issues experienced during completion of the change initiative were discussed within the team and reported to senior management. More than once, senior management did not directly engage in resolving the issues but instead assigned a committee, not directly involved in the change initiative, to help resolve issues. Other participants pointed out that the experience of not being heard or acknowledged was frustrating, leading to increased feelings of stress when nothing was done to address or reconcile employees' concerns with the company's change in direction.

Study Finding 2: Bargaining / Kübler-Ross Stage 3: Bargaining

Although categories two and three (Bargaining and Acceptance) are tied for second place in the findings—based on prevalence of occurrence across the study data—the researcher next discusses Bargaining because, in terms of the stages of grief in the Kübler-Ross construct, Bargaining (third stage) appears prior to Depression (fourth stage). Furthermore, in the context of the grief construct, Acceptance is the fifth and last stage. Kearney and Hyle (2003) defined Bargaining as "attempts to trade one action for avoidance of the change event" (p. 114). This theme encompassed the following coded descriptors: bargaining, deal making, schedule slippage, no end date, ongoing, trade, avoidance, handling expectations, go-back, and negotiation. Study participants took part in Bargaining as a response to completion of a task or delivery of work toward a hardware, software, or solution release to another internal customer (a group within the organization receiving input or support from the study participant) or an external customer.

Bargaining was associated with negotiation. When a task that was necessary to be completed during the change event could not be completed, or could not be completed within the timeframe allotted in the schedule, then bargaining of what could be completed and when it could be completed, was negotiated. Negotiation and bargaining also occurred with resourcing and availability of infrastructure (i.e., hardware or software) when a specific environment would not be available for use because it could not be properly configured, tested and delivered; or when a resource was not available to complete a task due to other commitments – work or tasks – within or outside of the change initiative. While some of the research participants engaged in or experienced Bargaining as a response to a change event, other participants indicated that such a practice or response was not acceptable by the enterprise or agency.

Cara stated that there was negotiation on what could be scheduled and completed within the project timeline from initiation of the project until delivery. Every time a new task was added to the project schedule or a change was made to the direction of the change initiative to accommodate for everything that needed to be accomplished, some bargaining had to occur. Additionally, Cara stated, to accommodate one person or group involved with a specific task to complete the change initiative, a deal had to be made with another person or group. And Cara did not have any direct support as it applied to resources or others who performed the same role as her. Cara stated:

Bargaining, I had to negotiate as I learned more. Even though they wanted a year, I had to come back and say, 'Well, based on what we've learned, we think it's XYZ, and we think it needs to be a phased approach.' There was lot of the back and forth. (Larry, 2017, p. 119)

In addition to having to negotiate to get things done, Cara was anxious for several reasons, including the timeline associated with the change initiative schedule and having the resources to support tasking associated with the change project. The balance between getting it done and having the resources to support the effort, while being a contractor not directly responsible for enforcing the completion of work, was a difficult task which required patience and perseverance to ensure that others felt they were being heard when they stated they did not feel the need for a change and/or understand how it would benefit them; and to ensure there was an understanding that a change was necessary and would benefit everyone. Cara was also experiencing the first stage of Bridges' Transition theory (Ending, Losing, Letting Go) while serving as a change agent, handling others concerns and issues and continuously bargaining. Cara also stated, "They're trying to abuse the resources though. No, that's the negotiation, and that's been shifting on a weekly basis. I'm very anxious about that" (Larry, 2017, p. 120).

Another example of ongoing and continuous negotiation/bargaining, at a lower level within the corporation is with Donna who was assigned the task of verifying new enhancements and modifications to the existing solution code base in support of a major change initiative to move insured record/data entry and records management from a mainframe system to a Web interface. Per Donna, the change was massive. Line-by-line verification was needed for every data field in the old system to ensure the new system data entry form mapped to the fields in the old system. There was multi-team, cross-team involvement over a two year period.

Bargaining and negotiation were never ending tasks through the course of the revolutionary change. As stated by Donna, "Bargaining—that is an ongoing thing, bargaining. When we need two weeks to get this done, it's going to be maybe five days. Just, okay fine. Well, as long as you can get it to me here, then I could get this done here" (Larry, 2017, p. 121).

Across the data, research participants expressed the need to negotiate when inadequate time was given to complete a task or deliver a solution. They talked about dealing with layers of customers and managing input from entities such as external oversight committees and senior leadership; all this, in addition to interacting with internal customers in other groups within the organization, as well as dealing with those customers who consume the solutions and services offered by the enterprise. Overall, Bargaining occurred in response to feelings of anxiety associated with daunting, undefined, and/or under-resourced tasks along with associated deadlines and expectations of compliance on the part of leadership.

Study Finding 3: Acceptance / Kübler-Ross Stage 5: Acceptance

As a study category, Acceptance represents the fifth and last stage of the Kübler-Ross grief construct. Yet, it emerged as the second most frequently experienced feeling/behavior (tied with Bargaining) associated with responses to change in the information technology environment. The coded descriptors that mapped to the stage of Acceptance resonated as emotionless responses from participants, such as "it is what it is," and acceptance. All study participants experienced this feeling, by default, according to the data. In other words, each participant indicated that, ultimately, compliance with change was inevitable if she/he expected to retain her/his position in the enterprise. As such, if a change event was thrust upon them, or if they were assigned to carry out tasks associated with a major change, participants concurred that they had to accept the change.

As a contractor, Deepak led a major IT change project to accommodate for the handling of more and larger data sets, as existing databases were overflowing with data, and a relational database storage system that would grow with data (a data warehouse) was needed to expand as data grew. Deepak was responsible for leading the effort, bringing on and training additional resources in support of the change initiative, providing support for other internal teams, and providing Tier 2 and 3 support for external vendors providing the databases and infrastructure (servers) that the data resided on, all while determining how to accomplish the tasks necessary to successfully complete the change initiative. Deepak's original role was simply to lead the effort from a technical perspective, not to participate in the actual hiring and development in support of the change initiative. Acceptance occurred before there was time to think about it, but there was still work to do. Deepak stated, "Yes, then there was no other way, so it was more like okay, you just had to accept it" (Larry, 2017, p. 123).

As indicated by the data, Acceptance "by default" actually underscored the overarching theme of Acceptance. To clarify, participants knew, based on enterprise practices, that employees and contractors were expected to do as they were instructed and by any means necessary; that is, within policy or governmental regulations. For contracting staff, the expectation was that tasking and the approaches necessary to implement a major change event had to be accomplished because that was their charge as the contractors. However, some of the participants described treatment of the contractor, along with the need for additional resources to reach the end goal, as stressful because of the extended hours (overwork) necessary to complete tasking; and the additional (and often times undefined) responsibilities added to their assigned roles. Consequently, while there was acceptance as expressed by contracting and employee staff, it was given by default as they felt there was no other choice.

Study Finding 4: Isolation / Kübler-Ross Stage 1: Isolation

The fourth category to emerge from the analysis of interview data was Denial and Isolation. The researcher coded the following descriptors in association with Denial and Isolation: denial, disbelief, isolation, limited or no support, no training, no help, limited resources, and one-to-many. Several study participants described experiences of Isolation in relation to the following scenarios: (a) when they were the only person in the role, (b) when they were establishing a new role within the organization, and (c) when they had limited to no support from management/leadership in the change event. Not all study participants experienced isolation; however, two study participants used the term isolation to describe their experiences during the initiation of change while a total of four study participants described feeling isolated (establishing a new/unique role without direction or support), without using the term or suggesting that what was experienced was isolation. All who experienced Isolation first had the feeling upon initiation of the change event at the beginning prior to moving on to Anger and other phases of loss.

Angela, a team lead for a testing group responsible for insurance enrollment verification, took on a new role as a team lead for a testing group that was split into two teams with different testing and support paths. Angela was initiated into the change event without information on the new role or the responsibilities associated with the new role. Angela's title did not change, but everything around her did. Angela's responsibilities to staff changed but were not documented or shared with her. Angela shared:

Anger that the whole project will go forward, and it wasn't clearly defined to everyone. I would think mostly, even isolation, because I felt like there was a lot on me that I was supposed to get done because it wasn't clearly communicated. That is where the anger and isolation came from. (Larry, 2017, p. 126)

Lei was an IT contractor who was assigned to be a technical lead for a contract to transition manual pricing to a web-based, automated solution for a government agency. Upon initiation to the project, the person who hired Lei left the agency and Lei was thrown into a new role. A very visible and unique role, taking on some responsibilities associated with the departed chief information officer (CIO), some responsibilities of the resourcing officer, and spokesperson responsibilities for the agency – in this revolutionary transformation that impacted multiple customer agencies. There wasn't anyone else who was having the same experience. Lei stated:

I was the technical lead and also the technical manager of the project. Before I joined the project, the former CIO was fired. A new CIO had just joined, and he brought us in. So, I was chosen, and he asked me if I would be the technical lead for the people to help them implement the project. So, I was more helping with the transition, re-architecture; and re-design; and, also, I had to do some hands-on work as well. (Larry, 2017, p. 128)

Isolation was a concern for participants who had been thrust into new roles in order to accommodate their respective firms' decisions to implement revolutionary change events. In those situations, each of the individuals had been charged with taking on a new role and new responsibilities without the provision of historical reference and resources to aid her/him in moving forward. For participants supporting both internal and external customers, the experience or feeling of isolation was an issue because the time and backing needed to accomplish some tasks internally, while also providing external customer support, was lacking; as such, others had to be brought in, and this was not easily done. Although isolation was not acknowledged by some of the participants, it was experienced based on observation of the participant and review of the data.

Study Finding 5: Depression / Kübler-Ross Stage 4: Depression

Representing the fourth stage of the Kübler-Ross grief construct, Depression emerged as one of the third most experienced feelings associated with responses to change in the IT work environment (along with Isolation). The coded descriptors that mapped to the Depression category include: overwhelmed, helpless, tired, loss, low, and depression. Only one participant (Lei) acknowledged depression during the course of a revolutionary change event in the workplace, but a second participant (Angela) experienced depression as observed by the researcher during the interview data collection process. Angela stated she felt "low" or "down" and experienced depression when faced with no alternative other than to proceed forward with a particular change event without direction or support; and Lei acknowledged feeling depressed while taking on multiple roles across agencies while fighting to move forward with the change initiative as originally planned. Both participants, Angela and Lei, experienced that depression was a response to feeling overwhelmed.

Angela, as previously described, was not provided with a description of responsibilities associated with the team lead role and did not know what tasks were the responsibility of the Team Lead role and which were not; nor was there anyone in the role aside from the Angela, initially. Without leadership, direction or support from the supervisor or senior management, the response was to take on all tasks. There was a lot to do causing continuous overwork in the office and at home in a home office for the first year. Some definition of responsibilities did not occur until the change initiative was in year two of the transformation. Angela, who did not acknowledge depression, was thrust into a major change effort without direction or support from her employer. It was a "learn as you go" and "more information to be provided" experience. According to Angela, it took at least one year to get some clarity about the new role and its associated responsibilities. The change in direction took a toll on the individual—personally and professionally. Angela stated, "I was upset. I was feeling down because I didn't know which direction to go or what my responsibilities were" (Larry, 2017, p. 130).

Lei, as a contractor taking on multiple roles (technical lead and Acting CTO), working across agencies as a change agent and spokesperson, performing human capital development and management responsibilities for a growing team; while completing hands on design and development for the revolutionary change, as the technical guru, was overwhelmed by the tasking and support that had to be given to internal project resources and external vendors and agencies. Lei acknowledged feeling depressed during the course of a revolutionary change event at his firm. Lei stated, "Initially, I was somehow depressed after [so] much pressure really [quite often]. After I made progress, I really felt good as [there was] acceptance of [the new] culture" (Larry, 2017, p. 131).

Study Finding 6: Ending, Losing, Letting Go / Bridges Transition Model Phase 1

The first phase in Bridges transition model (Ending, Losing, Letting Go) was evident during review of the Depression theme that emerged from the data. The observed feelings were frustration, stress, and anxiety. All eight participants experienced one or many of the listed phase 1 Transition feelings (frustration, stress and anxiety) as observed by the researcher in the data analysis stage of this study.

It is significant to note that several participants used the term, anxiety, in lieu of the term depressed/depression. Anxiety is defined as "a feeling of worry, nervousness, or unease about something with an uncertain outcome" (Oxford University Press, n.d.). These participants cited anxiety as a feeling they had experienced during past and present change events, pointing to situations that induced ongoing stress and cycles of loss during major, revolutionary transition efforts in the IT workplace. Cara did an excellent job of expressing what it felt like to act as a change agent with expanded responsibilities beyond those initially imposed without support and feeling anxiety while interviewing staff and answering their concerns about why the change initiative was necessary and how it would benefit them. Cara stated:

The hardest part of the project was convincing people of the Why? Fears and anxiety over their job, why do I have to learn something new? And why this solution when we've always done it this way? We have tried this before; how is this going to be better? There was a lot of doubt. We've seen this before. It's not going to work from the get-go. Of course, and I was new to the organization, so you're the change agent. You're marked the enemy right away. I felt like I was being put in a tough spot... there was a lot of resentment. A lot of unknown; a lot of anxiety... Currently going through that—a lot of anxiety, a lot of unknowns, and the messaging keeps changing every other day. That's currently what I'm going through. (Larry, 2017, p.132)

In addition to anxiety, stress was a response associated with feelings of depression, or actually communicated in lieu of depression. Stress is defined as "a state of mental or emotional strain or tension resulting from adverse or demanding circumstances" (Oxford University Press, n.d.). Several research participants cited stress as the result of a lack of understanding on the parts of both leadership and customers regarding what needed to be accomplished in what time frame and with limited resources to support the effort. Overall, the lack of a clearly defined role and its associated responsibilities, along with not having sufficient amounts and types of resources to support the major change effort, led to overwork and a generally stressful work environment.

Angela expressed these thoughts in the following interview excerpt:

When it started up, it was very rough, and it was just very stressful for me. But as it's been going along, it has become better. They're more defining what the roles are... When you're in the transition phase, just having a role clearly defined would be helpful. Because my role wasn't clearly defined, it created a lot of confusion and stress. Just making sure that everything is defined before you go to your transitional phase, or before you go in the project, helps the entire team. (Larry, 2017, p. 133)

Some of the study participants shared how the stress associated with longer work hours and heavier responsibilities impacted their personal lives. Deepak and

Lei spoke to the demands of work changes in conjunction with the quality of their personal lives. Deepak stated there was not enough home or family time during the major change initiative. There were long work days in the office and then more research and planning at home after work. Deepak could be called any time, day or night, to support vendors who were a part of the change initiative in trouble shooting and resolving issues found with the infrastructure, database or solution.

Study Finding 7: The Neutral Zone / Bridges' Phase 2

Acceptance, as it relates to the Bridges transition model, is the stage of transition that occurs when an individual begins to think of things in a new way and prepares for a new way of doing things. Per data analysis using, Bridges' definition of Acceptance occurred for only one study participant (Deepak). Deepak began thinking of things in a new way at the end of the change initiative, while determining new processes and procedures and documenting the way forward as part of the cleanup effort involved with a very chaotic 15-month period. Deepak had time to breath, he was able to move forward and move things toward a new order that included following policy, processes and procedures. Deepak was mentally and emotionally ready to move forward.

Study Finding 8: The New Beginning / Bridges' Phase 3

Excitement, Happiness and Confidence are feelings experienced during phase 3 of the Bridges transition model. These feelings were experienced by four study participants: Cara, Donna, Gina and Vishal. All four were excited and happy prior to initiation of the change initiative and this does not follow the Bridges transition phases in the order represented. Since the experience of this particular feeling occurred prior to the initiation of change, the researcher has termed it Pre-Change and has inserted it prior to the initial Transition phase – Ending, Losing, Letting Go. This experience of excitement or anticipation prior to the start of a change initiative and then a change in feelings as change begins has been described in the Hype Cycle in the Trough of Disillusionment stage (Fenn & Raskino, 2008). The Hype Cycle is described as when a new innovation is introduced, excitement builds and organizations jump on the bandwagon to incorporate new technologies, thus causing the change acceptance curve to slope up. The Trough of Disillusionment occurs as negative feelings occur (Kearney, 2013) and the change curve begins to slope down as issues are found and multiple iterations of the new innovation are introduced to resolve problems. The Trough of Disillusionment may be used as the basis for a precursor to the first phase of the Bridges transition model as it expresses how technical staff experienced transition as associated with the initiation of change.

In addition to Excitement and Happiness, Confidence was experienced by two study participants (Donna and Vishal) after they were able to reach individual goals associated with a revolutionary change effort. Both felt they had accomplished a great deal and that their work was above average. Because tasking was difficult and they were each able to provide great support for the change effort, Donna and Vishal felt confident that they could accomplish a lot more. Donna went on to retire and extend (fully start) a new business, and Vishal moved on to another, new and different, project/change initiative.

Study Finding 9: Change Link: Outcome Successful

An additional code emerged from the data, *Success*. Success was the code associated with completion of the final stage of the change initiative, regardless of whether the overall change effort was considered a good or bad experience by the research participant. The additional code was not included in the initial list of codes but emerged during data analysis as it mapped to a consistent theme across all eight study participants. Success was surrender or resignation that the change event had reached some form of completion; Success equated to completion.

SUMMARY

Findings from the data analysis indicated that the information technology workers who participated in this study experienced emotions/reactions associated with the stages of grief as represented in the Kübler-Ross grief construct and Bridges transition model during transition processes directly related to major, revolutionary change events in the workplace. Findings also showed that IT workers' experiences of the stages of grief spanned changing work roles, prior work experiences, and types of technology. Some of the participants experienced most stages of grief, while others appeared to be stuck in certain phases for extended periods of time—or repeated stages—depending on the length and success of the change event. While any change event that reached some form of completion—known as an end state—was considered successful, there was no evidence supporting the goodness or positive improvement provided by the change.

Change events that occur within technology-driven organizations position IT workers as front-line staff charged with the responsibility of dealing with both people and systems in order to facilitate the mandated change and move the organization forward. Thus, tasked with handling multiple areas of technological concern and interacting with a variety of people, IT teams face intensified demands when implementing and supporting change while, at the same time, they are transitioning through the change event themselves. Therefore, the findings of this research study are potentially significant to administrators, IT teams (practitioners), and scholars because they offer empirical evidence regarding the actual lived experiences of individuals who have navigated change and transition in the IT environment. On this point, the findings of this study might offer insights into the following areas: (a) how to more effectively introduce and prepare workers for change in the workplace (administrators), (b) how to navigate the transition process in terms of mandating, promoting, and supporting the change effort (IT teams/practitioners), and (c) how to extend scholarship and promote advanced research in support of the technology field.

RECOMMENDATIONS FOR FUTURE RESEARCH

Based on the findings yielded by this study, the researcher offers six recommendations intended to address the following concerns: (a) how to better understand and extend knowledge on the experiences of IT staff members/teams during major change events, (b) how to expand awareness and knowledge of IT staff-based change issues among management and leadership so that they might better support staff in moving through change and transition within the organization, (c) how IT staff might better transition through change, and (d) the use of pre-risk governance for IT staff (undergoing transition due to change). Additionally, the researcher proffers the following recommendations to address concerns and/or gaps in the theories used as the lens (the Kübler-Ross grief construct) and focus (the Bridges transition model) for this study: (e) determine if and how the Kübler-Ross grief construct might be expanded to cover those "fuzzy" responses to change that occur between the stages of loss, and (f) extend Bridges' theory to include a *Pre-Transition* phase to accommodate for what is experienced prior to the initiation of change.

Recommendation 1: Extend Knowledge on IT Staff

There is a lack of information on how leadership and management staff in IT and HIT companies prepare resources for and support IT staff members and teams through revolutionary change events. Therefore, the researcher recommends that this particular area of IT research be expanded in order to acknowledge, validate, and normalize the transition experiences of IT workers as a common phenomenon across the industry. By enlarging and adding credibility to this currently understudied area, new research could provide valuable information and insights that would support truly successful change initiatives for both human resources and the enterprises in which they work.

Recommendation 2: Enterprise Support for IT Staff

Per researcher observations, the participant descriptions (and data), for those from China the expectation is to do what is necessary and beyond; for those from India, the expectation is to work together and help one another to the advantage of the team—and normally within the culture; and for other cultures there is a variation of expression based on the individual. Per Lei, "I would do whatever was necessary for the success of the project" (Larry, 2017, p. 158). Per Deepak, "I worked across roles and helped my team members although I was the lead" (Larry, 2017, p. 158). As an extension of recognizing and addressing the reality of change and transition issues for IT workers, findings indicated the need to conduct future research specific to how companies might best support the skills and training necessary for those individuals and IT teams directly responsible for supporting major change efforts. In other words, study participants collectively communicated the point of view that, as human resources, they are expected to have and/or be ready to apply the knowledge and expertise necessary to implement the mandated change. However, they maintained that they are, typically, not given the training or additional education needed to do so effectively and within the timelines associated with the change event. In other words, they indicated a "learn on your own" mentality that was very apparent in the data collected from HIT staff specifically.

To close the gap and respond to issues communicated during this research study, organizations should: (a) include IT staff in decision making and planning as they are the experts in their fields and leadership depends on IT staff to determine how change will occur and how to best support change initiatives, (b) provide ongoing training to extend IT workers knowledge so they can complete tasking in support of change based on feedback from the IT worker on what training and education is needed, and (c) communicate the need/reason for the change and the overall impact to the enterprise often and simply to all staff concerned with the change event or initiative to ensure there is understanding and buy in from those involved – possibly aiding in keeping change initiative/event attributes (e.g., schedule, budget) in control. These three suggestions will begin to remedy the concerns shared by study participants in interviews and observed through analysis of data by the researcher.

Recommendation 3: IT Staff Vocalization/Response to Change

To better transition through change, IT workers must be vocal about what is necessary in order to support current and future change. Vocalization must be consistent and handled in multiple communication streams, verbally/orally and in writing. While IT staff is responsible for leading change as mandated by leadership and management, they must also prepare for future demands brought about in support of new company direction and updating infrastructure and solutions. Some research participants shared what they needed to support the change initiative while others did not express what was needed but did express what the problems were. One approach to getting the necessary support for change and the associated transition effort is to be clear about what is needed (training, better communication, additional resources, more experienced resources, etc.) and to map needs to what is required of the individual during change – in ongoing communications.

Recommendation 4: Pre-Risk Governance

The use of pre-risk governance in the information technology arena is to plan for future change initiatives by determining possible risks to the success and on-time delivery of a solution, product or service by listing the concerns/risks and possible mitigation responses prior to the start of the change as part of the project/product/ program management effort. Risks are then presented to involved technical staff and stakeholders (those who benefit from and/or consume the change). This allows for resolutions or responses to any risks prior to change initiation and continuous tracking of risk resolutions until they are complete and risks are mitigated. The researcher recommends that leadership/management and IT staff work together to utilize a pre-risk governance process to determine and address the needs of the IT organization and associated staff members prior to the start of change.

Recommendation 5: Kübler-Ross Grief Construct Phase Fuzziness

The Kübler-Ross grief construct provides stages of loss associated with transition once it has been determined that a change is coming. The stages of loss are: (a) denial and isolation, (b) anger, (c) bargaining, (d) depression, and (e) acceptance. The stages of loss may occur cyclically, simultaneously and in a non-linear fashion. As the stages of loss/transition may be non-linear in nature, there may be gaps between phases where the experience is fuzzy and may overlap. This fuzziness needs further investigation as it applies to IT staff. As Kübler-Ross has been expanded and extended in multiple applications in response to the experiences of nursing staff, it would be useful to do the same for IT staff in order to get a better representation of the stages of loss/ transition during change. While studying nursing staff, Perlman and Takacs (1990) expanded the Kübler-Ross grief construct to 10 stages as follows: 1. equilibrium, 2. denial, 3. anger, 4. bargaining, 5. chaos, 6. depression, 7. resignation, 8. openness, 9. readiness, and 10. Reemergence" (p. 33). This may be used as a starting point to determine if IT staff have a transition experience similar to that represented for nursing staff using Kübler-Ross.

Recommendation 6: Pre-Transition Phenomenon

There is a pre-transition phenomenon that was teased out of the data where IT staff was happy and excited to see change coming prior to the initiation of the change event. Per data from this study, the feelings associated with the pre-transition phase of change are represented in Bridges' Transition phase 3 (The New Beginning) but occurred prior to phase 1 (Ending, Losing, Letting Go). To more fully express the feelings associated with transition as they relate to IT staff and provide additional awareness regarding this yet defined phase, further investigation should be done to explore the phenomenon and possibly expand Bridges' theory to accommodate for the experience prior to change initiation.

With the addition of the new Pre-Transition phase, the Bridges transition model would be represented as follows:

1. Preparing for highly anticipated change;
2. Letting go of the old ways;
3. Going through an in-between time when the old is gone, but the new isn't fully operational; and
4. Coming out of the transition and making a new beginning.

It may be that the feelings experienced from the additional Pre-Transition phase that was teased out of the data is a closeout for/a remnant of a previous change effort and thus it truly is the Bridges transition model phase 3 (The New Beginning) but without further, more extensive study, the researcher cannot pinpoint how it was initiated. Additional research is warranted in response to this data.

CONCLUSION

There appears to be an understanding that IT workers are there to complete and support change and thus are not a variable in the change process. The researcher believes the reverse is true, that IT workers are a variable in change initiatives and thus should be considered during major change efforts. To address these gaps in current research, the researcher offers recommendations based on the conviction that studies of this nature would provide additional practical and scholarly data in support of change and transition at the individual level. Moreover, they hold the potential of providing a wealth of information that could, both directly and indirectly, support many of the industries supported by IT staff in 21st century, technology-driven work environments.

REFERENCES

Agarwal, R., & Prasad, J. (1999). Are individual differences germane to the acceptance of new information technologies? *Decision Sciences, 30*(2), 361–391. doi:10.1111/j.1540-5915.1999.tb01614.x

Bennis, W. G. (1966). Changing organizations. *The Journal of Applied Behavioral Science, 2*(3), 247–263. doi:10.1177/002188636600200301

Brailer, D., & Thompson, T. (2004). *Health IT Strategic Framework*. Washington, DC: Department of Health and Human Services.

Bridges, W. (2004). *Transitions: Making sense of life's changes*. Cambridge, MA: De Capo Press.

Bridges, W. (2010). *Managing Transition: Making the most of change*. Philadelphia, PA: Accessible Publishing Systems.

Bridges, W. (2013). *Managing Transition: Bridges transition model*. Philadelphia, PA: Accessible Publishing Systems.

Bridges, W., & Bridges, S. M. (2016). *Managing Transitions: Making the most of change*. Hachette Books.

Burke, W. W. (2013). *Organization Change: Theory and practice*. Sage Publications.

Burke, W. W. (2017). *Organization Change: Theory and practice*. Sage Publications.

Chaudhry, B., Wang, J., Wu, S., Maglione, M., Mojlca, W., Roth, E., ... Shekelle, P. G. (2006). Systematic review: Impact of health information technology on quality, efficiency, and costs of medical care. *Annals of Internal Medicine, 144*(10), 742–752. doi:10.7326/0003-4819-144-10-200605160-00125 PMID:16702590

Fenn, J., & Raskino, M. (2008). *Mastering the Hype Cycle: How to choose the right innovation at the right time*. Stamford, CT: Harvard Business Press.

Filej, B., Skela-Savič, B., Vicic, V. H., & Hudorovic, N. (2009). Necessary organizational changes according to Burke–Litwin model in the head nurses system of management in healthcare and social welfare institutions—The Slovenia experience. *Health Policy (Amsterdam), 90*(2), 166–174. doi:10.1016/j.healthpol.2008.09.013 PMID:18996612

Garfoot, A. (2001). Learning to live with change. *IT Training, 11*, 20–24.

Goodman, E., & Loh, L. (2011). Organizational change: A critical challenge for team effectiveness. *Business Information Review*, *28*(4), 242–250. doi:10.1177/0266382111427087

Green, F. (2012). Employee involvement, technology and evolution in job skills: A task-based analysis. *Industrial & Labor Relations Review*, *65*(1), 36–67. doi:10.1177/001979391206500103

Kearney, K. S. (2002). *A study of the emotional effects on employees who remain through organizational change: A view through Kübler-Ross (1969) in an educational institution* (Doctoral dissertation). Retrieved from ProQuest Dissertations and Theses. (276207296)

Kearney, K. S., & Siegman, K. D. (2013). The emotions of change: A case study. *Organizational Management Journal*, *10*(2), 110–119. doi:10.1080/15416518.2013.801744

Kübler-Ross, E. (1969). *On Death and Dying*. New York, NY: Touchstone.

Larry, L. (2017). *A qualitative study of the experience of individuals within information technology teams during transition using the Kübler-Ross grief construct and the Bridges transition model* (Doctoral dissertation). Retrieved from ProQuest Dissertations & Theses. (1944510678)

Leavitt, H. J., & Whisler, T. L. (1958). Management in the 1980s. *Harvard Business Review*, *36*, 41–48.

Levasseur, R. E. (2001). People skills: Change management tools – Lewin's change model. *Interfaces*, *31*(4), 71–73.

Lewin, K. (1951). Field theory in social science: Selected theoretical papers. In D. Cartwright (Ed.), New York, NY: Harper & Row.

Lippitt, W., & Watson, J. (1958). *Westley, the dynamics of planned change*. New York, NY: HBJ.

Litwin, A. S. (2011). Technological change at work: The Impact of Employee Involvement on the Effectiveness of Health Information Technology. *Industrial & Labor Relations Review*, *64*(5), 863–888. doi:10.1177/001979391106400502

McDonagh, J., & Coghlan, D. (2006). Information technology and the lure of integrated change: A neglected role for organizational development? *Public Administration Quarterly*, *30*(1), 22–55.

Oxford Press Dictionary. (2017). *Oxford Dictionaries*. Retrieved from https://www.oxforddictionaries.com/

Oxford University. (2015). *A Dictionary of Physics* (6th ed.). New York, NY: Oxford University Press.

Perlman, D., & Takacs, G. T. (1990). The 10 stages of change. *Nursing Management, 21*(4), 33–38. doi:10.1097/00006247-199004000-00010 PMID:2330180

Saldaña, J. (2011). *Fundamentals of Qualitative Research*. New York, NY: Oxford University Press.

Saldaña, J. (2015). *The Coding Manual for Qualitative Researchers*. Thousand Oaks, CA: Sage.

Scheuer, F., & Smetters, K. (2014). Could a website really have doomed the health exchanges? Multiple equilibria, initial conditions and the construction of the fine (w19835). Cambridge, MA: National Bureau of Economic Research.

Van de Ven, A., & Poole, M. (1995). Explaining development and change in organizations. *Academy of Management Review, 20*(3), 510–540. doi:10.5465/amr.1995.9508080329

Zell, D. (2003). Organizational change as a process of death, dying, and rebirth. *The Journal of Applied Behavioral Science, 39*(1), 73–96. doi:10.1177/0021886303039001004

KEY TERMS AND DEFINITIONS

A priori **Emotion Coding:** Relating to or denoting reasoning or knowledge that proceeds from theoretical deduction of feelings or mood in qualitative studies (Saldaña, 2015, pp. 45-182).

Grief Construct: A normative way, or means, of mourning/transitioning; the feelings associated with the transition process (Kübler-Ross, 1969, p. 59).

Health Information Technology: The application of information processing involving both computer hardware and software that deals with the storage, retrieval, sharing, and use of health care information, data, and knowledge for communication and decision making; a sub-grouping of IT (Brailer & Thompson, 2004, p. 46).

Hype Cycle: When a new innovation is introduced, excitement builds and organizations jump on the bandwagon to incorporate new technologies, thus causing the change acceptance curve to slope up (Fenn & Raskino, 2008, pp. 103-104).

Information Technology: The study, design, development, implementation, support, and management of computer-based knowledge; the application of computers to store, retrieve, transmit and manipulate data, often in the context of a business or other enterprise (Leavitt & Whisler, 1958, p. 34).

Organizational Change: When a company or organization is going through a transformation, organizational change occurs when business strategies or major sections of an organization are altered (Bennis, 1966, p. 23). Also known as reorganization, restructuring and turnaround (Burke, 2002, pp. 1, 20-22).

Planned Change: Initiatives driven from the top down (Lippitt, Watson, & Westley, 1958, p. 2).

Transition: A three-phased process that people go through as they internalize and come to terms with the details of the new situation that a change brings about (Bridges, 2010, p. 4).

Trough of Disillusionment: Experience of excitement or anticipation prior to the start of a change initiative and then a change in feelings as change begins (Fenn & Raskino, 2008, p. 104).

Chapter 2
Re-Defining Work-
Life Boundaries:
Individual, Organizational, and
National Policy Implications

Donna Weaver McCloskey
Widener University, USA

ABSTRACT

Technology has radically changed the way we live and work. This chapter explores the boundaries that knowledge workers employ to delineate work and personal time and the resulting outcomes. Based on scholarly research, the author proposes redefining the work-life boundary into three dimensions: flexibility, work boundary permeability, and home boundary permeability. While no longer able to control the time and place factors that once defined our work and personal time, employees can use behavioral and communicative tactics to maintain balance. These individual policy decisions and potential work-life balance tools are discussed. Organizations can support new boundary controls through education, support, and training. Finally, technology has resulted in cultural and societal changes, which may continue to be supported through national policy.

INTRODUCTION

The ubiquitous nature of mobile computing has dramatically altered the way knowledge workers live and work. Portability and communication speeds have eradicated the temporal (time) and physical boundaries that used to exist between work and home.

DOI: 10.4018/978-1-7998-2235-6.ch002

Employees work during times and settings that are typically considered personal time, such as while enjoying leisure activities, while traveling and on vacation and while with family. Likewise, personal activities such as socializing, reading, entertainment and shopping can be done while in the traditional work setting. The blurring of these boundaries has had both positive and negative impacts on knowledge workers. This chapter explores the dimensions of the work-life boundary and the resulting work and personal outcomes. The mobile work environment disrupted how we balance our work and personal commitments. Grounded in the research on the positive and negative aspects of these boundary changes, individual, organizational and national policy considerations are proposed.

REVIEW OF WORK-LIFE BOUNDARY RESEARCH

Boundary theory suggests individuals create physical, temporal (time), behavioral and communicative barriers between their work and personal life (Kreiner, Hollensbe, & Sheep, 2009). Prior to the internet-age, boundaries were pretty clear for knowledge workers – the workplace was defined by the office setting and business hours and there was little spillover from one domain to another. Internet access in the workplace changed the boundary that existed between our work and personal life. While most office workers would never do physical personal activities in the workplace, such as watching TV or reading a book, online access made entertainment, shopping and socialization accessible during work time. Over 72% of North American respondents have indicated they shop online while at work (Adams, Weinberg, Jarrett, & Surette, 2005). An Australian study found that nearly 74% of calls and 88% of text messages exchanged during the work day were not business related (Wajcman, Bittman, & Brown, 2008). A 2012 survey of 3,200 working adults by Salary.com reported that 64% visit non-work related websites every day during work hours and 21% reported spending up to 5 hours per week doing personal tasks during work time. Some individuals were able to personally regulate their use of the internet for personal reasons, such as only logging into social media and other forms of entertainment during a lunch break. Many organizations found it necessary to enforce a work-personal boundary by either monitoring usage or eliminating access to non-work related sites.

Internet access in the workplace changed the work boundary but portable computers and home networks lead to an explosion of new work models. Knowledge workers were now able to work from other physical locations, ushering in the growth of remote work, primarily referred to as telecommuting. Researchers examined the impact of this integration of work and home life and found both positive and negative outcomes (McCloskey, 1998). A meta-analytic examination of 46 research studies by Gajendran and Harrison (2007) concluded that telecommuting had beneficial impacts on autonomy, work-family conflict, job satisfaction and performance. High intensity telecommuting (> 2.5 days per week) had a beneficial impact on reducing work-family conflict but at the expense of relationships with co-workers. This second wave of work-life integration fostered a series of new organizational policies and cultural norms. Organizations set limits on telecommuting frequency, tolerance of childcare responsibilities while working and expectations on availability. Whether through formal training or personal experimentation, employees found ways to define work time when working outside of the physical office (Hilbrecht, Shaw, & Johnson, 2008; Hill, Ferris, & Martinson, 2003; Tietze, 2003), such as setting aside a designated work space, limiting chores or entertainment distractions when working and dressing for work and following a routine that delineated their work and home life.

Technology has continued to become more portable. The next wave of work-life integration occurred with the widespread adoption of the smart phone. With laptops, employees potentially faced work-life conflicts while in the home. For example, they could hear emails pinging from their home workspace while having dinner with the family or relaxing in the evening. Smart phone adoption exponentially increased this work-life conflict since distractions can occur literally anytime and anywhere (Prasopoulou, Pouloudi, & Panteli, 2006). Powering off a work laptop was a relatively easy way of eliminating a work conflict during personal time, but this does not easily translate to mobile devices. Since the cell phone can be the primary means of both work and personal communication, there is a reluctance to power off. For many 24/7 access has irrevocably shattered the boundary between work and personal time.

The mobilization of technology has resulted in a significant change in boundary research. Since a physical location no longer determined the role, we could no longer simply research personal tasks in the workplace and work tasks in the home, therefore the concept of the work-life boundary needed to be redefined. The initial definition was based on the extent to which employees segmented or integrated their work and personal lives (Ashford, Kreiner, & Fugate, 2000; Bulger, Matthews, & Hoffman, 2007; Kirchmeyer, 1995; Kossek, Ruderman, Braddy, & Hannum, 2010; Tremblay & Genin, 2008). Ultimately this one-dimensional definition was found lacking and unable to capture to nuances in the evolving work-life boundary. To fully understand how we use technology to effectively set boundaries between our personal and professional lives, we must consider both boundary flexibility and permeability.

The concept of flexibility is how much control the individual has over when and where work is completed. Work schedule flexibility can be a formal program, such as flex-time or telecommuting, or an informal ability to change work hours as needed. Flexibility has been found to be negatively related to forms of work-family conflict (Bulger et al., 2007; Carlson, Grzywacz, & Kacmar, 2010; Kattenbach, Demerouti, & Nachreiner, 2010; Kossek, Lautsch, & Eaton, 2006; Porter & Ayman, 2010). The ability to alter the work schedule or location makes it easier to juggle competing demands. Schedule flexibility has also been found to contribute to higher job satisfaction (McCloskey, 2016), lower intention to quit (Porter & Ayman, 2010) and reduced depression (Kossek et al., 2006).

Flexibility appears to be beneficial in balancing work and non-work commitments, but mobile technology is a knife that cuts both ways. While it offers the flexibility to work at different times and locations, it also blurs the lines between our work and personal roles. When considering the work-life boundary, in addition to flexibility, permeability must also be considered. Boundary permeability is the extent to which an individual integrates the obligations of one role when in the other role. Permeable boundaries allow one to be physically located in one domain and psychologically or behaviorally involved in another role (Olson-Buchanan & Boswell, 2006). Permeability needs to be examined directionally since it can vary for the home and work boundary (Eagle, Icenogle, Maes, & Miles, 1998; Kasper, Meyer, & Schmidt, 2005; Kossek & Lautsch, 2012). If the home border is permeable it means work tasks can intrude on personal time whereas when the home border is not permeable, work is limited to work time. If the work border is permeable it means non-work tasks can intrude on work time whereas when the work border is not permeable, personal tasks are limited to personal time. Researchers have examined the permeability of both the work and home boundary and have, generally, found negative outcomes. Home boundary permeability, allowing work tasks to be done during personal time, results in higher work-family conflict (Hecht & Allen, 2009; Kossek et al., 2012; McCloskey, 2016; Olson-Buchanan & Boswell, 2006; Schieman & Glavin, 2008; Wepfer, Allen, Brauchli, & Bauer, 2018). Likewise a permeable work boundary, one in which home responsibilities intrude during work time, has been found to contribute to higher home®work conflict (Hecht & Allen, 2009; Kim & Hollensbe, 2017; Kossek et al., 2012).

Researchers have recognized that the initial segmentation/integration continuum does not capture the nuances and variations in the work-life boundary (Kossek & Lautsch, 2012). An individual could work from home (integration) but keep a firm boundary separating work and personal time (segmentation). In a mobile technology world the work-life boundary is a multi-dimensional construct comprised of schedule flexibility, home boundary permeability and work boundary permeability. Table 1 briefly describes the eight possible boundary configuration combinations among these three dimensions (McCloskey, 2016). Given the strong evidence that work-family conflict contributes to many negative outcomes, including exhaustion (Boles, Johnston, & Hall, 1997; Golden, 2011), job dissatisfaction (Carlson et al., 2010) and turnover intentions (Porter & Ayman, 2010), it is imperative that individuals, organizations and society consider re-defining what a work-life boundary means in a digital age.

Table 1. Description of boundary types

Flexible	Work Boundary Permeable	Home Boundary Permeable	Description
Yes	Yes	Yes	This combination offers the most work-life integration. The timing of work can shift and demands from one role are allowed to intrude when in the other role.
Yes	Yes	No	The time when work is done may shift but the home boundary is firm and work is not done during personal time. Personal tasks may be done at work.
Yes	No	Yes	The time when work is done may shift but the work boundary is firm. While work tasks may be done during personal time, personal tasks are not done during work time.
Yes	No	No	Work and personal life are compartmentalized but the timing of work can be shifted to meet changing demands.
No	Yes	Yes	Work and non-work times are set and rarely altered. Permeable boundaries for both work and home means that work activities are sometimes done at home and personal activities are sometimes done at work.
No	Yes	No	Work occurs during scheduled time. While work may intrude on personal time, the opposite does not happen.
No	No	Yes	Work occurs during scheduled time. While work may intrude on personal time, the opposite does not happen.
No	No	No	This combination offers the most work-life segregation.

ADDRESSING WORK-LIFE BOUNDARIES: INDIVIDUAL POLICY PERSPECTIVE

From an employee perspective, the first step in developing and maintaining effective work-life boundaries is self-awareness of existing levels of flexibility and work/home boundary permeability. Just as organizations monitored internet use at work

(Arnesen & Weis, 2007), individuals should monitor their time and technology boundary crossings. A time log, as prescribed by Vanderkam (2015), may reveal insights into the current boundary between work and home. Researchers have found employees perceive their use of time differently from reality (Ferreira & Esteves, 2016) so committing to tracking for at least a week can offer useful insights. Once aware of their current work-life boundary, employees can be reflective of the boundary they would like to have. Some employees prefer to have more role integration and thrive on technology connectivity (Adkins & Premeaux, 2014). Through a time log, others may realize there is too much integration and can become more conscious about how they intend to maintain a different boundary through behavioral and communicative tactics. Ultimately, the employees who are most satisfied are those who have congruence between their desired and enacted work-life boundary (Chen, Powell, & Greenhaus, 2009).

Technology has altered the time and place factors that once defined work and personal time. Two additional ways that a boundary can be delineated is through behavioral and communicative tactics (Kreiner et al., 2009), which are largely in the control and prevue of the individual. A behavioral boundary tactic means consciously enforcing preferred boundaries by leveraging technology, invoking triage and deflecting tasks to other people or a more appropriate time. Just as telecommuters and home-workers have been coached to set boundaries with physical objects, routines and rules (Myrie & Daly, 2009), so too should we coach knowledge workers. A conscious decision to use separate devices for work and home, transitional routines for entering and leaving roles, scheduling leisure or "unplugged" time and negotiated rules with the both the organization and family members will allow workers have more control of boundary permeability.

In addition to behavioral boundary controls, communicative boundary tactics, setting expectations and confronting violators, can be employed. For boundaries to be effective access and expectations need to be clearly communicated to both colleagues/clients and friends/family. In interviews employees have acknowledged the importance of communicating work and personal time (Adisa, Gbadamosi, & Osabutey, 2017; Cousins & Robey, 2015). If an employee has defined Sunday as being a day for personal time, they are enacting a temporal boundary. In order to make that a reality they will need to reaffirm that boundary with their behavior and communication. For example, the employee may choose to turn off their work devices. If they use one shared mobile device for work and personal tasks they could mute work-related notifications. An auto response to email indicating that they are unavailable that day and will respond on Monday morning communicates the enacted temporal boundary. If a colleague or client breaches that boundary for a non-critical reason, they should be directed to another on-call employee or deferred until work time. Effectively communicating boundaries is a strategy that deserves greater attention. While almost all employees reported using behavioral boundary strategies, most did not use any communicative methods. In a survey of working mothers 50% reported setting availability expectations, 46% negotiating boundary expectations in advance and only 19% corrected a violator (Araujo, Tureta, & Araujo, 2015). While this has organizational implications, discussed in the following section, the strategy of defining a border and using behavioral and communicative tactics to defend it applies to the work boundary as well. Family expectations and preferences has an impact on boundary setting (Ashforth et al., 2000). Setting expectations with family and friends about work time and preserving those boundaries is as important as managing organizational expectations.

Research has shown that schedule flexibility allows employees to balance their work and family commitments, yet flexibility is the very thing that makes boundary maintenance so difficult. Because work time and place can shift, it is hard for others to know when an employee is in the work or personal role. A client calls on a Tuesday afternoon not knowing that you're chaperoning a school field trip. A friend texts on Wednesday night to get together, not knowing you're working to make up for the time spent on the field trip. The combination of availability and flexibility means others have difficulty knowing when you are available for which role. Mobile technology has created many challenges regarding work-life conflicts but it can also be a tool to mitigate these challenges. A behavioral boundary is the proactive use of technology to define work and personal time. As summarized in Table 2, smart phone companies and app developers offer ways to manage the use of mobile technology so that individuals can proactively minimize the potential negative outcomes.

Table 2. Select iPhone settings and apps to manage the work-life boundary

iPhone Function / Feature	Description
Do Not Disturb	Settings → Do Not Disturb Silences calls/notifications. Can be configured to still accept calls from certain numbers (spouse, children's school, etc.) OR can be overcome if a second call comes within 3 minutes, thus limiting distractions but still be reachable in an emergency
Screen Time	Settings → Screen Time Provides weekly reports on your iphone/ipad usage and allows you to set daily downtime and app category limits.
Email Notifications	Settings → Notifications Allows you to customize notifications for various apps, including your work and personal email
Apps for monitoring time and tracking/limiting connectivity	Highly rated apps include Atracker, Space, Life Cycle, Rescue Time and Week Plan
Apps for improving focus and productivity	Highly rated apps include Focus Booster, Strides, OmniFocus and Things 3

While available tools for work-life boundary management should be utilized, employees are calling for additional support. In a survey of work-life boundary issues of 172 knowledge workers (McCloskey, 2018) respondents indicated they needed additional technological support in the form of time management, improving focus, maintaining a holistic calendar and simplifying communication. Of the new features and functions requested, summarized in Table 3, employees were asking for help controlling the very conflicts that technology has created.

Table 3. Requested features/functions to improve work-life boundary management

Function / Feature	Comments
Time Management	App that suggests boundaries for various activities and reminds you when you are over-scheduling yourself or access work apps after hours too much.
	Something that would enable me to keep an easy electronic to-do list, calendar and way to "log" time and almost track how much time is being devoted to different aspects of my life.
	An app that can figure out when I am spending time on work vs not, and charts to show me how I'm spending that time.
Focus / Control Interruptions	An app to stop me multitasking everywhere and gets me to focus on one thing at a time
	One that keeps me focused on whatever I'm supposed to be doing at the moment.
	Work email would become inaccessible during family time
	An app that blocks Facebook, Pinterest, and personal email during specified work hours, and blocks work email during specified personal hours
Integrated Calendar	A one stop calendar app that would input everything from all disparate calendars for me (work, personal, kid school and activities, birthday reminders, garbage pickup days, home
	A comprehensive to-do list & calendar that easily separates work & family
	Being allowed to combine my work and home calendars. Government does not allow that currently.
	A side by side calendar of work related tasks and family related tasks. This pops up daily to show the two different columns
	One that could integrate my work calendar (Outlook) with my personal calendar (Cozi)
	I would love an app that can be used for personal and work functions but belongs to you and not your employer. Something that can be used with any employer. As often as people change jobs now it would have to be interchangeable and compatible with multiple systems.
Communication	Why can't I easily set my cell phone to work, non-work, both or neither mode to control notifications, calls and texts?
	A shared calendar for co-parents that actually works. Everything I've used has been clunky and useless
	Multi-functional calendar that is easy to update, coordinate with multiple phones, individuals
	I'd like to do a better job of collaborating and keeping calendars between mine, my partner and kids schedules so it is visible to all of us.

Like a fitness tracker, employees felt that would make better decisions if they could easily see how they were spending their time and be able to set controls to limit multi-tasking and distractions. The recognition that maintaining separate work and personal calendars no longer reflects the reality of how we manage our work and life time was illuminating. McKechnie and Beatty (2015) suggest that calendars should be considered along two different dimension: segmentation/integration and personal/public, which is exactly what these knowledge workers were requesting.

Through flexibility and permeability there is no longer a firm line between our work and personal life, which means time needs to be managed more holistically. An integrated calendar in which the employee can manage both work and personal demands while maintaining privacy in each domain would be an acknowledgment of new work-life boundaries. If employees were able to define their work and personal time in one inclusive calendar and then have the ability to share work/personal delineation with friends/family and colleagues, there could a dramatic decrease in the role conflicts that occur and, presumably, a reduction in the resulting stress and negative outcomes.

ADDRESSING WORK-LIFE BOUNDARIES: ORGANIZATIONAL POLICY PERSPECTIVE

Kanter (1977) identified that organizations deal with their employee's non-work demands by either ignoring that they exist or allowing for integration, such as onsite recreation or childcare. Hall and Richter (1988) added a third organizational response that was to respect that employees had non-work commitments and supporting that through flexible work options. Both integration and respect organizational responses have a positive correlation with employee organizational commitment (Kirchmeyer, 1995). Organizations must now recognize that boundary management involves more than flexibility and should be proactive in acknowledging and addressing both boundary flexibility and permeability.

While some organizations are active in helping employees find a successful work-life harmony (Montanez, 2018), widespread adoption is slower. Given the research that shows achieving work-life balance contributes to positive outcomes such as well-being, reduced stress and more organizational commitment (Tomazevic, Kozjek, & Stare, 2014; Zheng, Molineux, Mirshekary, & Scaparo, 2015), organizations should be more involved in helping employees define their optimal boundary. The first step is to assess the extent to which core competencies, regulations and other limitations will allow for a non-traditional work-life boundary. Even within one organization, there may be some roles or job types that have different requirements for availability and physical presence. The implementation of flexibility and acceptance of permeability should be seen as equitable and based on job design, not individual factors (Putnam, Myers, & Gailliard, 2014). Among those who can manipulate their boundary, education and coaching should be initiated. Mobile business intelligence apps and collaboration tools, such as Slack, provide real-time insights and team communication. In addition to security, mobile app deployment should also consider technological and non-technological controls for boundary management. Empowerment initiatives that provide employees with the knowledge and skills to manage multiple life roles have been found to have a significant positive impact on satisfaction (work, home, community and self) and performance (home and self domains) (Friedman & Westring, 2015). In addition to the daily management of work-life boundaries, the organization should consider policies and procedures regarding vacation and mandated time off. Human Resources should proactively promote policies to encourage employees to periodically "switch off" from work to focus on non-work relationships and activities (Adisa et al., 2017).

Organizational policies can only go so far in counterbalancing our "always available" culture. Managers need to be aware of the way they model (or fail to model) effective boundaries. Managerial support is critical to employees using and reaping the benefits of organizational policies (Breaugh & Frye, 2007; Haines, St-Onge, & Archambault, 2002; Higgins & Duxbury, 2005; Lautsch, Kossek, & Eaton, 2009; Putnam et al., 2014). Even the most boundary-disciplined employee will feel a pang of guilt over not seeing a weekend email from a supervisor until Monday morning. Managers should be clear in their expectations about availability during non-work times and should demonstrate that by communicating and enacting their own work-life boundary.

While the research summarized in this chapter makes an important contribution in expanding our understanding of how work-life boundaries should be operationalized, it is important to note that most of it was conducted in the United States and may not be generalizable to broader national and international audiences. While some research on work-family conflict (Kinnunen & Mauno, 1998; Scholarios & Marks, 2004; Wepfer et al., 2018) and boundary spanning (Tremblay & Genin, 2008) has been conducted in non-US countries, there have been little cross-cultural comparisons. Loh, Restubog, and Gallois (2010) did find cross-cultural differences in boundary permeability with Singaporeans (collectivists) having less permeable workgroup boundaries than Australians (individualists). Culture and regional social norms could impact not only how work-life boundaries are breached and maintained but also the resulting consequences on stress and satisfaction. This would be important for multinational companies to understand when developing boundary policies and procedures and is an area that should be addressed by researchers.

ADDRESSING WORK-LIFE BOUNDARIES: NATIONAL POLICY PERSPECTIVE

Employees can be more aware and proactive in managing their work-life boundary and employers can assist in validating and respecting a boundary between work and personal life, but effective re-definition requires more. There needs to be a societal acknowledgement that technology has changed the way we work and live and the evolution of cultural norms. As alluded to in employee demands for more controls over calendar management, summarized in Table 3, it is only when the culture at large can see and understand work and personal roles will we be able to effectively maintain boundaries in a time fluid world.

To some extent this could be done through legislative action. Legislation on cell phone usage has been focused on safety. In the United States, most states have regulations regarding texting or using a cell phone while driving (O'Reilly & Richards, 2012) and at least one state is considering a ban on texting while walking (Anthony, 2019). Legislation has also addressed boundary setting in direct marketing. There are national, state, and local restrictions on when and how marketers can reach consumers, including requirements for opting-out and limiting communication. Legislation could, potentially, require that organizations set limits on how much work can be done during non-work time. France has led the way with a Right to Disconnect law, which requires businesses to establish hours when staff should not send or answer emails (Morris, 2017). If organizations are not more proactive in helping people manage 24/7 access, it is likely that controls will be imposed legislatively.

The Organization for Economic Co-operation and Development (OECD) has conducted the Better Life Index for nearly a decade. In this index, 40 countries are ranked on work-life balance, operationalized as the percentage of the population working 50 or more hours per week and the percentage of time spent in personal endeavors. The United States ranks 28th—directly behind the United Kingdom, Brazil and Poland—well behind the Netherlands (#1), Italy (#2) and Denmark (#3). Even cultures that have been very focused on growth are questioning the need for balance. There have been protests and debates in China over the tech sector's 996 culture, working 9 a.m. to 9 p.m. 6 days per week (Barrett, 2019). Continued research on work-life balance and the ways other culture address the conflict will likely spur cultural changes in boundary definition.

CONCLUSION AND DIRECTIONS FOR FUTURE RESEARCH

Our understanding of the work-life boundary has been expanding along with the growth of mobile technologies. Instead of defining the boundary along one integration-segmentation continuum, research has re-defined the boundary based on three dimensions: flexibility, home permeability and work permeability. Generally schedule flexibility has resulted in positive outcomes and permeability has resulted in more negative experiences. Researchers have questioned whether individual traits, such as role identity, and work style preferences can impact the enacted boundary and outcomes (Kossek et al., 2012; Kossek & Lautsch, 2012; Kreiner et al., 2009). Role identity theory says that we identify with certain roles, considering them defining components of ourselves, and that this affiliation impacts the time and energy we dedicate to that role (Ashforth & Mael, 1989; Lobel, 1991). Individuals who identify stronger with their personal life than their work, maintain a strong boundary in the home domain so that work does not interfere during personal time (Hecht & Allen, 2009). McCloskey (2019) found knowledge workers with stronger work identity experienced less work-family conflict when they maintained a permeable work boundary. In addition to differences in role identity, employees also have different preferences. Rothbard, Phillips, and Dumas (2005) found that when employees who prefer segmentation had organizational policies that supported integration, their job satisfaction and organizational commitment was negatively impacted. The way in which individual characteristics may moderate the relationship between boundary dimensions and outcomes requires additional research. In addition to role identity, the impact of job responsibilities, work hours, and work/family demands should be examined.

While related work-family conflict research in other cultures (Powell & Craig, 2015; Schieman & Glavin, 2008; Shanmugam & Agarwal, 2019) has been consistent with US-based studies, it cannot be assumed. Future research should examine the boundary decisions of professionals with larger and broader samples from around the world. This will contribute to the understanding and needs of organizational policy for multinational corporations. Likewise, researchers should seek to examine the impact of cultural and legislative controls on boundary definition on the work and personal outcomes.

Having advocated for an expansion in boundary operationalization, moderating variable examination and samples, perhaps it is also time to expand the definition of work-family conflict. Individuals have more roles than just worker and spouse/parent. By limiting the scope to conflict between work and family other important personal realms, such as volunteering, recreation, leisure, political activism, spirituality and even sleep, are ignored. Some researchers have broadened the definition to work-to-home conflict (Schieman & Glavin, 2008), work-life conflict (Boswell & Olson-Buchanan, 2007) and work-to-leisure conflict (Son & Chen, 2019). Researchers should continue to work towards broadening the definition beyond family conflict to be more inclusive and recognize that a balanced life is more holistic.

The adoption of mobile technology occurred without thoughtful consideration on how it would impact our lives. Having realized that the boundary between work and personal time has been breached and the resulting negative outcomes, we can consider how to react at the individual, organizational or national level. Through powerful networks and mobile devices, individuals have the ability to both work and play anytime and anywhere. Without the physical and temporal (time) boundaries that used to separate our work and personal lives, there has been conflict. Employees are calling for more technological assistance in managing, delineating and communicating in a world without defined boundaries. Without waiting for lagging organizational policy, employees can be proactive in defining their preferred boundary and then using behavioral and communicative tactics to enforce it. Formally and informally, organizations can assist in boundary management. Whether through education or supervisors modeling behavioral and communicative boundary tactics, employees need assistance in traversing this evolving work environment. Several countries have made work-life balance and working hours part of their legislative agenda. Ultimately, we need a cultural change in recognizing and honoring boundaries that support work-life harmony.

REFERENCES

Adams, S. M., Weinberg, B. D., Masztal, J. J., & Surette, D. M. (2005). This time it is personal: Employee online shopping at work. *Interactive Marketing*, *6*(4), 326–336. doi:10.1057/palgrave.im.4340301

Adisa, T. A., Gbadamosi, G., & Osabutey, E. L. (2017). What happened to the border? The role of mobile information technology devices on employees' work-life balance. *Personnel Review*, *46*(8), 1651–1671. doi:10.1108/PR-08-2016-0222

Adkins, C., & Premeaux, S. (2014). The use of communication technology to manage work-home boundaries. *Journal of Behavioral and Applied Management*, *15*(3), 82–100.

Anthony, A. (2019). *New York might make it illegal to text while walking*. Retrieved from https://www.cnn.com/2019/05/20/us/new-york-walking-while-texting-trnd/index.html

Araujo, B., Tureta, C., & Araujo, D. (2015). How do working mothers negotiate the work-home interface? *Journal of Managerial Psychology*, *30*(5), 565–581. doi:10.1108/JMP-11-2013-0375

Arnesen, D. W., & Weis, W. L. (2007). Developing an effective company policy for employee internet and email use. *Journal of Organizational Culture, Communication and Conflict*, *11*(2), 53–65.

Ashforth, B. E., Kreiner, G. E., & Fugate, M. (2000). All in a days work: Boundaries and micro role transitions. *Academy of Management Review*, *25*(3), 472–491. doi:10.5465/amr.2000.3363315

Barrett, E. (2019). *China's '996' overwork culture fueled its tech engine – Why workers are burning out.* Retrieved from https://fortune.com/2019/04/24/china-996-overwork-culture-tech/

Boles, J. S., Johnston, M. W., & Hair, J. F. (1997). Role stress, work-family conflict and emotional exhaustion: Inter-relationships and effects on some work-related consequences. *Journal of Personal Selling & Sales Management, 17*(1), 17–27.

Boswell, W. R., & Olson-Buchanan, J. B. (2007). The use of communication technologies after hours: The role of work attitudes and work-life conflict. *Journal of Management, 33*(4), 592–610. doi:10.1177/0149206307302552

Breaugh, J. A., & Frye, K. N. (2007). An examination of the antecedents and consequences of the use of family-friendly benefits. *Journal of Managerial Issues, 19*(1), 35–52.

Bulger, C. A., Matthews, R. A., & Hoffman, M. E. (2007). Work and personal life boundary management: Boundary strength, work/personal life balance, and the segmentation-integration continuum. *Journal of Occupational Health Psychology, 12*(4), 365–375. doi:10.1037/1076-8998.12.4.365 PMID:17953495

Carlson, D. S., Grzywacz, J. G., & Kacmar, K. M. (2010). The relationship of schedule flexibility and outcomes via the work-family interface. *Journal of Managerial Psychology, 25*(4), 330–355. doi:10.1108/02683941011035278

Chen, Z., Powell, G., & Greenhaus, J. (2009). Work-to-family conflict, positive spillover and boundary management: A person-environment fit approach. *Journal of Vocational Behavior, 74*(1), 82–93. doi:10.1016/j.jvb.2008.10.009

Cousins, K., & Robey, D. (2015). Managing work-life boundaries with mobile technologies. *Information Technology & People, 28*(1), 34–71. doi:10.1108/ITP-08-2013-0155

Eagle, B. W., Icenogle, M. L., Maes, J. D., & Miles, E. W. (1998). The importance of employee demographic profiles for understanding experiences of work-family interrole conflicts. *The Journal of Social Psychology, 138*(6), 690–709. doi:10.1080/00224549809603255 PMID:9872064

Ferreira, A. I., & Esteves, J. D. (2016). Perceptions of time at work: When the clock ticks differently for men and women when they are not working at work. *Personnel Review, 45*(1), 29–50. doi:10.1108/PR-02-2014-0033

Friedman, S. D., & Westring, A. (2015). Empowering individuals to integrate work and life: Insights for management development. *Journal of Management Development*, *34*(3), 299–315. doi:10.1108/JMD-11-2012-0144

Gajendran, R. S., & Harrison, D. A. (2007). The good, the bad, and the unknown about telecommuting: Meta-analysis of psychological mediators and individual consequences. *The Journal of Applied Psychology*, *92*(6), 1524–1541. doi:10.1037/0021-9010.92.6.1524 PMID:18020794

Golden, T. D. (2011). Altering the effects of work and family conflict on exhaustion: Telework during traditional and nontraditional work hours. *Journal of Business and Psychology*, *27*(3), 255–269. doi:10.100710869-011-9247-0

Haines, V. Y. III, St-Onge, S., & Archambault, M. (2002). Environmental and person antecedents of telecommuting outcomes. *Journal of End User Computing*, *14*(3), 32–50. doi:10.4018/joeuc.2002070103

Hall, D. T., & Richter, J. (1988). Balancing work life and home life: What can organizations do to help? *The Academy of Management Perspectives*, *2*(3), 213–223. doi:10.5465/ame.1988.4277258

Hecht, T. D., & Allen, N. J. (2009). A longitudinal examination of the work-nonwork boundary strength construct. *Journal of Organizational Behavior*, *30*(7), 839–862. doi:10.1002/job.579

Higgins, C., & Duxbury, L. (2005, July). Saying 'no' in a culture of 'hours,' money and no-support. *Ivey Business Journal*, 1-5.

Hilbrecht, M., Shaw, S. M., Johnson, L. C., & Andrey, J. (2008). 'I'm home for the kids': Contradictory implications for work-life balance of teleworking mothers. *Gender, Work and Organization*, *15*(5), 454–476. doi:10.1111/j.1468-0432.2008.00413.x

Hill, E., Ferris, M., & Märtinson, V. (2003). Does it matter where you work? A comparison of how three work venues (traditional office, virtual office, and home office) influence aspects of work and personal/family life. *Journal of Vocational Behavior*, *63*(2), 220–241. doi:10.1016/S0001-8791(03)00042-3

Kanter, R. M. (1977). *Work and family in the United States: A critical review and agenda for research and policy*. New York: Russell Sage Foundation.

Kasper, H., Meyer, M., & Schmidt, A. (2005). Managers dealing with work-family-conflict: An explorative analysis. *Journal of Managerial Psychology*, *20*(5), 440–461. doi:10.1108/02683940510602978

Kattenbach, R., Demerouti, E., & Nachreiner, F. (2010). Flexible working times: Effects on employees' exhaustion, work-nonwork conflict and job performance. *Career Development International, 15*(3), 279–295. doi:10.1108/13620431011053749

Kim, S., & Hollensbe, E. (2017). Work interrupted: A closer look at work boundary permeability. *Management Research Review, 40*(12), 1280–1297. doi:10.1108/MRR-02-2017-0025

Kinnunen, U., & Mauno, S. (1998). Antecedents and outcomes of work-family conflict among employed women and men in Finland. *Human Relations, 51*(2), 157–177. doi:10.1177/001872679805100203

Kirchmeyer, C. (1995). Managing the work-nonwork boundary: An assessment of organizational responses. *Human Relations, 48*(5), 515–536. doi:10.1177/001872679504800504

Kossek, E. E., & Lautsch, B. A. (2012). Work–family boundary management styles in organizations: A cross-level model. *Organizational Psychology Review, 2*(2), 152–171. doi:10.1177/2041386611436264

Kossek, E. E., Lautsch, B. A., & Eaton, S. C. (2006). Telecommuting, control, and boundary management: Correlates of policy use and practice, job control, and work-family effectiveness. *Journal of Vocational Behavior, 68*(2), 347–367. doi:10.1016/j.jvb.2005.07.002

Kossek, E. E., Ruderman, M. N., Braddy, P. W., & Hannum, K. M. (2012). Work-nonwork boundary management profiles: A person-centered approach. *Journal of Vocational Behavior, 81*(1), 112–128. doi:10.1016/j.jvb.2012.04.003

Kreiner, G. E., Hollensbe, E. C., & Sheep, M. L. (2009). Balancing borders and bridges: Negotiating the work-home interface via boundary work tactics. *Academy of Management Journal, 52*(4), 704–730. doi:10.5465/amj.2009.43669916

Lautsch, B. A., Kossek, E. E., & Eaton, S. C. (2009). Supervisory approaches and paradoxes in managing telecommuting implementation. *Human Relations, 62*(6), 795–827. doi:10.1177/0018726709104543

Loh, J., Restubog, S. L. D., & Gallois, C. (2010). Attitudinal outcomes of boundary permeability. *Cross Cultural Management, 17*(2), 118–134. doi:10.1108/13527601021038697

McCloskey, D. W. (1998). A review of the empirical research on telecommuting and directions for future research. In M. Igbaria & M. Tan (Eds.), *The Virtual Workplace*. Hershey, PA: Idea Group.

McCloskey, D. W. (2016). Finding work-life balance in a digital age: An exploratory study of boundary flexibility and permeability. *Information Resources Management Journal*, *29*(3), 53–70. doi:10.4018/IRMJ.2016070104

McCloskey, D. W. (2018). An examination of the boundary between work and home for knowledge workers. *International Journal of Human Capital and Information Technology Professionals*, *9*(3), 25–41. doi:10.4018/IJHCITP.2018070102

McKechnie, S. P., & Beatty, J. E. (2015). Contemporary calendar management: Exploring the intersections of groupware and personal calendars. *Management Review*, *26*(3), 185–202.

Montanez, R. (2018). T*he highest-rated companies for work-life balance in 2018*. Retrieved from https://www.forbes.com/sites/rachelmontanez/2018/10/01/the-2018-highest-rated-companies-for-work-life-balance/#7849faab7cb1

Morris, D. Z. (2017). *French law bars work e-mail after hours*. Retrieved from https://fortune.com/2017/01/01/french-right-to-disconnect-law/

Myrie, J., & Daly, K. (2009). The use of boundaries by self-employed, home-based workers to manage work and family: A qualitative study in Canada. *Journal of Family and Economic Issues*, *30*(4), 386–398. doi:10.100710834-009-9166-7

O'Reilly, J. S., & Richards, B. (2012). *Texting and cell phone use while driving: Summary of state laws*. Retrieved from https://www.carinsurancelist.com/texting-and-cell-phone-use-while-driving-summary-of-state-laws.htm

Olson-Buchanan, J. B., & Boswell, W. R. (2006). Blurring boundaries: Correlates of integration and segmentation between work and nonwork. *Journal of Vocational Behavior*, *68*(3), 432–445. doi:10.1016/j.jvb.2005.10.006

Organization for Economic Co-operation and Development. (2019). *Better life index*. Retrieved from http://www.oecdbetterlifeindex.org/topics/work-life-balance/

Porter, S., & Ayman, R. (2010). Work flexibility as a mediator of the relationship between work–family conflict and intention to quit. *Journal of Management & Organization*, *16*(3), 411–424.

Powell, A., & Craig, L. (2015). Gender differences in working at home and time use patterns: Evidence from Australia. *Work, Employment and Society*, *29*(4), 571–589. doi:10.1177/0950017014568140

Prasopoulou, E., Pouloudi, A., & Panteli, N. (2006). Enacting new temporal boundaries: The role of mobile phones. *European Journal of Information Systems*, *15*(3), 277–284. doi:10.1057/palgrave.ejis.3000617

Putnam, L. L., Myers, K. K., & Gailliard, B. M. (2013). Examining the tensions in workplace flexibility and exploring options for new directions. *Human Relations*, *67*(4), 413–440. doi:10.1177/0018726713495704

Rothbard, N. P., Phillips, K. W., & Dumas, T. L. (2005). Managing multiple roles: Work-family policies and individuals' desires for segmentation. *Organization Science*, *16*(3), 243–258. doi:10.1287/orsc.1050.0124

Salary.com. (2018). *Why and how your employees are wasting time at work*. Retrieved from https://www.salary.com/articles/why-how-your-employees-are-wasting-time-at-work/

Schieman, S., & Glavin, P. (2008). Trouble at the border? Gender, flexibility at work, and the work-home interface. *Social Problems*, *55*(4), 590–611. doi:10.1525p.2008.55.4.590

Scholarios, D., & Marks, A. (2004). Work-life balance and the software worker. *Human Resource Management Journal*, *14*(2), 54–74. doi:10.1111/j.1748-8583.2004.tb00119.x

Shanmugam, M. M., & Agarwal, B. (2019). Support perceptions, flexible work options and career outcomes. *Gender in Management*, *34*(4), 254–286. doi:10.1108/GM-12-2018-0157

Son, J. S., & Chen, C. (2019). Does using a smartphone for work purposes "ruin" your leisure? Examining the role of smartphone use in work-leisure conflict and life satisfaction. *Journal of Leisure Research*, *48*(3-5), 236–257. doi:10.1080/00222216.2018.1534074

Tietze, S., & Musson, G. (2003). The times and temporalities of home-based telework. *Personnel Review*, *32*(4), 438–455. doi:10.1108/00483480310477524

Tomazevic, N., Kozjek, T., & Stare, J. (2014). The consequences of work-family (im)balance: From the point of view of employers and employees. *International Business Research*, *7*(8), 83–100. doi:10.5539/ibr.v7n8p83

Tremblay, D. G., & Genin, É. (2008). Permeability between work and non-work: The case of self-employed IT workers. *Canadian Journal of Communication*, *33*(4), 701–720. doi:10.22230/cjc.2008v33n4a1994

Vanderkam, L. (2015). *I Know How She Does It: How professional women make the most of their time*. New York: Penguin Random House.

Wajcman, J., Bittman, M., & Brown, J. E. (2008). Families without borders: Mobile phones, connectedness and work-home divisions. *Sociology*, *42*(4), 635–652. doi:10.1177/0038038508091620

Wepfer, A. G., Allen, T. D., Brauchli, R., Jenny, G. J., & Bauer, G. F. (2017). Work-life boundaries and well-being: Does work-to-life integration impair well-being through lack of recovery? *Journal of Business and Psychology*, *33*(6), 727–740. doi:10.100710869-017-9520-y

Zheng, C., Molineux, J., Mirshekary, S., & Scarparo, S. (2015). Developing individual and organisational work-life balance strategies to improve employee health and wellbeing. *Employee Relations*, *37*(3), 354–379. doi:10.1108/ER-10-2013-0142

KEY TERMS AND DEFINITIONS

Behavioral Boundary: Acting in a way that enforces a boundary between work and home. Behavioral boundary tactics include using technology to automatically alert clients/co-workers to unavailability and deferring non-critical tasks and communication to work time.

Boundary Integration: Employees assimilate their work and personal time and have both flexibility and permeability. Boundary Theory originally defined boundaries as lying on an integration/segmentation continuum.

Boundary Segmentation: Employees separate their work and personal time and have little flexibility and permeability. Boundary Theory originally defined boundaries as lying on an integration/segmentation continuum.

Communicative Boundary: Setting availability expectations, communicating them clearly to colleagues/clients and family/friends and confronting violators.

Flexibility: How much control an individual has over when and where work is completed. Generally flexible schedules have resulted in positive outcomes.

Permeability: The extent to which an individual integrates the obligations from one role when in the other role. Permeability may differ for the home and work boundary. A permeable home boundary means work responsibilities can intrude on personal time whereas a non-permeable home boundary means work tasks are limited to work time. A permeable work boundary is where personal communication/tasks intrude on work time.

Physical Boundary: Work is assigned to a particular location. When the workplace is a separate location from the home there is an obvious physical boundary. Some telecommuters designate a part of their home as a workspace to create a physical boundary.

Telecommuting: A form of remote work in which organizational employees work from other physical locations. Telecommuting offers a degree of flexibility in where work is completed but may or may not involve flexibility in terms of time.

Temporal (Time) Boundary: Work is assigned to designated days and times. When an employee consciously stops checking email at 7 pm or on the weekend, they are enacting a temporal boundary.

Work-Family Conflict: Occurs when an individual experiences incompatible demands between work and family roles, causing participation in both roles to become more difficult. Researchers have examined the time, strain and behavioral dimensions of work-family conflict as well as directionality (home ® work and work ® home). It is associated with negative outcomes, such as stress, burnout, lower organizational commitment and intention to quit.

Chapter 3
User-Created Online Learning Videos:
Collaborative Knowledge Construction Through Participatory Design

Adesola Olulayo Ogundimu

(iD) https://orcid.org/0000-0003-2813-1873

Carey Business School, Johns Hopkins University, USA

ABSTRACT

Through digital technologies, learning has become more flexible in terms of location and mode of delivery, as well as open opportunities for inquiry, discourse, extension, and application towards the creation of new knowledge. A tendency towards a lack of uniformity in the quality of knowledge produced as well as deviation from the norms that guide content creation and sharing have been envisioned with new modes of knowledge creation and sharing in general. This chapter will synthesize research and strategies on designing high value, engaging online video content, with the aim of equipping creators within participatory, informal learning contexts with approaches for becoming more responsible and effective contributors to the digital ecosystem.

INTRODUCTION

Learning is usually regarded as an experience involving the transfer of information to produce knowledge or elicit the performance of an action or behavior. The nature of learning in the present digital society has taken a form distinct from one in which knowledge was accessed through mediums, artifacts, repositories and knowledge

DOI: 10.4018/978-1-7998-2235-6.ch003

infrastructures that are bound by space and location. Knowledge is no longer seen as residing in the minds of a select few—usually scholars and experts who have been certified credible through an enduring system of appraisal. Channels for the dissemination of information, once administered by educational institutions, libraries and publishers are freer and more open than ever before (Edwards et al., 2013). Enabled by the mechanism of digital media, collective discovery has taken the place of traditional sources of expertise and channels of dissemination.

As information and communication technologies evolve, long-established approaches to learning are increasingly being augmented with digital, technology-driven modes of communication and knowledge sharing. This has given rise to a networked kind of knowledge, which holds much promise for a progressive, information-driven society, but also challenges established ways of understanding and handling knowledge with much uncertainty and complexity. Much of the uncertainty surrounds the difficulty in applying long-standing principles and standards that guide the intellectual value of knowledge towards these new, often networked knowledge forms. While these values and principles for establishing the worth of information and credibility of sources serve as vital gatekeepers for preserving quality and integrity, at the same time, these ideals place limitations on creativity and the true dynamic nature of knowledge.

Just as formal learning has been transformed through digital technologies and media, informal learning opportunities are also becoming increasingly abundant. Learning is even more interest-driven, socially constructed and readily accessible than ever before. Up to 70 percent of millennial users watched YouTube for learning purposes in 2017, with a thirty-eight percent growth in viewing time for learning videos focused on professional, career-related skills alone. Over one million learning videos are shared across the platform each day (YouTube, 2018). In their discourse on the influence of new knowledge forms on conventional learning approaches, Edwards et al. (2013) state that, "networked social forms permit many more participants to comment publicly on knowledge products, bypassing traditional credentialing and certification mechanisms" (p. 7).

Learning according to the U.S. Department of Education, Office of Educational Technology (2017), is now:

both 'lifelong,' happening at all stages throughout a student's life; and 'lifewide,' occurring not just in an educational setting, but at multiple kinds of organizations, such as community or non-traditional providers of education, in their homes, at their places of employment, and in other settings enabled by mobile and portable technology. (p. 8)

Learning (whether formal or informal) can therefore no longer be limited to the forms, mediums and learning spaces that educational institutions and other stakeholders are familiar with and regard as ideal, authentic or safe.

As a corollary, what remains is to encourage methods and techniques for generating and managing new knowledge that support creativity and active involvement in inquiry and vibrant discourse among creators and the consumers of their content. Regarding this, Edwards et al. (2013) emphasize that the changing nature of knowledge requires a response that would "debalkanize scholarship by assembling a methodological repertoire that can match the geographic and temporal scale of emerging knowledge infrastructures" (p. 19). In the face of concerns with preserving the integrity of knowledge, it becomes imperative to help individuals develop the ability to better understand and navigate the changing landscape that new digital information modalities present.

Unlike print media with its mechanisms of appraisal in place as well as rules guiding knowledge creation and distribution, with digital media, much of the focus lies on the responsibility of the information consumer to make judgements regarding the quality of the content. The sheer amount of user-generated content on the web warrants for optimal design, creation and use of the content. It thus becomes crucial to encourage methods and techniques for generating and managing new knowledge that support creativity and active involvement in inquiry and vibrant discourse among creators and consumers of digital content. This chapter continues by examining learning afforded through online video in informal, participatory learning environments. The discourse then moves on to focus on instructional videos created by active contributors within these environments, with the intent of imparting content relevant to viewers' learning needs. Emphasis will be on the importance of good multimedia design from a participatory design perspective, for the creation of relevant, effective and engaging learning videos, as well as the value these considerations have on the quality of the learning objects and the informal collaborative learning experiences they enable.

The Nature of Networked Learning in Participatory Knowledge Spaces

Frameworks for learning in online spaces have emerged to accommodate the shifting dynamics that digital technologies introduce into the nature of learning and more importantly, the social learning relationships that materialize. Indeed, the growth of collective learning paradigms like participatory culture (Jenkins, Clinton, Purushotma, Robison, & Weigel, 2006) and networked learning, also holds much value for informal learning online as well as for integrating media from informal sources within formal learning settings. Based on social theories of learning, the concept of networked learning draws on the relationship that is activated between the affordances that digital information technologies provide, and the processes by which people learn. Steeples and Jones (2002) and subsequently Jones (2015) define networked learning as "learning in which information and communications technology (ICT) is used to promote connections: between one learner and other learners; between learners and tutors; between a learning community and its learning resources" (p. 5).

Here, the network is not necessarily the technology or other digital elements that enable the interchange of information (Jones, 2015; Sloep, 2016). Rather, the focus is on the actors and the interrelationships that form between these individuals. On the information network side of things, the technology does play a crucial role of on one hand facilitating connections but more importantly, mediating these relationships between people and people, as well as the connections between people and information (Goodyear, Banks, Hodgson, & McConnell, 2006; Gourlay & Oliver, 2016). Thus, the technology complements the social learning interactions that take place.

In fact, Markham (2003) describes the Internet as a tool, a place and a way of being (as cited in Gerber, Abrams, Curwood, & Magnifico, 2016, p. 32). An online social network (Facebook, for instance) may be regarded as a learning tool when considering all the nodes, connections and functionalities that enable information sharing. It may also be considered a learning place by examining the interactions that occur within that space to support communication and collaboration. Finally, it may be regarded as a way of being by focusing on the individual and collective actions that members engage in, as well as the influence these actions have on learning-related behavior both online and offline.

At the foundation of the development of information and communication technologies in human society is the need for efficiency in the interchange of knowledge between sources. Therefore, at the core of networked learning is the quality that learning is a dynamic process that involves engaging with others in the network and finding connections within and across networks. This relational view of learning is rooted in foundational theories of learning, particularly, connectivist schools of thought (Jones, 2015). Regarding the parallels between networked learning and connectivism, Jones (2015) writes that:

Connectivism argues that the starting point for learning occurs when knowledge is actuated through the process of a learner connecting to, and providing information in, a networked learning community... Connectivism stresses two important skills that contribute to learning, namely the ability to seek out information, and the ability to filter information. (p. 65)

Learners by virtue of being able to connect to a network (of individuals), are able to share information, while accessing new information relevant to their needs or interests. In fact, in many discussions of connectivism, opportunities to learn or contribute new information are near limitless, and are prized as being more important than the static nature of what is known at any one time (Anderson, 2016; Couros & Hildebrandt, 2016).

Connecting, finding information, and sharing within and across networks all require the elements of self-directedness and individual responsibility that an information user requires to demonstrate digital literacy. As Anderson (2016) puts it, the requirements of an ever evolving digital society "demands that education move beyond instructing and testing for learner competencies, and toward supporting learners in a journey to capacity rather than competency" (p. 42). This is especially important when considering the relative ease and subtlety with which a learner can combine, connect and shift between information sources.

With the multitude of networked digital media and media-sharing spaces available on the web, the need for individuals to develop new media literacies and skills for understanding and using digital media, as well as for participating in a multimedia rich environment has been emphasized (Jenkins et al., 2006). Building upon and extending traditional literacy and information literacy principles, this new set of skills and attitudes is applicable to the use of new media and the engagement of individuals in collective meaning making. These skills equip individuals to be critical consumers of information, but also enable them to be active and creative contributors to our digital ecosystem (Jenkins et al., 2006). Media creators as contributors should therefore have the ability to employ a deliberate and systematic approach to creating content that is capable of adequately meeting the needs of their intended audience.

A distinction however exists between the design elements this chapter will examine and the instructional design approaches typically implemented in the development of formal learning content and experiences. What is covered in this chapter relates more to learning design than instructional design. The former encompasses the type of design that Sloep (2016) makes a case for through their emphasis on the learner-centered nature of networked learning by stating that "learning design seeks to put the learner at the focus of the attention while instructional design focuses more on the instructor role" (p. 44). Under learning design, the creative process of crafting learning content and experiences in this case is more open, pedagogically informed based on learning needs and preferences and is supported by judicious technology use (Conole, 2012).

The informal nature of many participatory online learning networks makes the responsibility for selecting learning content, platforms and experiences more user-defined. Individuals as learners are able to chart their own learning course, select content and media that interests them, and make decisions on the quality and relevance of such content, all while taking cues from the conversations and contributions of other individuals within their network/networks. As content creators and co-producers, their approach to producing learning content is more prescriptive and would benefit from alignment with the needs of their audience. The design of learning treated in the following sections is targeted at supporting the advancement of the learning goals of participants in the learning network.

Multimedia Learning Through Video

Much of the research on multimedia learning attempts to explain the elements that make multimedia—including but not limited to video—a compelling and often effective medium for learning. Simply put, multimedia learning is learning that is based on the development of meaning from a combination of words and pictures (Mayer, 2014). When used alone, words (in text or verbal form) or pictures (in still or moving form) can be an effective medium of communication and representation. However, a combination of both leverages the cognitive capabilities of the human mind to integrate both forms towards faster and more powerful information processing (Butcher, 2014; Mayer, 2014). Following this rationale, with multimedia, the presentation of visual and verbal cues if complementary, amplifies the ability of the human mind to comprehend and retain information. Thus, for such a combination to be effective in its delivery of the intended learning message, an understanding of the cognitive processes that underlie multimedia learning and the application of suitable multimedia learning design techniques is crucial.

Bétrancourt and Benetos (2018) employ a tri-fold representational, cognitive (perceptual) and instructional treatment to address the elements and conditions in instructional video that stimulate learning. Instructional videos in this case are intended to support learning about specific topics or skills and are therefore distinct from entertainment videos (de Koning, Hoogerheide, & Boucheix, 2018; Fiorella & Mayer, 2018). Regarding the representational nature of the video format as mode of communication and expression, Bétrancourt and Benetos (2018) indicate that the "dynamic visualizations" in video enable "depictions that change continuously over time and represent a continuous flow of motion" (p. 472), and are therefore effective for conveying a combination of visual and verbal learning content to the viewer.

Even more recognized in the literature on multimedia learning through video is the cognitive perspective. The continuous flow of information in video places a demand on cognitive resources and mechanisms, such that for learning to result, sufficient capacity is required for information processing and working memory (Paas & Sweller, 2014). A variety of instructional approaches have emerged around the use of video for learning particularly in both formal and informal contexts including lectures, tutorials used to demonstrate specific tasks or procedural steps, animation and so on.

Within formal learning environments, educators have used a variety of video content sources and formats to support instruction in face-to-face, hybrid and fully online learning modalities. This may be in the form of instructor-created content shown in class or made available for independent viewing by students via a dedicated platform or via video hosting and sharing platforms. Original instructional content created by individuals, organizations or a third-party source other than the teacher may also be adapted to augment classroom instruction (Alpert, 2016).

Alternately, content originally intended for non-education-related purposes but which possess instructional value or relevance can be repurposed to function as stand-alone or supplemental units of instruction to provide an illustration of real life events or rare occurrences. For instance, a documentary on a historical event may serve as a valuable artifact to facilitate understanding of the history of a specific time period. In any of these instances, the responsibility is usually on the teacher to evaluate content and choose media that align with their learning objectives (Jones & Cuthrell, 2011).

Approaches for educational video use within formal learning typically depend on the learning goal, the subject area, recognition of the usefulness of multimedia for driving student engagement, availability of relevant third-party created content or willingness to devote the time, effort and skill towards creation of original content in addition to other pedagogical considerations (Alpert, 2016). Within informal learning, digital literacy skills for finding and connecting to learning content are the learner's responsibility. The individual thus determines what content will best support the achievement of self-determined goals, whether those are merely interest-based or more directed towards developing skills that are directly transferable to specific personal or work life needs.

Regardless of the learning context, the design of learning content should be focused on the creation of resources that are relevant to the problems and issues individuals are interested in learning how to tackle. Also, effective video designs for learning have been shown to combine that which is known about human cognitive processes and the human memory, with multimedia principles to achieve a compelling information presentation. The application of these principles tailored towards specific content types and learning goals has been proven as holding value for learning effectiveness (Guo, Kim, & Rubin, 2014; van der Meij & van der Meij, 2013).

Video-Based Learning in Participatory Spaces

A combination of technology development factors have spurred the ubiquity of video creation and consumption in the 21st century, including the greatly improved functionality and affordability of digital video production equipment, particularly mobile devices. The evolution of the internet with exponential gains in access, capacity and speed, attended by the emergence of various platforms for creative expression and video streaming, have also aided the hosting of video content online, thus furnishing easier channels for access and seamless redistribution.

Numerous participatory knowledge spaces, which leverage video hosting and sharing capabilities for learning, now exist via online video platforms such as YouTube and Vimeo, social media platforms like Facebook, Instagram and LinkedIn and even cMOOCs (Connectivist Massive Open Online Courses). Some of these video hosting platforms initially emerged as technical solutions for sharing video and other multimedia content online. However, this purpose gradually evolved from merely serving as a technical platform for digital media transfer and sharing, to serving a more social purpose, by opening up opportunities for an online community (and eventually multiple communities) to be formed.

The participatory features of these media-sharing sites allow for multimedia expression, while drawing on the power of the collective intellect to create an abundance of media for a variety of purposes, but more particularly, learning media. These features, while social in nature are enabled and mediated by technical functionalities which may include a content rating system of likes or dislikes as well as a commenting feature which in particular lends itself as an avenue for interaction and building collective intelligence through critical discourse. Other features may include an embeddable video player that functions well for integration into web pages or external platforms as well as sharing options to multiple other social media platforms. Even more functionalities that bolster easy access include autogenerated recommendations of related videos and a system for content organization through channels within which playlists can be compiled around specific topics, such that creators can curate related videos into categories and recommendations of related videos. The latter set of features are beneficial for helping viewers find additional sources for extending learning or where applicable, comparing sources to establish credibility.

Of the aforementioned platforms, YouTube is perhaps the video platform with the widest reach, and has become one of the most widely recognized online environments for multimedia expression. Individuals and groups all around the world often rely on videos on this multimedia-friendly social platform for meaningful learning. From scientific curiosities, self-improvement tutorials, in-depth "do it yourself" guides, homework help created and shared by private individuals providing detailed content regarding a subject or step-by-step guidance for solving a problem; to educational content, webinars and training materials and even full courses or standalone learning modules put together by educational institutions and business corporations, a variety of learning media exists on the platform.

The combination of media production and dissemination as well as social networking capabilities within a single location affords an ideal creative and sociotechnical space, which often embodies several of the characteristics of participatory culture as described by Jenkins et al. (2006). The relative ease with which individuals are able to access the platform and interact as viewers or contributors poses little to no restrictions on creative expression. When combined with the potential of receiving some form of recognition and acknowledgement, individuals' motivation to engage in various forms of intellectual, civic and artistic expression is heightened.

The nature of interactions within these online environments is such that members are able to experience a sense of connectedness and community from the support and feedback they receive for their work in the form of likes or dislikes, comments and shares, as well as from providing support and feedback to content created or shared by others. User engagement thus varies from passive viewing of content, to more active forms of engagement by providing feedback that may influence other users' interaction with such media, or establishing an online presence by communicating with others. Even more active participation takes place when users engage in the creation of content.

Also, a system of informal mentorship as described by Jenkins et al. (2006) can be said to exist with media created and made available to others with the intent of providing information on a specific subject or guiding others to perform an action based on personal experience or expertise. Content that is instructional or educational in nature may be produced by expert individuals or groups for an intellectually enhancing or skill-building purpose directed at novices. This is especially true in the case of educators seeking to extend their instruction beyond the formal classroom or online course environment through custom-created videos, as well as other professionals with specialized training, experience or facility with a skilled area. Such content may emerge based on a felt need on the part of the creator or as a result of an expressed need from viewers or subscribers within the online community.

Recognizing the value these educational videos have for informal learning, platforms like YouTube have put together resources to support the creative process for educational video creators. *YouTube Learning*, an initiative to support the platform's community of educational content creators was announced in July of 2018. In addition to providing funding support, a dedicated *Learning* channel, partnerships with other online learning platforms as well as conferences and courses for creators are all resources offered under this initiative (YouTube, 2018). The development of programs like this signals the value of resources that support educational media creators towards achieving success in their creative endeavors and increasing the presence and value of multimedia content for learning.

When digital media is created with an instructional goal, it becomes even more crucial for creators to engage in content creation and design approaches that combine sound, authoritative knowledge of the content with clear delivery that employs relevant illustrations and purposeful applications of the technology. Much of the research and evaluation of video content in participatory digital environments has focused on the informational value of the content. Focus has been on the authority and credibility of creators from the standpoint of their content expertise (Bloom & Johnston, 2010; Jones & Cuthrell, 2011; ten Hove & van der Meij, 2015), and not so much on creators' facility with the planning and delivery of the content from a design standpoint. Even within formal learning designs, the application of design approaches informed by research and best practices in multimedia design in the creation of instructional video is limited (de Koning, Hoogerheide, & Boucheix, 2018).

CHARACTERIZING VIDEO DESIGN IN PARTICIPATORY LEARNING SPACES

The need for content creators and prosumers to realize the far-reaching impact of their creations on their audience has been emphasized in the research literature. Jenkins et al. (2006) express the importance of being "more reflective about the ethical choices they make as participants and communicators and the impact they have on others" (p. 17). New media skills are therefore highly crucial for both knowledge consumers and producers in participatory knowledge spaces. These skills although reminiscent of traditional information literacy skills are extensions that lend special applicability to the rather dynamic nature of networked knowledge in a digital age.

Generally, the research on media literacies for contributing to participatory media environments address skills for engaging with media forms in participatory spaces like play, simulation and performance; skills for using and adapting content ethically like appropriation, multi-tasking, distributed cognition, and judgment; as well as relational skills like collective intelligence, judgment, transmedia navigation, networking and negotiation (Jenkins et al., 2006). While these provide a broad treatment of relevant social skills and cultural competencies, they focus less on key multimedia learning design principles and the broader science on how learning through media occurs.

Knowledge creation within participatory learning spaces thus presents opportunities for design principles and practices to emerge to match the dynamic nature of learning and learners in these spaces. While a participatory design approach has been recommended as holding much potential for ensuring alignment between the needs of consumers and the goals of creators of content in participatory creative spaces (Edwards et al., 2013), well-grounded design frameworks dedicated to media design, specifically for online video within participatory informal learning contexts are scarce.

The design considerations addressed in this chapter integrate fundamental multimedia design principles and research on key elements of engaging instructional video with the form of participatory design that is typical of participatory learning spaces. The design of content in these spaces is based in part on the motivations of creators as active members who are privy to the learning interests, goals and needs of other participants. The result is an integrative approach that is rooted in sound design principles and draws on empirical research (Conole, 2012; Fiorella & Mayer, 2018; Kiili, 2006; Mayer, 2008) but more importantly, is more readily transferable to participatory learning contexts to inform creative endeavors that are geared towards achieving learning content that is appealing to the intended audience.

Effective learning is often measured via assessments of how well learners are able to master and demonstrate the knowledge and skills identified as the goal of learning (typically presented as learning objectives). Such measures that capture the progression from contact with the content to successful application of knowledge or skills performance are harder to gather in informal, participatory contexts in which the media serves an instructional purpose. Instead, metrics such as views, likes, comments and shares are used as key measures for assessing users' reception of the content, engagement, and to some extent, perceptions of utility. Such metrics are also useful for identifying successful online instructional videos but more importantly, for highlighting the attributes that make such videos valuable and engaging for viewers. Therefore, the extension of relevant multimedia design principles and research-based best practices for effective video-based multimedia learning is fitting to support the creation of informal online instructional videos. Viewing time—the length of time expended while viewing video content—has been identified as an indicator of engagement in a study of student engagement in MOOC videos by Guo et al. (2014). Short videos (six minutes or less) were found to have longer viewing times relative to the video length, and were therefore more engaging for learners. One explanation they provide for this is the fact that short videos are more content-rich due to the planning and scripting required to cut down on filler content, making them more valuable to viewers. Related to succinctness in length, segmenting of longer videos into meaningful parts that support learner control (Fiorella & Mayer, 2018) and pacing (van der Meij & van der Meij, 2013) have been identified as key features that enhance learning through video. Relatively fast-paced narrative speed in terms of the number of words spoken per minute by the narrator (upwards of 160 words per minute) is also a recognized attribute of engaging MOOC videos (Guo et al., 2014) and popular instructional YouTube videos (ten Hove & van der Meij, 2015).

All three of these attributes operate on the consideration of the cognitive load for the viewer. Recalling the discussion of the cognitive conditions under which learning occurs in the previous section on multimedia learning through video, it is known that due to the dynamic manner in which information is presented via video, information processing capacity is quickly used up. Good design of learning videos therefore takes this "cognitive load" (Mayer, 2008; Paas, 2014) into account, by planning the content in advance and using techniques that highlight the most salient information, hence the value of conciseness and segmentation.

A relational component has also been noted as having the potential to elicit connections between the viewer and the instructor or speaker. Guo et al. (2014) recommend that talking head videos make the viewing experience more relatable with gains in student engagement being recorded in their study. The efficacy of this measure has been questioned by Fiorella and Mayer (2018) on the basis of possible increases on cognitive load, where the viewer is faced with the choice of focusing on the instructor's face and facial cues, or devoting their mental processes towards understanding and visualizing actual content. However, the use of a human voice for narration has been recommended by van der Meij and van der Meij (2013).

The video format in terms of structure and approach has also been shown to be impactful on engagement. Lecture-style recordings, screen captures, step-by-step demonstrations and animation are among the most common formats in use. The choice of an ideal format would primarily be determined by the nature of the content as either declarative (conceptual or factual) or procedural (involving the presentation of steps for completing a task), and the kind of illustrations and visuals necessary to support such content. Just as important as relevance is the ease of finding and accessing video content. Learners in need of specific content will often perform a search for suitable resources using key terms that are relevant to the concepts or skills they are interested in learning about. Using video titles that make judicious use of key terms is therefore key to supporting easy access (van der Meij, & van der Meij, 2013).

A Participatory Approach to Video Design

Participatory design is user-focused design with opportunities in place that enable the end user to engage with the creative process. The focus here is on co-creation with the intent of enhancing usability. While this approach has its origins in the Human-Centered Computing or Human Computer Interaction domain, it is not entirely new in the learning sciences especially when considering models like user-design, co-design and similar frameworks in the instructional design domain that place emphasis on a design partnership between designers and users of the design (Hoadley, 2017a). Participatory approaches have been recommended for the design of learning content, tools and activities to involve collaboration between the designer and the teacher, as well as learners who are typically the target users of the new or improved learning intervention (Hoadley, 2017b; Kiili, 2005; Kiili, 2006; Könings, Seidel, & van Merriënboer, 2014).

Unless expressly determined as the design approach of choice prior to the beginning of the design effort, the application of participatory design towards the creation of learning content is rare and may often be retrospective. Often, in traditional educational contexts, the content and activities have a clear, readily definable learning audience, a specified curriculum, clear assessments and measures of learning, as well as definite channels for instruction, interaction and engagement. These predefined attributes are often based on inferences drawn from prior instructional practice and at best, may have a research-basis. However, they in many ways reinforce the suboptimal design approaches that Conole (2012) describe as belief-based and therefore implemented in support of implicit goals. Rather, learning design approaches that are explicit and are rooted in reflection and collaboration between stakeholders have been recommended as holding more promise.

Participatory meaning making and knowledge construction in particular are not at all new within informal collaborative learning settings. Several of the examples of collaborative learning environments introduced earlier in this chapter demonstrate elements of collaborative design in an integral form. The design of learning in cMOOCs makes a good case in point. This category of MOOCs is driven by principles of learner autonomy, diversity, openness and interactivity (Downes, 2013). Here, learners are also active contributors to the learning content and activities either through direct creation of tutorials or indirectly as they interact with peers through discussion forums and peer feedback on shared content. The dual identity of the media creator as the designer, but equally as an active participant in the learning community blurs out some of the barriers, tensions and power dynamics that may be more evident in formal instances of participatory learning design. In fact, in such instances, the user may perceive their agency to be subordinate to the agency of the designer or teacher (Hoadley, 2017b). Thus the informal nature of the learning environment in cMOOCs, media-sharing sites, social media and other participatory learning spaces is well suited for a participatory design approach.

In video designs for informal participatory learning therefore, the needs and interests of learners should be central to the design and development process. Designing for a target audience for which specifics about prior knowledge and learning needs are so diverse thus requires careful deliberation. This audience may likely include new and existing members of the learning network as well as visitors whose point of connection to the network may be select videos that are relevant to specific goals or needs. Within the context of networked learning and participatory learning environments however, the creator's identity as a member of the network and their interests as a producer or co-producer, actively engaged in creating useful and meaningful learning media, may often be indicative of the interests of other members of the network. This may therefore provide a starting point for deciphering the interests of the audience. As Figure 1 illustrates, the interests and expertise of the creator play into the choice of the topic and learning goals for the media to be designed. While the relevance of the content to potential learners is certainly key, the media creator's grasp of the content is of importance. Since the goal is to create useful and meaningful content, the successful execution of this goal would to a significant degree depend on whether the subject is within the creator's sphere of knowledge or expertise.

Figure 1. Design considerations for user-created online learning videos

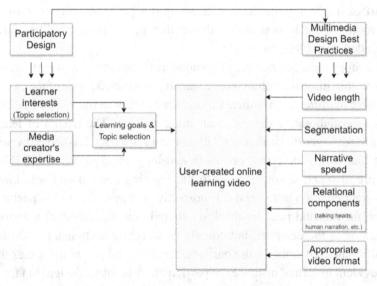

A participatory design approach when employed correctly should however take the task of topic selection beyond speculation on possible interests of the audience. This is where the creator's identity as a member of the learning community serves as an opportunity to engage the other members in the design process. While the creator can set the parameters and confines of the content within a specific area of focus or expertise, the goals of other learners may differ. The task of selecting a topic or content area should be informed by input from active participants in the learning environment.

Knowing the interests of the members of the learning network to whom the content will be delivered is key to designing content that is relevant and therefore, useful for helping users achieve their learning goals. Engaging other participants in defining the content choice and scope also raises questions of expertise and credibility early on in the knowledge creation and sharing process. Since learning in these environments is interest based, the end-user selects content that fits their learning needs and a video format or style that best supports their learning. Participatory design is thus key to deciphering several of the other key video characteristics previously identified in this chapter.

CONCLUSION

This chapter's discourse supports participatory knowledge construction in informal learning environments by outlining complementary strategies for the design of multimedia content and videos. The goal here is to expand opportunities for the transfer of knowledge from individual cognitive processes to a collectively constructed setting within a connected information-sharing environment. Serrat, 2017 explains this as follows:

The units of knowledge production are both the individual and the collective. Learning organizations understand that while knowledge is created in the minds of individuals, knowledge development thrives in a rich web of social contact among individuals, groups, and organizations. (Serrat, 2017, p. 61)

For the participants and co-contributors this chapter has focused on, the individual cognitive process entails identifying an area of expertise for which there is a shared common interest or need by other members of the network. Here, individual knowledge is parsed and processed into units of knowledge to be shared at the social group level. Then follows the individual learning through multimedia, in which each member of the learning network engages in the process of parsing, processing and making meaning out the learning content to support knowledge acquisition or the performance of a productive activity where applicable.

Expounding on the relation of cognitive and social systems, Cress and Kimmerle (2017) explain that cognitive systems are made up of sending and receiving cognitive entities—in our case both the media creator and their audience—each of which may be exclusive in their own processes of thinking, understanding of cognitive stimuli and meaning making. They write:

Understanding is contingent upon what a sender selects and how he/she puts it into words and it is contingent upon the way in which a recipient observes and understands the message. Because communication is so unpredictable, a receiving cognitive system tries to ensure that its own interpretation of the other's message is approximately congruent with the information the sender initially wanted to express. The best way to achieve this is further communication. (Cress & Kimmerle, 2017, p. 134)

Chinn and Sandoval (2018) regard this as an epistemic cognition involving social processes that begin with knowledge construction at the individual level, progressing to analyses and discussions between individuals, which further expand to community or system-wide interactions. The latter not only entails the dispersion of ideas, but also an informal system of peer review in which constituent members of the network weigh-in and offer critique on shared knowledge. These system-wide interactions function as a mechanism for the social-regulation of legitimacy by which individuals are held accountable for their contributions.

As digital age knowledge practices open up opportunities and challenge our understanding and approach towards the processes through which knowledge is created or spread, questions of quality, intellectual worth and value of content in collaborative knowledge spaces remain. The answers are often limited and somewhat inscrutable in their reach. One reaction would be to impose limitations on the growth of participatory channels of knowledge creation or to regard such channels as entirely lacking in value and credibility. Limitations of this form would not only be ineffective, but would also undervalue the rich informal learning interactions individuals engage in within participatory environments. While the majority of these interactions take place beyond the confines of formal educational systems, the vibrant interactions and collective intellectual processes that take place, serve to validate shared learning towards the enhancement of the knowledge, skills and abilities that emerge from the learning process for all participants.

FUTURE RESEARCH DIRECTIONS

Since the advent of participatory online environments, concerns regarding the place and value of learning in these spaces have been raised. The need to empower individuals to develop digital and new media literacy skills has been central to these concerns. As established in this chapter, much progress has been made in the research on multimedia design within traditional frameworks of learning, a considerable proportion of which is translatable to informal learning environments. However, an understanding of the form and direction that these design approaches take within actual informal participatory contexts is still mostly speculative. Further inquiry is needed into how and to what extent creators consciously engage in a deliberative design process prior to content development. The key questions that such research endeavors should examine include: How might intending producers and co-producers recognize the need for conscious, participatory design? How should they design for a largely unknown audience of learners and information users? How might they encounter the support and resources they need? What effects are observable or measurable from participatory designs that would help inform future work on the subject? How might these findings inform participatory design in formal educational contexts?

REFERENCES

Anderson, T. (2016). Theories for learning with emerging technologies. In G. Veletsianos (Ed.), *Emergence and Innovation in Digital Learning: Foundations and applications* (pp. 35–50). Edmonton, Canada: Athabasca University Press.

Bétrancourt, M., & Benetos, K. (2018). Why and when does instructional video facilitate learning? A commentary to the special issue "developments and trends in learning with instructional video". *Computers in Human Behavior*, *89*, 471–475. doi:10.1016/j.chb.2018.08.035

Bloom, K., & Johnston, K. M. (2010). Digging into YouTube videos: Using media literacy and participatory culture to promote cross-cultural understanding. *The Journal of Media Literacy Education*, *2*(2), 113–123.

Burgess, J., & Green, J. (2009). *YouTube: Online video and participatory culture*. Cambridge, UK: Polity Press.

Butcher, K. (2014). The multimedia principle. In R. Mayer (Ed.), *The Cambridge Handbook of Multimedia Learning* (pp. 174–205). Cambridge, UK: Cambridge University Press. doi:10.1017/CBO9781139547369.010

Chau, C. (2010). YouTube as a participatory culture. *New Directions for Youth Development*, *128*(128), 65–74. doi:10.1002/yd.376 PMID:21240954

Chinn, C., & Sandoval, W. (2018). Epistemic cognition and epistemic development. In F. Fischer, C. E., Hmelo-Silver, S. R., Goldman, & P., Reimann, (Eds.), International Handbook of the Learning Sciences (pp. 24-33). New York: Routledge. doi:10.4324/9781315617572-3

Conole, G. (2012). *Designing for Learning in an Open World*. New York: Springer.

Couros, A., & Hildebrandt, K. (2016). Designing for open and social learning. In G. Veletsianos (Ed.), *Emergence and Innovation in Digital Learning: Foundations and applications* (pp. 143–161). Edmonton, Canada: Athabasca University Press.

Cress, U., & Kimmerle, J. (2017). The Interrelations of individual learning and collective knowledge construction: A cognitive-systemic framework. In S. Schwan & U. Cress (Eds.), *The Psychology of Digital Learning*. New York: Springer. doi:10.1007/978-3-319-49077-9_7

de Koning, B. B., Hoogerheide, V., & Boucheix, J. M. (2018). Developments and trends in learning with instructional video. *Computers in Human Behavior, 89,* 395–398. doi:10.1016/j.chb.2018.08.055

Downes, S. (2007). Models for sustainable open educational resources. *Interdisciplinary Journal of Knowledge and Learning Objects, 3,* 29–44.

Downes, S. (2013). The quality of massive open online courses. In International Handbook of e-learning (pp. 65-77). New York: Routledge.

Edwards, P. N., Jackson, S. J., Chalmers, M. K., Bowker, G. C., Borgman, C. L., Ribes, D., ... Calvert, S. (2013). *Knowledge Infrastructures: Intellectual frameworks and research challenges*. Ann Arbor, MI: Deep Blue.

Fiorella, L., & Mayer, R. E. (2018). What works and doesn't work with instructional video. *Computers in Human Behavior, 89,* 465–470. doi:10.1016/j.chb.2018.07.015

Gerber, H. R., Abrams, S. S., Curwood, J. S., & Magnifico, A. M. (2016). *Conducting Qualitative Research of Learning in Online Spaces*. Thousand Oaks, CA: SAGE.

Goodyear, P. M., Banks, S., Hodgson, V., & McConnell, D. (Eds.). (2006). *Advances in Research on Networked Learning* (Vol. 4). Boston, MA: Kluwer Academic Publishers.

Gourlay, L., & Oliver, M. (2016). It's not all about the learner: Reframing students' digital literacy as sociomaterial practice. In T. Ryberg, C. Sinclair, S. Bayne, & M. De Laat (Eds.), *Research, Boundaries, and Policy in Networked Learning* (pp. 77–92). New York: Springer. doi:10.1007/978-3-319-31130-2_5

Guo, P. J., Kim, J., & Rubin, R. (2014). How video production affects student engagement: An empirical study of MOOC videos. *Proceedings of the First ACM Conference on Learning @ Scale Conference* (pp. 41-50). New York: Association for Computing Machinery. 10.1145/2556325.2566239

Hoadley, C. (2017a). Conversation: Viewing participatory design from the learning sciences and the field of design. In Participatory Design for Learning: Perspectives from practice and research (pp. 28-42). New York: Routledge.

Hoadley, C. (2017b). How participatory design has influenced the learning sciences. In Participatory Design for Learning: Perspectives from practice and research (pp. 22-27). New York: Routledge. doi:10.4324/9781315630830-4

Ito, M., Gutiérrez, K., Livingstone, S., Penuel, B., Rhodes, J., Salen, K., ... Watkins, S. C. (2013). *Connected Learning: An agenda for research and design*. Irvine, CA: Digital Media and Learning Research Hub.

Jenkins, J., Clinton, K., Purushotma, R., Robison, A. J., & Weigel, M. (2006). *Confronting the Challenges of Participatory Culture: Media education for the 21st century*. Cambridge, MA: MIT Press.

Jonassen, D., Spector, M. J., Driscoll, M., Merrill, M. D., van Merrienboer, J., & Driscoll, M. P. (2008). *Handbook of Research on Educational Communications and Technology: A project of the association for educational communications and technology*. New York: Routledge. doi:10.4324/9780203880869

Jones, C. (2015). *Networked Learning: An educational paradigm for the age of digital networks*. New York: Springer. doi:10.1007/978-3-319-01934-5

Jones, C., & Healing, G. (2010a). Learning nests and local habitations. *Proceedings of the 7th International Conference on Networked Learning*, L. Dirckinck-Holmfeld, V. Hodgson, C. Jones, D. McConnell, & T. Ryberg (Eds.). Aalborg, Denmark: Conference on Networked Learning.

Jones, T., & Cuthrell, K. (2011). YouTube: Educational potentials and pitfalls. *Computers in the Schools*, *28*(1), 75–85. doi:10.1080/07380569.2011.553149

Keppell, M., Suddaby, G., & Hard, N. (2015). Assuring best practice in technology-enhanced learning environments. *Research in Learning Technology*, *23*(1), 1–13. doi:10.3402/rlt.v23.25728

Kiili, K. (2005). Digital game-based learning: Towards an experiential gaming model. *The Internet and Higher Education*, *8*(1), 13–24. doi:10.1016/j.iheduc.2004.12.001

Kiili, K. (2006). Towards a participatory multimedia learning model. *Education and Information Technologies*, *11*(1), 21–32. doi:10.100710639-005-5711-7

Könings, K. D., Seidel, T., & van Merriënboer, J. J. (2014). Participatory design of learning environments: Integrating perspectives of students, teachers, and designers. *Instructional Science*, *42*(1), 1–9. doi:10.100711251-013-9305-2

Mayer, R. (2014). Introduction to multimedia learning. In R. Mayer (Ed.), *The Cambridge Handbook of Multimedia Learning* (pp. 1–24). Cambridge, UK: Cambridge University Press.

Mayer, R. E. (2008). Applying the science of learning: Evidence-based principles for the design of multimedia instruction. *The American Psychologist, 63*(8), 760–769. doi:10.1037/0003-066X.63.8.760 PMID:19014238

Nye, D. E. (2006). *Technology Matters: Questions to live with*. Cambridge, MA: MIT Press.

Paas, F., & Sweller, J. (2014). Implications of cognitive load theory for multimedia learning. In R. Mayer (Ed.), *The Cambridge Handbook of Multimedia Learning* (pp. 27–42). Cambridge, UK: Cambridge University Press. doi:10.1017/CBO9781139547369.004

Reigeluth, C. M., Beatty, B. J., & Myers, R. D. (Eds.). (2016). Instructional-design Theories and Models: Vol. IV. *The learner-centered paradigm of education*. New York: Routledge.

Serrat, O. (2017). *Knowledge Solutions: Tools, methods, and approaches to drive organizational performance*. New York: Springer. doi:10.1007/978-981-10-0983-9

Sloep, P. B. (2016). Design for networked learning. In The Future of Ubiquitous Learning: Learning designs for emerging pedagogies (pp. 41-58). New York: Springer. doi:10.1007/978-3-662-47724-3_3

Steeples, C., & Jones, C. (Eds.). (2002). *Networked Learning: Perspectives and issues*. New York: Springer. doi:10.1007/978-1-4471-0181-9

ten Hove, P., & van der Meij, H. (2015). Like it or not. What characterizes YouTube's more popular instructional videos. *Technical Communication (Washington), 62*(1), 48–62.

U.S. Department of Education, Office of Educational Technology. (2017). *Reimagining the Role of Technology in Higher Education: A supplement to the national education technology plan*. Retrieved from https://tech.ed.gov/netp/

van der Meij, H., & van der Meij, J. (2013). Eight guidelines for the design of instructional videos for software training. *Technical Communication (Washington), 60*(3), 205–228.

Weinberger, D. (2011). *Too Big to Know: Rethinking knowledge now that the facts aren't the facts, experts are everywhere, and the smartest person in the room is the room*. New York: Basic Books.

YouTube. (2018). *Learning Best Practices*. Retrieved from http://services.google.com/fh/files/blogs/youtube_learning_best_practices.pdf

YouTube. (2018). *YouTube Learning: Investing in educational creators, resources, and tools for edutubers*. Retrieved from https://youtube.googleblog.com/2018/10/youtube-learning-investing-in.html

KEY TERMS AND DEFINITIONS

Informal Learning: A form of learning in which individuals engage with content and activities outside of the context of classrooms, schools and similar educational structures.

Learning Design: A process for designing learning content and experiences that places emphasis on the needs, goals and attributes of the learner.

Media Literacy: The collection of knowledge, skills, and attitudes required for engaging in ethical use of digital media for learning, creative expression and productive activity.

Multimedia Learning: Learning that combines words and pictures towards the representation of meanings.

Networked Learning: A relational type of learning in which digital technologies not only support information exchange, but also enable social learning interactions.

Participatory Culture: A culture that affords individuals dual roles as members and active contributors through opportunities to exercise creative agency.

Chapter 4

A Composite Risk Model for Optimizing Information System Security

Yahel Giat

iD https://orcid.org/0000-0001-7296-8852
Jerusalem College of Technology, Israel

Michael Dreyfuss
Jerusalem College of Technology, Israel

ABSTRACT

This chapter describes a two-step decision-support risk model that focuses on investment in information technology security. In the first step, the risk level of each of the system's components is mapped with the goal of identifying the subsystems that pose the highest risk. In the second step, the model determines how much to invest in various technological tools and workplace culture programs to enhance information security. The mode is applied to an information system in an academic institution in Israel. This system comprises 10 subsystems and the three that are responsible to most of the risk are identified. These findings are then used to determine the parameters of the investment allocation problem and find the optimal investment plan. The results of the model's application indicate that monetary incentives and grade cheating are the greatest threats to the system's security. In addition, the results provide support to the claim that information security officials tend to overinvest in security technological tools and underinvest in improving security workplace culture.

DOI: 10.4018/978-1-7998-2235-6.ch004

INTRODUCTION

The task of strengthening information security poses a serious dilemma for universities. On the one hand, universities store valuable and personal information in their systems that must be protected diligently. On the other hand, universities are missioned with promoting inclusiveness, openness and the dissemination of information and knowledge (Doherty, Anastasakis, & Fulford, 2009; Mensch & Wilkie, 2011). Increased security protocols inevitably hinder these missions. Furthermore, being public institutions the challenges that universities face with information security are exacerbated by budgetary and regulatory constraints. The budget, therefore, must be used efficiently to pursue strategies and purchase technological tools that achieve the "best bang for the buck".

In order to determine the optimal investment scheme while avoiding an overreaching security system, it is important for the security staff to identify the riskiest elements of their information system and determine the best tools to improve the security of these elements. Doing so provides the following benefits to the institution:

1. It enables the dissemination of academic knowledge without allowing malicious entities from exploiting this welcoming environment. This is achieved by strengthening security only on the riskiest and most sensitive modules, leaving the majority of the information system less restrictive to users;
2. It enables the information technology (IT) department's management to place higher emphasis on the technological tools and security policies that affect mainly the components that are in the most need of improved security;
3. It allows university managers to use this knowledge to improve their understanding of the nature of the information-related threats that they face. For example, it is possible that student hacking and cheating may pose a bigger threat to the university than issues of propriety rights ownership (i.e. industrial espionage), people's privacy and so forth.

The study described in this chapter has two main goals:

1. The first goal is to develop a two-step IT risk-management decision support model. This model emphasizes breaches and risks that are related to the human factor, with further stress on inside-users;
2. The second goal is to apply the decision support model to an academic institution in Israel to identify the security-related investment needs according to the model's results. To achieve this goal, a two-step risk management model to identify the critical components of an academic institution's information system is proposed. In the first step, the subsystems of the institution's information system are

identified with the riskiest subsystems further highlighted using a composite risk index model. In the second step, a mixed-integer optimization problem is developed. The goal of the problem is to determine the budget allocate that maximizes the IT security. The model is then applied in a technology-oriented academic institution and its output is used to help security managers identify the riskiest components of their system and decide on how to distribute their investment in improving their system security.

The main finding of the study is the practical recommendation of how to allocate investment among the menu of possible technological tools and workplace culture programs. In addition, two theoretical contributions can be made based on the results of the application. First, the results indicate that student-related hacking is a major security concern to the organization together with the more "traditional" risks motivated by monetary reasons. Second, by comparing the current investment scheme with the model's recommended investment scheme the results suggest that security officers place more emphasis on technological tools rather than improve workplace culture.

BACKGROUND

University Information Technology Security

Due to the universities' role as knowledge-intensive organizations, protecting their information is a public policy priority (Mok, 2005). Despite the value of the informaabletion stored in their systems, Mensch and Wilkie (2011) find that "universities openly share a substantial amount of information and data, web sites are rarely banned and message content is not filtered" (p. 91). Beyond the need to prevent the theft of valuable information, universities must also deal with the growing problem of student cheating. Three of four college students reported cheating at some point during their studies (Dick et al., 2003), with student cheating including hacking into the information systems to change grades (Smith, 2014). Chapman, Chinnaswamy, and Garcia-Perez (2018) analyzed cyber security-related data from many universities in the United Kingdom and found students' motivation for hacking goes beyond cheating and may result from boredom, disgruntled feelings, as well as a sense of euphoria that is associated with hacking.

The importance of IT security in universities has led to the development of a variety of models. Sridhar & Ahuja (2007) present an implementation of security management infrastructure in a business school in India and Drevin, Kruger, & Steyn (2007) describe a similar project in a South African university. Kvon et al.

(2018) demonstrate the complexities of IT systems and the risks of implementing new systems in universities in central Russia (Republic of Tatarstan) and Kurniawan and Riadi (2018) who use the ISO 27002 standard to assess the system's security level in universities in Indonesia.

Researchers have investigated the student features that affect the likelihood of computer-related crime and cheating. This research was conducted in a college in which the majority of the student body is orthodox (religious) Jews pursuing computer sciences and related engineering degrees. Interestingly, Cronan, Foltz, and Jones (2006) reports that computer-savvy students are more likely to commit computer crime whereas Burton, Talpad, and Haynes (2011) find that a high level of religiosity is associated with less academic cheating. Lastly, Alshare, Lane, and Lane (2018) study information security policy compliance in a university in the US. They argue that the importance of information security must be embedded within the organizations' workplace culture and that management must hand down strict and swift measures when it is violated.

IT Risk Management

The issue of IT security is at its core a problem of risk assessment and management (Blakley, McDermott, & Geer, 2002) which requires the ability to assimilate new information regularly and use a variety of tools ranging such as decision-analysis, technical data and expert assessment (Collier et al., 2014). Straub and Welke (1998) develop a three-step model for IT security. The first step is the security risk planning model that includes the recognition of the problems, the risk analysis, the generation of alternatives and the decision and implementation of solutions to the problems. The second step is the security awareness program that trains managers and employees to be proactive and to look forward to potential threats. In the last step, the effectiveness of different security options is evaluated using the model's four countermeasures: deterrence, prevention, detection and remedies. Sumner's (2009) model surveys perceived impact, probability and preparedness to IT threats. Each threat is mapped into an information security risk grid, whose axes are the impact and the probability for the threat. The threats that are identified as high impact and high probability are considered to be the riskiest. Sumner (2009) compares whether the reported risks are aligned with the IT professionals' perceived preparedness and finds that this is not generally the case. Dreyfuss and Giat (2016) identify the risky subsystems and modules of the information system using a similar approach. These studies use a composite risk index approach, which is frequently used in the fields of medicine (e.g., Stephan, Tang, & Muniz-Terrera, 2016), finance (e.g., Agliardi, Pinar, & Stengos, 2014) and engineering (da Silva, Castro, & González-Fernández, 2016).

Another approach to assessing risk is breaking down the system hierarchically and assessing each subsystem and its sub-subsystems separately. In the model described in this study, the hierarchical approach is coupled with the composite risk index to assess the system's overall risk. Other examples for the use of hierarchy modeling are Zhou, Pan, Mao, and Huang (2018) who base their IT risk analysis on the information-state transition theory, and Yang & Yao (2018) who incorporate fuzzy evaluations of risk for each hierarchical level in order to assess the risk of accounting information disclosures.

The foundation of information security is controlling access to the systems (Chaudhry, Chaudhry, Reese, & Jones, 2012). Human factor is the real cause to most security breaches, with insider threats by employees or users as the main source of these breaches (Bishop et al., 2014; Posey, Bennett, & Roberts, 2011). Lowry and Moody (2015) explain that employees are the biggest concern because they are the most frequent source of information security breaches, and Hashem, Takabi, GhasemiGol, and Dantu (2015) claim that attacks by employees could cause more damage than any other attacks. These breaches are not necessarily intentional; however, the breaches may be easily exploited by other actors with malicious intent. Consequently, it is possible to approximate the probability of a breach by the number of users of the system itself and the systems connected to it. In contrast to the view emphasizing prevention, Ahmad, Maynard, and Park (2014) claim that organizations should also consider these strategies: deterrence, surveillance, detection, response deception, perimeter defense, compartmentalization, and layering.

Notably, many of the security breaches are not motivated by malice (Greitzer et al., 2014). Instead, these are sourced by a lax security culture that must be addressed by management. Indeed, Wang and Lu (2018) stress the role of management claiming that "unclear authority, unclear responsibilities, chaotic management, and unsound management systems all pose major security risks" and argue that people are the central element of IT security. Following research about the importance of security culture (e.g., Alnatheer, 2015; Tu & Yuan, 2014), the model in this study emphasizes both the technological tools and the organization's security culture.

Optimization

Once the security needs and safety requirements are understood other steps must be implemented such as budgeting tools and workplace culture programs. Special emphasis must be placed on the workplace culture (e.g., Shedden, Smith, & Ahmad, 2010; Tang, Li, & Zhang, 2016) and managerial support (e.g., Knapp, Marshall, Rainer, & Ford, 2006) both of which are essential to improving the organization's IT risk (Shedden et al., 2010). A methodical approach to investing in IT security is offered by Huang, Behara, and Goo (2014) who apply their model in the health industry. Other approaches include constructing a relationship between improvement and investment to allow gradual, optimal investment as in Giat (2013), or using mixed-integer-programming (e.g., Goel & Lauria, 2010; Sawik, 2013). This study's two-step model of first identifying the risky subsystems and then optimizing investment with integer programming is similar to Chorppath and Alpcan (2012) who assume dynamic risk. They first consider the various complexities of the organization and in the next step use integer programming to mitigate these risks.

Verendel (2009) claims that there is insufficient empirical evidence to corroborate the hypothesis that computer and information "security can correctly be represented with quantitative information" (p. 37). Ekelhart et al. (2015) use, instead, simulation to assess the risk of the system. The modeling approach of this study follows the numerous researchers attempting to quantify IT security risks (e.g., Feng & Li, 2011; Rebollo, Mellado, Fernández-Medina, & Mouratidis, 2015; Ryan et al., 2012). Many models use fuzzy logic tools to quantify risks. Recent examples include Yao (2018) using the fuzzy comprehensive evaluation method, Zhu and Wang (2019) using fuzzy neural networks and Yang and Yao (2018) and Zhou et al. (2018) combining fuzzy logic with hierarchy analysis of risk.

RISK MANAGEMENT DECISION SUPPORT MODEL

Model Overview

The model that is described serves as a decision support tool for managers in their need to improve their IT security. It comprises of two steps. The first is to quantify the risk of each component of the IT system and map the riskiest components. The second step is an optimization model that determines how to invest in different security tools and approaches. To weigh correctly the effects of the security tools one must first have a methodical understanding of the IT system. Therefore, the optimization model can be effectively used only after considering the results of the first step of the support tool.

Step 1: Identifying the System's Risky Components

To identify the risky components of the system one must first start with identifying the different systems of the organizations' IT system. Table 1 describes the variables used to evaluate the risk of each subsystem. These variables address security-related questions that were developed together with the IT staff.

Table 1. Subsystem variables

Variable	Addresses the question
S_1	To what degree will exposing or corrupting the information in the subsystem result with higher operational costs?
S_2	To what degree will exposing or corrupting the information in the subsystem cause work delays?
S_3	To what degree will exposing or corrupting the information in the subsystem result with damages to customers, other organizations or other systems related to the school?
S_4	To what degree will exposing or corrupting the information in the subsystem result with giving the school's competitors a considerable advantage?
S_5	To what degree will exposing or corrupting the information in the subsystem hinder future plans or operations of the school?
S_6	To what degree will exposing or corrupting the information in the subsystem cause panic among the public?
S_7	To what degree will exposing or corrupting the information in the subsystem result with severe disruption to the schools activities?
S_8	To what degree will exposing or corrupting the information in the subsystem hurt the school in the event of a state of emergency?
S_9	Does this subsystem contain sensitive information requiring protection according to Protection of Privacy Act?
S_{10}	Does this subsystem contain sensitive business information on which the organization's viability depends?
S_{11}	How many people use the subsystem?
S_{12}	How many people are authorized to make changes or edit the subsystem?

Each of the variables is assigned a value by the subsystem's manager. The value of the first eight variables range between 1 (no adverse effect) to 5 (very severe) and the ninth and tenth variables are binary (zero or one).

The subsystem's *Severity* is the weighted average of $S_1, ..., S_{10}$ in the following manner:

$$S = 0.1 * \left(\frac{1}{8} \sum_{i=1}^{8} S_i + S_9 + S_{10} + 3 \right) \quad (1)$$

In the above, the maximal possible value of S is 1 and the minimal possible value is 0.4. In accordance with research that stresses that insider human factor is the greatest source of risk (Bishop et al., 2014; Posey et al., 2011) it is assumed that the subsystem's risk exposure to depend on the number of people who have access to it (S_{11} and S_{12}). The answers to these items are normalized to be in the range $[0,1]$ by taking it as a percentage of the subsystem with the biggest value of each item.

The subsystem's *Exposure* is now given by:

$$E = \frac{Normalized\,S_{11} + Normalized\,S_{12}}{2} \quad (2)$$

The subsystem's *Impact* is given by:

$$I = S^{1-E} \tag{3}$$

That is, Impact increases with the Severity and the Exposure (recall, $S < 1$) and ranges between 0.4 and 1.

Identifying a Subsystem's Risky Components

It may be the case that certain subsystems are so large or complex that it would be beneficial to consider their own components (i.e., sub-subsystems) individually. Typically, this should be done for subsystems with the highest risk scores and which can be broken to up to more than a handful of sub-subsystems. For brevity, this chapter presents the analysis for only the riskiest subsystem that has been identified in the application. The approach to evaluating the risk level of the sub-subsections is similar to that of the assessment of the subsystems themselves in that a composite risk score is derived in both cases. The specifics of the scores however, are determined in a somewhat different manner and may changes depending on the nature of each subsystems and its components. This is described in detail in the application section of this chapter.

Step 2: Risk Optimization

Once the risk components of each subsystem (and perhaps, sub-subsystems) are determined the IT managers have a better understanding of the system's weaknesses and needs. The objective of the second step is to utilize this understanding to determine how to optimally enhance the system's security. Specifically, a mixed-integer programming model that minimizes the IT system's overall risk subject to a budget constraint is developed. Table 2 describes a categorized list of technological solutions constructed by the IT managers and describes the different tools they were considering. Obviously, this list is not comprehensive, as there are other categories and tools that could be considered. In light of the rapid changes in this field such a list must be reviewed periodically.

Table 2. Technological measures and security tools

Category	Variable	Technological Tool
Storage	X_1	Cloud Storage
	X_2	Private Storage Server
	X_3	External Storage Server
Data Transfer	X_4	Hard drives
	X_5	USB
	X_6	Mail
	X_7	Shared Folders
	X_8	Safe
Data Protection	X_9	Control Center
	X_{10}	Data Classification Tools
	X_{11}	Data Security Tools
	X_{12}	Closed network
	X_{13}	Backup data

Consider the Storage category. This category contains several technological solutions that address the issue of where to locate the information. In this category three possible solutions are allowed: cloud storage, an in-house server or an off-campus server. Each of these solutions has a different cost to implement as well as a different effect on the system's security. This effect is denoted by assigning a value to each of the solutions. These values are determined by the IT managers according to the system's needs and how the technological solution addresses those needs.

In the Data Transfer and Storage categories the safety levels obtained by different technological tools do not accumulate. Instead, the overall effect on safety behaves as the average safety obtained by each solution. In contrast, for the Data Protection category, the positive effects of the technological tools accumulate and therefore the more tools that are purchased the higher levels of safety that are obtained. Furthermore, each category may have different rules with regard to the relationships between the solutions and other constrains that require different tools to be used simultaneously or exclusively. Therefore, the objective function and constraints must be done with IT personnel taking into account not only the systems' specific requirements but also the interplay between the various tools themselves.

To this end, the following variables and constants are defined:

- **Decision Variables:** X_k denotes the decision whether to implement the technological solution $k = 1,...,13$. X_{10} and X_{11} are continuous variables between 0 and 1, whereas the other X_k are binary variable (0 or 1) is a bulleted term;

- **Cost Constants:** c_k^X, $k = 1,...,13$ be the cost of implementing technological solution;

- **Value Constants:** v_k^X, $k = 1,\ldots,13$ be the value of implementing solution k. It is assumed that v_k^X is an integer between 0 and 5;
- **Default Value Constants:** d_k^X, $k = 1,\ldots,13$ be the default value when not implementing solution k. It is assumed that d_k^X is an integer between 0 and 5, and that $d_k^X + v_k^X \le 5$. The value of the binary variables X_k is set endogenously to optimize the system's security. In contrast, c_k^X, v_k^X and d_k^X are constants whose values are determined by the IT managers.

The technological safety factor (TSF) is defined as follows:

$$TSF = \frac{1}{3}\left(\frac{\sum_{k=1}^{4}\left(d_k^X + v_k^X * X_k\right)}{5*\sum_{k=1}^{4}X_k} + \frac{\sum_{k=5}^{8}\left(d_k^X + v_k^X * X_k\right)}{5*\sum_{k=5}^{7}X_k} + \frac{\sum_{k=9}^{13}\left(d_k^X + v_k^X * X_k\right)}{25} \right)$$

In the above, the TSF is the average of the safety scores of each of the categories of Table 2. Notice that the first two categories are defined differently than the third category, reflecting the aforementioned assumptions about the different categories.

In addition to deciding upon which technical solutions are to be implemented, the IT management team can implement programs and procedures to improve the institution's IT workplace culture. Table 3 lists various programs and schemes to enhance IT workplace culture in the organization. The programs, with the exception of Regulation, are listed in order such that program k may be implemented only after program $k-1$ has been (at least partially) implemented. This is formalized in the problem's constraints. Here, too, the list was compiled with the IT managers and reflects the various programs that they considered at the specific point the list was compiled. Therefore, Table 3, too, must be reviewed periodically and adapted to the specific needs of the organization employing the model.

Table 3. Workplace security culture procedures and programs

Variable	Procedures and Programs
Y_1	Data Security Department: Establishing a department dedicated to the system's data security.
Y_2	Data Security Procedures: Developing and implementing system security procedures and rules.
Y_3	Employee training.
Y_4	Workshops: about security awareness and policies.
Y_5	Testing: Performing periodical tests examining the system's security.
Y_6	Security-related conferences.
Y_7	Enforcement Policy: Developing a safety enforcement policy.
Y_8	Enforcement officers.
Y_9	Regulations: ISO certifications (ISO9001 and ISO27001)

The following variables and constants are used:

- **Decision Variables:** Y_k, $k = 1, \ldots, 8$ is a continuous variable between 0 and 1, describing the level of implementation of the k'th training program;
- **Regulation Decision Variable:** Y_9 is a binary decision variable denoting whether or not Regulations are met;
- **Implementation Cost Constants:** c_k^Y, $k = 1, \ldots, 9$ be the cost of implementing the workplace culture programs;
- **Implementation Value Constants:** v_k^Y, $k = 1, \ldots, 9$ be the value of implementing solution k. It is assumed that v_k^Y is an integer between 0 and 5.

The CSF represents the cultural safety factor that results from applying the workplace culture programs. It is given by:

$$CSF = \frac{\sum_{k=1}^{9} v_k^Y Y_k}{\sum_{k=1}^{10} v_k^Y}$$

As stated above, there are many interactions between the different tools and procedures affecting their efficacy in achieving IT security. Accordingly, the constraints described in Table 4 are added to the definition of the problem.

In conclusion, the optimization problem is $min\ Risk = 1 - \dfrac{TSF}{2} - \dfrac{CSF}{2}$ subject to the budget constraint $\sum_{k=1}^{13} c_k^X + \sum_{k=1}^{9} c_k^Y = B$ and the constraint set in Table 4.

Table 4. Problem constraints

Variable	Procedures and Programs
Y_1	Data Security Department: Establishing a department dedicated to the system's data security.
Y_2	Data Security Procedures: Developing and implementing system security procedures and rules.
Y_3	Employee training.
Y_4	Workshops: about security awareness and policies.
Y_5	Testing: Performing periodical tests examining the system's security.
Y_6	Security-related conferences.
Y_7	Enforcement Policy: Developing a safety enforcement policy.
Y_8	Enforcement officers.
Y_9	Regulations: ISO certifications (ISO9001 and ISO27001)

MODEL APPLICATION

This research was conducted in an academic institution in Israel with a student body of approximately 6,000 in four campus locations. The school offers bachelor degrees mainly in engineering, exact sciences and management, and has graduate programs in physics, computer science, data science and business.

Identifying the Risky Subsystems

The model described above is used to provide the school's IT staff with a decision support tool as to how to invest in improving the IT security. As a first step, the institution's different information subsystems were identified together with the head of the institution's IT department. In the next step, the manager of each of the subsystems was asked to assign values to $S_1, ..., S_{12}$ (see Table 1). The validity of the results depends on the ability to assign these values adequately. To enhance the validity, therefore, the study's researchers were actively involved with the managers' completion of the questionnaires. Table 5 describes the Impact and its components (Severity and Exposure) for each subsystem. It can be seen that the subsystem with the highest impact is the Student Administration subsystem. Indeed, this subsystem is large and complex, and involves many aspects of the school's activities. There are two more subsystems that require additional attention due to their risk characteristics. These systems are Salaries & Personnel and Student Employment.

Table 5. The risk components of the institution's IT subsystems

Variable	S Severity	E Exposure	I Impact	Rank
Domitories	57.50%	4.38%	58.91%	7
Student Administration	82.50%	55.00%	91.71%	1
Endowments & Contributions	61.25%	4.59%	62.64%	5
Parking	53.75%	4.60%	55.31%	10
Procurement	70.00%	4.79%	71.21%	4
General Maintenance	50.00%	19.00%	57.04%	9
Student Employment	72.50%	47.92%	84.58%	3
Salaries & Personnel	72.50%	57.50%	87.23%	2
Library	47.50%	25.58%	57.47%	8
Computer Services	50.00%	25.83%	59.80%	6

The Student Administration subsystem was found to have the highest risk factor (82.5%). Not surprisingly, this subsystem is probably the most complex subsystem in the institutions information system. It is therefore advantageous to take Student Administration and examine each of its components to identify wherein lies most of the risk. The Student Administration comprises eighteen sub-subsystems as detailed in Table 6. For each sub-subsystem data for the twelve items ($S_1,\ldots,S_{12}$) defined in Table 1 was collected. Here, S_{11} and S_{12} were redefined as follows:

- **Connectivity:** S_{11} is the number of connection tables between the sub-subsystem and other subsystems;
- **Permissions:** S_{12} is the number of people with permission to access the sub-subsystem.

Here, too, *normalized* S_{11} and *normalized* S_{12} are defined to be items in the range $[0,1]$ by taking S_{11} and S_{12} as a percentage of the subsystem with the maximum value of each item. The following additional risk variables are defined (these definitions may differ from the definitions for the subsystems):

- **Exposure:** E is defined as the average of *normalized* S_{11} and *normalized* S_{12} By definition, it is a number between 0 and 1;
- **Severity:** $S := 0.2*(S_9 + S_{10} + 3)$. Its range is between $[0.6, 1]$;
- **Probability:** P is defined as the average of the items ($S_1,\ldots,S_8$).

The sub-subsystem's risk score is the variable *Impact*, which is defined as $I := P * S^{1-E}$. Table 6 details the risk variables (Exposure, Severity, and Probability) and the risk score (Impact) of each of the sub-subsystems of Student Administration. Interestingly, only three sub-subsystems have a risk score that is greater than 50%, revealing that the risk posed Student Administration is concentrated in these three sub-subsystems. This is an important result that guides administrators to where exactly they should target their efforts of improving information system's security.

Optimization Model

Having achieved a better understanding about the risk posed by each of the system's component managers are better equipped to decide how to allocate funds in improving the system. Table 7 details the cost and risk values of the technological tools' solutions. It also describes the current investment policy as well as the policy that is proposed. Table 8 details for each workplace culture variable its cost and possible

Table 6. The risk components of the institution's IT subsystems

Variable	S Severity	E Exposure	P Probability	I Impact	Rank
Personal Details	90.00%	62.50%	60.0%	57.68%	3
Course Registration	62.50%	21.32%	52.5%	36.27%	8
Grades	85.00%	43.38%	82.5%	75.25%	1
Test Registration	51.25%	15.44%	87.5%	49.72%	4
Approval Letters	48.75%	2.50%	50.0%	24.82%	11
Exam Appeals	48.75%	37.50%	57.5%	36.70%	6
Appeals and Requests	62.50%	50.00%	45.0%	35.58%	9
Final Day Form	42.50%	15.44%	37.5%	18.19%	17
Forms	40.00%	2.50%	25.0%	10.23%	18
Surveys	53.75%	2.50%	40.0%	21.84%	14
Credit Payments	70.00%	7.94%	52.5%	37.81%	5
Account Details	82.50%	15.44%	72.5%	61.62%	2
Tuition and Payment Invoices	66.25%	12.50%	52.5%	36.62%	7
Printing	45.00%	2.50%	52.5%	24.10%	12
Extra-Curricular Attendance	47.50%	5.00%	42.5%	20.95%	15
Registration – Dormitories	61.25%	5.00%	50.0%	31.38%	10
Registration – Sport facilities	43.75%	5.00%	40.0%	18.24%	16
Registration – Lockers	53.75%	5.00%	40.0%	22.18%	13

values. For example, Y_1 may be assigned the values 0, 0.25, 0.5, 0.75, and 1 only. If it is assigned 1 (i.e., it is fully implemented) then the cost is 720 thousand Israeli Shekel (ILS), whereas if it is assigned only 0.25 then the cost is only 180 thousand ILS. Table 7 also describes the current and proposed solution. The current annual IT security budget, B, is 3.51 million ILS and the current risk level is 39.6%. The proposed solution diverts 870 thousand ILS from the technological tools to the workplace culture programs and its risk level is 13.7%.

Table 7. Technological tools' parameter values and current and optimal solution

Category	Variable	c_k^X	d_k^X	v_k^X	Current value	Optimal
Storage	X_1	114	0	3	0	1
	X_2	2000	0	5	1	0
	X_3	2400	0	4	0	0
Data Transfer	X_4	400	0	3	0	0
	X_5	100	0	2	0	0
	X_6	50	0	4	1	1
	X_7	100	0	3	0	0
	X_8	1500	0	5	0	0
Data Protection	X_9	50	1	5	1	1
	X_{10}	500	1	5	0	0.68
	X_{11}	100	1	5	0	0.68
	X_{12}	2000	2	5	0	0
	X_{13}	1000	2	5	1	1

Table 8. Workplace culture parameter values and current and optimal solution

Variable	Cost	Possibilities	Utility	Current value	Proposed
Y_1	720	0/0.25/0.5/0.75/1	5	0.25	1
Y_2	50	0/0.5/1	3	0.5	1
Y_3	50	0/0.5/1	3	0.5	1
Y_4	50	0/0.5/1	3	0.5	1
Y_5	60	0/0.25/0.5/0.75/1	5	0.5	1
Y_6	50	0/0.5/1	2	0.5	1
Y_7	20	0/1	2	0	1
Y_8	180	0/0.5/1	3	0	1
Y_9	100	0/1	3	1	1

DISCUSSION

The analysis reveals that there are three subsystems with a high (above 80%) risk score. The riskiest subsystem is the Student Administration followed by Salaries & Personnel and Student Employment (see Table 5). A detailed analysis of Student Administration reveals that four sub-subsystems contribute to most of its risk. These are (in descending order) Grades, Account Details, Personal Details, and Test Registration (see Table 6). The common feature of all these system modules is that they relate to money or grades. Therefore, these results highlight that money and grades are the two major reasons for cyberattacks and hacking in academic institutions. Monetary incentives for cheating are a time old behavior of people and are not unique to academic institutions. In contrast, hacking for the purpose of changing grades is a phenomenon that is quite common in academic institutions spanning a wide range of ages and levels (Abrams, 2019; Gulezian, 2018; Hawes, 2014; Vaas, 2017).

The students of the academic institution in this study are characterized as highly religious. Therefore, in light of Burton et al.'s (2011) finding that a high level of religiosity is associated with less academic cheating, one would expect that cheating would not pose a significant risk. Nevertheless, Grades and Test Registration are the first and third riskiest sub-subsystems in the Student Administration subsystem, implying that cheating is in fact a major risk in the school. This may be explained by the fact that the school is engineering-oriented and engineering students were found by Cronan et al. (2006) to be more associated with computer hacking for the purpose of cheating. Student cheating is not limited to tertiary schools but happens as early as high school (see Abrams, 2019 and Gulezian, 2018, for recent examples). Indeed, the IT staff reported about a number of security breaches by students. In one event, engineering students used a phishing scam to retrieve a final exam. In another example, information science students used a Trojan horse malware to obtain a lecturer's password. Such behavior is not unprecedented and similar stories can be found in many news reports around the world. The finding that the current investment policy places more emphasis on tools rather than workplace culture is consistent with current research (e.g., Drevin et al., 2007; Shedden et al., 2010). Furthermore, the institution's current practice overspends on storage solutions where it is found that investment should be shifted towards data protection tools.

Sensitivity Analysis

The output of the model may be used to shed light on how risk changes with the budget size. Figure 1 displays the risk level as a function of the budget. The convex functional form implies that there is a decreasing return to investment. Therefore, if the institution cut its budget by 3 million ILS the risk level would rise by 31% to 45%, whereas if it were to increase the budget by the same amount the absolute reduction in the risk is only 9%.

Figure 1. The risk level as a function of the security budget

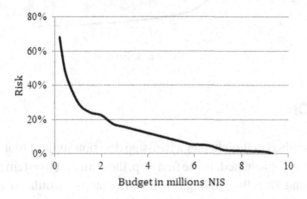

An alternative approach to the problem is to set a desired risk level, RL, and determine the budget required to attain this level. In this case, the problem to be solved is:

$$min\ B = \sum_{k=1}^{13} c_k^X + \sum_{k=1}^{9} c_k^Y$$

subject to meeting the target level:

$$1 - \frac{TSF}{2} - \frac{CSF}{2} \leq RL$$

and the set of constraints in Table 4. In Figure 2, the budget as a function of the risk level is displayed. The data in this figure can help management in the budgeting decision of the institution's IT security.

Figure 2. The budget needed to attain the desired risk level

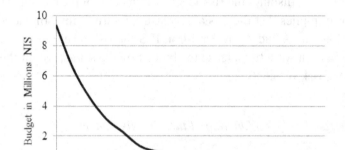

CONCLUSION

In the study described in this chapter a two-step decision support tool for enhancing IT system security is presented. In the first step, the critical subsystems are identified and in the second step the findings of the first step are utilized to develop an optimization problem that minimized risk subject to the budget and technological constraints. The model is applied to the IT system of a large college in Israel. The results of the first step show that there are three candidate subsystems that merit investment in improving their IT security. The results of the second step imply that the institution's current investment scheme is suboptimal and the output of this step is a recommendation of the optimal investment plan.

There are a number of limitations to this study that must be considered when generalizing its findings or applications. First, the validity of the results hinge on the IT staff's ability to complete the questionnaire correctly. Obviously, this is not always the case. To overcome this shortcoming, the person in charge of the subsystem was asked to complete the questionnaire while accompanied with the researchers of this study. In other situations, it may be better to consult with additional, experienced, IT staffers. Second, the model in this study follows research that emphasizes breaches originating from system users. This approach may be expanded to include external breaches as well as non-human-related sources of risk. Finally, it is worthy to re-stress that the systems and the questionnaires presented in the model must be continuously reviewed to address the rapid changes in the IT structure, technological solutions and sources of risk. The model, therefore, should be viewed by managers as a decision support tool when they face the problem of improving their IT system's security under a constrained budget. In lieu of spending the money in overall system improvement, they can use the model presented in this study for pinpointing the actual subsystems that need improvement, thus achieving effective improvement in their overall security while avoiding excessive spending.

FUTURE RESEARCH DIRECTIONS

Investments in information security are continuously increasing and are expected to continue to grow in the foreseeable future. Unfortunately, the advances in this field do not yet allow "one-size-fits-all" solutions and most research provide only local solutions that are tailored to address specific problems. While there are many attempts to create general frameworks, there is still a large gap, perhaps an abyss, between these theories and the specific applications in private and public institutions. Future research could be directed at trying to find commonalities. For example, in many countries public universities operate under similar government oversight and may use similar information systems. Developing a single framework for all public universities in such a country may be a feasible feat. Future research in this field is needed to improve the understanding of risk and ways to quantify it. This is an essential step for any optimization-based model for IT security.

ACKNOWLEDGMENT

A prior version of this manuscript appeared in the *Information Resources Management Journal*.

REFERENCES

Abrams, L. (2019). Students Hack School System to Change Grades and Attendance. *Bleepingcomputer.com*. Retrieved from https://www.bleepingcomputer.com/news/security/students-hack-school-system-to-change-grades-and-attendance/

Agliardi, E., Pinar, M., & Stengos, T. (2014). A sovereign risk index for the Eurozone based on stochastic dominance. *Finance Research Letters, 11*(4), 375–384. doi:10.1016/j.frl.2014.07.002

Ahmad, A., Maynard, S. B., & Park, S. (2014). Information security strategies: Towards an organizational multi-strategy perspective. *Journal of Intelligent Manufacturing, 25*(2), 357–370. doi:10.100710845-012-0683-0

Alnatheer, M. A. (2015). Information security culture critical success factors. In *Information Technology-New Generations* (pp. 731–735). ITNG.

Alshare, K. A., Lane, P. L., & Lane, M. R. (2018). Information security policy compliance: A higher education case study. *Information & Computer Security, 26*(1), 91–108. doi:10.1108/ICS-09-2016-0073

Bishop, M., Conboy, H. M., Phan, H., Simidchieva, B. I., Avrunin, G. S., Clarke, L. A., ... Peisert, S. (2014). Insider threat identification by process analysis. In *Security and Privacy Workshops* (pp. 251–264). SPW.

Blakley, B., McDermott, E., & Geer, D. (2002). Information security is information risk management. In *Proceedings of the 2001 workshop on new security paradigms* (pp. 97-104). New York: Association for Computing Machinery.

Burton, J. H., Talpade, S., & Haynes, J. (2011). Religiosity and test-taking ethics among business school students. *Journal of Academic and Business Ethics, 4*, 1–8.

Chapman, J., Chinnaswamy, A., & Garcia-Perez, A. (2018). The severity of cyber attacks on education and research institutions: A function of their security posture. In *ICCWS 2018 13th International Conference on Cyber Warfare and Security* (p. 111). Academic Press.

Chaudhry, P. E., Chaudhry, S. S., Reese, R., & Jones, D. S. (2012). Enterprise information systems security: A conceptual framework. In *Re-conceptualizing Enterprise Information Systems* (pp. 118–128). Berlin: Springer. doi:10.1007/978-3-642-28827-2_9

Chorppath, A. K., & Alpcan, T. (2012). Risk management for it security: When theory meets practice. In *2012 5th International Conference on New Technologies, Mobility and Security (NTMS)* (pp. 1-5). Academic Press.

Collier, Z. A., DiMase, D., Walters, S., Tehranipoor, M. M., Lambert, J. H., & Linkov, I. (2014). Cybersecurity standards: Managing risk and creating resilience. *Computer, 47*(9), 70–76. doi:10.1109/MC.2013.448

Cronan, T. P., Foltz, C. B., & Jones, T. W. (2006). Piracy, computer crime, and IS misuse at the university. *Communications of the ACM, 49*(6), 84–90. doi:10.1145/1132469.1132472

da Silva, A. M. L., Castro, J. F. C., & González-Fernández, R. A. (2016). Spinning reserve assessment under transmission constraints based on Cross-Entropy method. *IEEE Transactions on Power Systems, 31*(2), 1624–1632. doi:10.1109/TPWRS.2015.2418222

Dick, M., Sheard, J., Bareiss, C., Carter, J., Joyce, D., Harding, T., & Laxer, C. (2003). Addressing student cheating: Definitions and solutions. *Association for Computing Machinery SigCSE Bulletin, 35*(2), 172–184.

Doherty, N. F., Anastasakis, L., & Fulford, H. (2009). The information security policy unpacked: A critical study of the content of university policies. *International Journal of Information Management, 29*(6), 449–457. doi:10.1016/j.ijinfomgt.2009.05.003

Drevin, L., Kruger, H. A., & Steyn, T. (2007). Value-focused assessment of ICT security awareness in an academic environment. *Computers & Security, 26*(1), 36–43. doi:10.1016/j.cose.2006.10.006

Dreyfuss, M., & Giat, Y. (2016). Identifying security risk modules in a university's information system. *Proceedings of Informing Science & IT Education Conference, 2016*, 41–51.

Ekelhart, A., Kiesling, E., Grill, B., Strauss, C., & Stummer, C. (2015). Integrating attacker behavior in IT security analysis: A discrete-event simulation approach. *Information Technology Management, 16*(3), 221–233. doi:10.100710799-015-0232-6

Feng, N., & Li, M. (2011). An information systems security risk assessment model under uncertain environment. *Applied Soft Computing, 11*(7), 4332–4340. doi:10.1016/j.asoc.2010.06.005

Giat, Y. (2013). The Effects of Output Growth on Preventive Investment Policy. *American Journal of Operations Research, 3*(6), 474–486. doi:10.4236/ajor.2013.36046

Goel, S., & Lauría, E. J. (2010). Quantification, optimization and uncertainty modeling in information security risks: A matrix-based approach. *Information Resources Management Journal, 23*(2), 33–52. doi:10.4018/irmj.2010040103

Greitzer, F. L., Strozer, J., Cohen, S., Bergey, J., Cowley, J., Moore, A., & Mundie, D. (2014). Unintentional insider threat: contributing factors, observables, and mitigation strategies. In *System Sciences* (pp. 2025–2034). HICSS. doi:10.1109/HICSS.2014.256

Gulezian, L. A. (2018). Concord teen arrested after hacking into school grading system. *Abc7news*. Retrieved from https://abc7news.com/education/concord-teen-arrested-after-hacking-into-school-grading-system/3457995/ on June 19, 2019.

Hashem, Y., Takabi, H., GhasemiGol, M., & Dantu, R. (2015). Towards insider threat detection using psychophysiological signals. In *Proceedings of the 7th ACM CCS International Workshop on Managing Insider Security Threats* (pp. 71-74). 10.1145/2808783.2808792

Hawes, J. (2014). Jail time for university hacker who changed his grades to straight As. *Naked Security*. Retrieved from https://nakedsecurity.sophos.com/2014/02/28/jail-time-for-university-hacker-who-changed-his-grades-to-straight-as/

Huang, C. D., Behara, R. S., & Goo, J. (2014). Optimal information security investment in a healthcare information exchange: An economic analysis. *Decision Support Systems*, *61*, 1–11. doi:10.1016/j.dss.2013.10.011

Knapp, K. J., Marshall, T. E., Rainer, R. K., & Ford, F. N. (2006). Information security: Management's effect on culture and policy. *Information Management & Computer Security*, *14*(1), 24–36. doi:10.1108/09685220610648355

Kurniawan, E., & Riadi, I. (2018). Security level analysis of academic information systems based on standard ISO 27002: 2003 using SSE-CMM. *International Journal of Computer Science and Information Security*, *16*(1), 139–147.

Kvon, G. M., Vaks, V. B., Masalimova, A. R., Kryukova, N. I., Rod, Y. S., Shagieva, R. V., & Khudzhatov, M. B. (2018). Risk in implementing new electronic management systems at universities. *Eurasia Journal of Mathematics, Science and Technology Education*, *14*(3), 891–902.

Lowry, P. B., & Moody, G. D. (2015). Proposing the control-reactance compliance model (CRCM) to explain opposing motivations to comply with organisational information security policies. *Information Systems Journal*, *25*(5), 433–463. doi:10.1111/isj.12043

Mensch, S., & Wilkie, L. (2011). Information security activities of college students: An exploratory study. *Academy of Information and Management Sciences Journal*, *14*(2), 91–116.

Mok, K. H. (2005). Fostering entrepreneurship: Changing role of government and higher education governance in Hong Kong. *Research Policy*, *34*(4), 537–554. doi:10.1016/j.respol.2005.03.003

Posey, C., Bennett, R. J., & Roberts, T. L. (2011). Understanding the mindset of the abusive insider: An examination of insiders' causal reasoning following internal security changes. *Computers & Security*, *30*(6), 486–497. doi:10.1016/j.cose.2011.05.002

Rebollo, O., Mellado, D., Fernández-Medina, E., & Mouratidis, H. (2015). Empirical evaluation of a cloud computing information security governance framework. *Information and Software Technology*, *58*, 44–57. doi:10.1016/j.infsof.2014.10.003

Ryan, J. J., Mazzuchi, T. A., Ryan, D. J., De la Cruz, J. L., & Cooke, R. (2012). Quantifying information security risks using expert judgment elicitation. *Computers & Operations Research*, *39*(4), 774–784. doi:10.1016/j.cor.2010.11.013

Sawik, T. (2013). Selection of optimal countermeasure portfolio in IT security planning. *Decision Support Systems*, *55*(1), 156–164. doi:10.1016/j.dss.2013.01.001

Shedden, P., Smith, W., & Ahmad, A. (2010). Information security risk assessment: towards a business practice perspective. In *8th Australian Information Security Management Conference* (pp. 119-130). Academic Press.

Smith, G. (2014). Why study? College hackers are changing F's to A's. *The Huffington Post*. Retrieved from https://www.huffingtonpost.com/2014/03/05/student-hacking_n_4907344.html

Sridhar, V., & Ahuja, D. K. (2007). Challenges in managing information security in academic institutions: Case of MDI India. *Journal of Information System Security*, *3*(3), 51–78.

Stephan, B. C., Tang, E., & Muniz-Terrera, G. (2016). Composite risk scores for predicting dementia. *Current Opinion in Psychiatry*, *29*(2), 174–180. doi:10.1097/YCO.0000000000000235 PMID:26779863

Straub, D. W., & Welke, R. J. (1998). Coping with systems risk: Security planning models for management decision making. *Management Information Systems Quarterly*, *22*(4), 441–469. doi:10.2307/249551

Sumner, M. (2009). Information security threats: A comparative analysis of impact, probability, and preparedness. *Information Systems Management*, *26*(1), 2–12. doi:10.1080/10580530802384639

Tang, M., Li, M., & Zhang, T. (2016). The impacts of organizational culture on information security culture: A case study. *Information Technology Management, 17*(2), 179–186. doi:10.100710799-015-0252-2

Tu, Z., & Yuan, Y. (2014). Critical success factors analysis on effective information security management: A literature review. *Twentieth Americas Conference on Information Systems*, 1-13.

Vaas, L. (2017). Student charged by FBI for hacking his grades more than 90 times. *Naked Security*. Retrieved from https://nakedsecurity.sophos.com/2017/11/01/student-charged-by-fbi-for-hacking-his-grades-more-than-90-times/

Verendel, V. (2009). Quantified security is a weak hypothesis: a critical survey of results and assumptions. In *Proceedings of the 2009 workshop on new security paradigms workshop* (pp. 37-49). 10.1145/1719030.1719036

Wang, W., & Lu, N. (2018). Security risk analysis and security technology research of government public data center. In *2018 IEEE International Conference on Energy Internet (ICEI)* (pp. 185-189). 10.1109/ICEI.2018.00041

Yang, C. Q., & Yao, J. B. (2018). *Accounting Information Disclosure Risk Assessment Based on a Hierarchical Model. DEStech Transactions on Economics, Business and Management.*

Yao, X. (2018). Application research of optimized FCE method in information security risk evaluation model. In *2018 International Conference on Intelligent Transportation, Big Data & Smart City (ICITBS)* (pp. 456-459). 10.1109/ICITBS.2018.00121

Zhou, C., Pan, P., Mao, X., & Huang, L. (2018). Risk analysis of information system security based on distance of information-state transition. *Wuhan University Journal of Natural Sciences, 23*(3), 210–218. doi:10.100711859-018-1312-3

Zhu, G., & Wang, Y. (2019). Research on risk assessment of information system based on fuzzy neural network. *Advances on Economics, Business and Management Research (AEBMR)/ International Academic Conference on Frontiers in Social Sciences and Management Innovation (IAFSM 2018), 62*, 50-55. 10.2991/iafsm-18.2019.8

KEY TERMS AND DEFINITIONS

Composite Risk Model: A risk analysis model that identifies a limited number of factors whose combination predicts the adverse outcome.

Decision Support System: An information system (computer programs and the relevant data) that supports decision-making activities of the organization.

Human Factors: Incorporating psychological and physiological principles into the engineering and design of products, processes, and systems.

Integer Optimization or Integer Programming: A mathematical optimization (or feasibility) program in which some or all the variables are restricted to be integers.

Mixed Integer Optimization: A mathematical optimization (or feasibility) program in which the variables may be either real or integer numbers.

Risk Management: The practice of identifying and analyzing potential risks in advance and taking precautionary steps to limit risk.

Security Hacker: A computer expert who uses their technical knowledge to break into computer systems.

Chapter 5
Communication Matrices for Managing Dialogue Change to Teamwork Transformation

James Calvin
Johns Hopkins University, USA

ABSTRACT

New technology platforms continue to be introduced inside organizations in this digital age. Technology and generational diversity will have sustained impact on how business organizations consider and adapt to meet a number of technology and people challenges. The case discusses why it is to promote and sustain crucial conversations dialogue among team members to both enhance and strengthen team and teamwork practices. In the case, the change management process was essential to being able to go deeper through matrixed crucial conversations to achieve a desired organization goal. This case study chapter offers insight and outcomes that were achieved by building a dialogic approach and model, so a vital unit of the organization could begin taking advantage of future technology enhancements.

INTRODUCTION

There is broad general agreement that the current worldwide digital revolution is introducing new technology platforms that will have sustained impact on how business organizations consider and adapt to meet a number of technology and people orientation challenges while engaging in industries and business sectors (Segars, 2018). Concurrently, the role of developing and implementing change management practices to achieve human centered goals often requires methods and tools such

DOI: 10.4018/978-1-7998-2235-6.ch005

as appreciative inquiry, to promote and sustain crucial conversations dialogue among team members to both enhance and strengthen team and teamwork practices that are essential to the focus of this chapter and future application (Cooperrider, 2013). Specifically, in this chapter, it is a discussion about the potential of applied action-research based engagement involving teams and teamwork inside a business organization with the lens of focus on dialogue between team members for their teamwork capabilities, and process and culture. The premise is that new organizational capacity through crucial conversations can enable better team management together by establishing more effective communication matrices as new technology is introduced in the HR unit of a national business organization.

Action Research and Managing Dialogue in Change Management

This chapter discusses a multi-month action-research intervention process that was co-joined with appreciative inquiry to facilitate a crucial conversations organizational intervention. The chapter details and outlines key aspects and factors observed through a change management process that desired to overcome disparate conversations and voices of team members spanning multiple generations. Specifically the case is about the HR unit of a national business organization and the scenario to unfold seeks to illuminate the introduction and role of dialogue practice as a change method, approach and tool for adoption by the team members in the HR group. Briefly, the organization is interested in gaining knowledge and understanding of its current communication capacity matrices in order to erect an inclusive bridge and platform for all members of its HR group who represent four generations in the workplace (Fry, 2018). The swath of four generations presents cultural alignment as well as new technology challenges to unlock new potential for future achievement in the HR unit and overall organization. At the onset, it was determined by senior leadership that a stronger communication pathway is necessary to strengthen overall team performance. A desired outcome was to motivate and encourage the adoption of crucial conversations dialogue to build group capability and cohesion of the HR unit. An immediate objective for the unit and organization was how to get beyond communication gaps from a merger that happened several years ago by engaging in change management. In doing so the quest was to integrate a change model that began with Kurt Lewin's (1947) to whom is attributed three-step change model (Cummings, Bridgman, & Brown, 2016); or another accepted change model like John Kotter's (2012, 2014) eight step change model. Thus, the focus of this business case is two-fold: the first is to discuss how the HR group in an actual organization is actively pursuing the potential and possibility to invent and integrate a dialogue process that involves tools and methodology to unblock, enhance and improve communication quality by establishing a baseline of dialogue as a foundation.

A NEED FOR RECIPROCITY FOR CHANGE

Within the HR unit the assumption was that ongoing improvement could be influenced by dialogue that encourages communication and learning exchanges toward shared reciprocity. The purpose and fundamental role of reciprocation that Robert B. Cialdini (2007) mentions is give and take, and because "the rule says that we should repay, in kind, what another person has provided us" (p. 17). The HR unit views reciprocation as being essential as an enabler factor to be able to go beyond accuracy of flow, and more widely, into knowledge discovery and knowledge sharing, as business flows both within the unit and out from the HR group across the organization. Intertwined with communication quality and flow is the need to simultaneously address and realign cultural issues and challenges of pre-merger team member preference for analog communication norms and post-merger newer team member preference for digital communication norms and processes. The aforementioned use of reciprocation alludes to group dynamics that is present in many types of organizations that must grapple with conceptual change that is linked to change management tools and processes to adapt human systems.

In planning for change the seminal idea from Kurt Lewin (1947) is the standard – in it he lays the foundation for taking on organizational change in the phases of unfreeze, change, refreeze (also see Cummings et al., 2016). The original notion for advancing and managing change in an organization is attributed to Kurt Lewin who established that change for any individual or an organization is a complicated journey. Moreover, the journey toward change often involves several stages of transitions or misunderstandings before getting to a desired equilibrium or stability. This author also notes that Lewin's original theory has been has been the foundation for other theories of change and change models from its inception more than seventy years ago. John P. Kotter a foremost authority in *Leading Change* (2012) emphasizes the uniting of leadership and change. Concerning the rapid pace of discontinuity and disruption that impacts and effects all organizations must deal with constant waves and forces of change (Kotter, 2014). A further impetus for engaging and navigating change is that there is influence on organizations in a fourth industrial revolution time of advancing artificial intelligence (AI) and machine learning (ML). Change and change making is complex because there are other contributing internal factors along with other societal factors, and because the future is where innovation and technology would converge while centering on humanity and the need to serve broad public interests. AI and ML are also knowledge making tools that emerge from data acquisition and mining and what they can mean for the HR unit is still being surfaced. Still, the idea is that AI and ML can also become innovation sources for managing change and change processes in the organization. Thus, it was decided after consulting with senior leadership in the HR group to introduce a crucial conversations-difficult conversations modeling approach to start change and anchor that change by engaging in dialogue with fellow HR group members.

Dialogue for Change: Who Are the Dialogue Participants – Sequence One

At the start of crucial conversations-difficult conversations (CCDC) group communication full group work, it was necessary to assess perceived breaks and gaps in cross-group communication, and it was also necessary to identify the potential of a communication change model to emerge inside the organization. It was declared by senior leadership to both managers and team members in the HR group, that being able to go deeper through matrixed crucial conversation in a dialogic way would be necessary to achieve a desired organization goal. This case study chapter pertains to insight and outcomes arrived at by building a dialogic approach and model to introduce a dialogue structure to manage and facilitate communication bridges involving team and group members that range from the Silent/Greatest Generation to Baby Boomers, to Generation X and Millennials (Fry, 2018) in the HR unit. The introduction and applicability and utility of actor-network theory (ANT) from Michael Callon and Bruno Latour (1992) as well as John Law (1999, 2007) was another cornerstone for building a dialogue model approach for engaging the HR unit. In brief, ANT seeks to understand processes of technological innovation and scientific knowledge creation in a system. ANT when applied as theory enables consideration of all surrounding factors contextually because no one acts alone in a given infrastructure, how it is formed, and how and what a network does not connect. Actor-network theory allows for incorporating the principle of generalized symmetry for example the human factors as well as artifacts and organization structures.

Once more, the crucial conversations-difficult conversations (CCDC) sets of sessions with HR unit team members was conceptualized and planned as a multi-tiered change management engagement, as an adaptive learning process extended over a number of months with team members. The initial use of the Rush Hour Game was a structured getting started group communication activity where objectives and goals were announced to all participants. Some game participants held back, some were skeptical, while others seized on the ice breaking opportunity that was presented, with opportunities to be had individually and together. The Rush Hour game was also experiential learning at an intersection of culture in the Hofstede (1997) view that culture is "a collective phenomenon, because it is at least partially shared with people who live or lived within the same social environment, which is where it is learned" (p. 5). The assumption is that learning when coupled with dialogue would over time show up as influence and eventual impact. The dimension of power as per Foucault is another contributing factor; he purports the ubiquitous nature of power – that it is everywhere (Foucault, 1977, 1998).

Another baseline component toward erecting the proposed communication matrices for managing dialogue change model is masspersonal communication – a model that bridges the mass-interpersonal divide. The theoretical discussion and exchange that is taking place is that there is a false dichotomy between interpersonal and mass communication because of the emergence of recent digital communication tools at the intersections of interpersonal communication and mass communication (O'Sullivan & Carr, 2018). The masspersonal communications model concept enables traverse between older communication and newer communication technologies regarding perceived message accessibility and message practices. The implication is that mass communication and interpersonal communication are being linked together in new ways in the digital age. In the early work and evaluation of HR group and team member preferences and approaches, the possibility of bridge building communication methods was identified given generational differences and communication preferences. The chapter contextually seeks to present what emerged from focused communication artifacts relative to communication styles and preferences that links with group dynamics, yields insights, trends, further questions and areas for current and future change management consideration for both adoption and future implementation within the HR group.

Concerning baseline theory and practice of dialogue toward achievable outcomes attendant issues of depth and commitment to dialogue was advanced as an idea or potential building block. In doing so, there is system affect and impact because a company or organization is generally organized as a system often with different departments or groups that perform differing and specific functions, while often the expectation is to function together as a coherent system. Given the realities of the HR unit, the expressed need to was to utilize dialogue as a strategic tool and pathway forward to better cohesion. Given the organizational needs for the unit, Bohm (1996) provided a comprehensive approach toward realizing the potential of a communication dialogic process as a core element toward a sustainable foundation. Bohm (1996) notes that the application and reinforcement of dialogic principles through real-time dialogue practice is a purposeful approach that can lead to gradually deepened communication between people within and across groups in an organization. In brief, Bohm's (1996) view is that:

In a dialogue, each person does not attempt to make common certain ideas or items of information that are already known to him. Rather, it may be said that two people (or more people) are making something in common, i.e. creating something new together. But of course such communication can lead to the creation of something new only if people are able freely to listen to each other, without prejudice, and without trying to influence each other. (p. 2-3)

It became necessary in the use and application of a dialogic approach to add a second baseline theory from William Isaacs in congruence with David Bohm. In tandem, there are features and elements of another useful and practical dialogic approach and application that compliments Bohm's dialogue that is codified by William Isaacs (1999) who, in *Dialogue: The Art of Thinking Together*, asks the following questions: "How can we learn, as individuals, to take actions that might be conducive to evoking dialogue? How can we create dialogue in settings where people may not have initially been willing to engage in it? How can we broaden the dialogue process to include more people? How can we prevent retrenchment?" Further, Isaacs (1999) goes on to suggest three fundamental dimensions to be addressed as levels of action in a dialogue: "To produce coherent actions, the creation of fluid structures of interaction, and to provide wholesome space for dialogue."

Constructing a dialogue model for adoption and implementation incorporates many facets and for the HR unit the question of what was/is the current communication network communication structure was raised at the beginning of an ongoing dialogue building journey. In attempting to identify and assess the network communication structure that is operating the model of design has benefitted from review, the recognition of features, and some degree of validation when matched against two employee satisfaction surveys over multiple years. Furthermore, the validation emerged from individual interviews, full group interviews, and manager of group interviews. In the action-based research practice that was done, it was assessed with input from unit leadership that the communication network structure involved compliments of a chain, a circle and a wheel to some degree of accuracy. Given the aforementioned, the assumption made at the time was that a three forms of communication in small group model and theory offers a degree of promise for further clarification and elucidation for the HR group. The facilitator also offered to unit leadership that there were other theory into practice possible models that could also be considered for team communication matrices building and implementation purposes. Briefly, the three inter-connective features of the model assessment and review are: A chain network of formal small groups that follows the formal chain of command and helps to maintain communication accuracy; a circle network that has the leader/manager as the central person for conducting all communications within the group as well as great speed and accuracy; and, a wheel network features broad openness that enables joint communication by all members.

Figure 1. Three types of communication networks

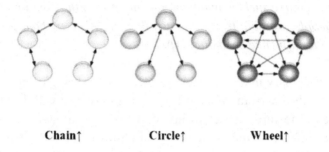

Chain↑   **Circle**↑   **Wheel**↑

Concerning the HR unit communication network structure, the senior leadership of the group referenced two interrelated categories of business organization goals during the initial full-day working session of the HR group. The first objective was to engage in action-research and inquiry to begin to explore the practicality of navigating crucial conversations/difficult conversations on a structured journey that would enhance and strengthen the overall capability and function of unit. A second crucial conversations objective required thinking and deepened conversation when thinking about how linking team and unit goals through dialogue could be carried over to the larger organization. Via crucial conversations it was beginning to reinvent internally driven communication processes that would be able to take advantage of new digital and problem-solving technologies to augment the skills inside the HR unit. The initial full day experience was also a time one sequence that featured team problem solving utilizing the Rush Hour experiential problem solving game matrix. The Rush Hour team experiential activity features dexterity and communication by grouped participants who were brought together in eight 10-member problem solving groups. At the last third of the all-hands day the talking together for problem solving debrief led to the following inquiry driven questions being asked in a full group conversation and discussion as a facilitation, and the debrief yielded data for analysis and some next steps for further inquiry and team member follow-up.

Day One Problem Solving Team Questions

1. How do you and colleagues currently have conversations about shared organizational information or a goal or purpose?
2. When in conversation with a member of your team do you suspend (reflective, remain open, generative) your point of view? Or do you defend a point of view (control, withhold, debate)?
3. When in a conversation do you listen to the other person or people in the group? Do you think that you are listened to the other person or people?

4.   How do you cultivate group, organization and system conversation that can lead to dialogue?

In the day-long set of activities, the author notes that responses were recorded from problem solving teams and members. The full HR unit was informed that more questions regarding how, what and why communication can become sustainable dialogue as part of HR unit culture. It was announced that the initial set of questions would be asked again individually, and also in unit teams at two other times over a multi-month period.

Dialogue for Change: Diving Deeper into Conversation – Sequence Two

The structured follow-on to the full day unit activity involved all members of the HR group who were next given a written dialogue tool to further introduce crucial conversations as becoming dialogue minded to spur team member interaction, and knowledge sharing. Over time with new dialogic practices there could emerge new understanding of how and why dialogue can bring about potentially better and more effective dialogue practices and approaches personally, and broadly into the culture of the unit. In diving deeper toward the introduction and facilitation of a dialogue capability and structure within the HR unit, there was a return to more underpinning provided by David Bohm and William Isaacs. As previously suggested by David Bohm and William Isaacs there is the following dialogue setting – from David Bohm (1996), the implication is that dialogue is a multi-faceted process that looks well beyond conventional ideas of conversational parlance and exchange. The view of the HR unit is that there is potential alignment with Bohm's principles that calls for a shared process that explores a wide range of human experience, from closely held values to the nature and intensity of emotions; the patterns of our thought processes and functions of memory. Bohm goes on to say…perhaps most importantly, dialogue explores the manner in which thought as a limited medium, rather than an objective representation of reality – is generated and sustained on a collective level (i.e. the organization). Such an inquiry calls into question deeply held assumptions about organizational culture, meaning, and identity.

   Accordingly, William Isaacs (1999) makes reference to Aristotle who offered that human beings are distinguished from other species by our ability to use language. As knowledge has progressed over many centuries we as a species have also learned that other species also have the ability for language. Isaacs suggests that individuals don't listen to one another because they are "invested in their own view"; they often "explain" when they should "inquire". Thus, by being caught up in our own preconceptions, feelings and fears are disguised and meaning is hidden. According to

Isaacs, talk in fact, drives individuals apart…dialogue is more than just the exchange of words, but rather, the embrace of different points of view—literally the art of thinking together. With a well-designed dialogue "container tool", one can create an atmosphere of shared awareness that can transform an organization-or a country." It is of vital importance to transition from a philosophical approach to the possibility of dialogue, to a personal self-generated reality. Still, the concept and framework of a container for communication is to begin with the Fire of Conversation which is to kindle the spark of conversation into a productive fire regarding core principles of dialogue to include participation, listening, respecting, suspending, unfolding, awareness, voicing and coherence. The art and act of creating a container is to move people toward a more profound conversational field where one becomes aware of and can influence the subtler aspects of a conversation. The potential extends to patterns of thought, the quality of the exchange and the comfort of discomfort a person feels regarding relationships, direction, and purpose in people pulling together.

Contextually for Isaacs it is also important to remember that people will shift fluidly in healthy conversations; however they get stuck in unhealthy conversations much like the Rush Hour problem solving activity that was led by this author at the first full day meeting. Subsequently over a one-month period each member of the HR unit was interviewed about their understanding and potential use of dialogue. The questions that were asked at the initial meeting were asked again of each person in the HR unit. In this case chapter, it is important to generally say that the individual responses were different in more than eighty percent of the time than was verbalized in the full-group setting. The reasons given by interviewees ranged from "I did not want to speak up in front of my manager" to "I really don't have real communication with one or more people in my group" as well as "I am not listened to nor are my ideas respected" and "something that was said was not truthful or accurate" and "I don't understand technology and young people".

At the start onsite of crucial conversations-difficult conversations (CCDC), it was stated to HR team members that in going deeper that any comments made would be kept confidential, and there would be no personal attribution made in a summary report to unit leadership. What follows is a summary of key points, observations, reflections and responses given by HR team members who participated in group conversations that averaged 65 minutes per group. The CCDC process took place over a combination of four full-day work sessions and several 65-minute conversations on several other days respectively. This case document presents a selective recollection of some of what was spoken and heard. Additionally, this summary document highlights possible ideas, themes and gaps as well as identifies other areas for more team building that could support improved business operations within the current functioning HR group system. This consultant contends that effective team building involves consistent communication and dialogue management in a workplace environment that supports and sustains higher level and stronger intra-group and inter-group performance. As previously stated, the summary to follow is not verbatim and is without direct attribution to any one participant in the HR unit or the larger organization. The document contextually seeks to present what emerged from focused communication relative to communication styles and preferences that links with group dynamics, yields insights, trends, further questions and areas for current and future change management consideration for implementation.

A major impression, reflection and take away gleaned from my concerted time with the HR team members is that I think that mutually beneficial strategic goals, for management and the HR team can be attained and sustained at a higher level by HR team members. The reflective practice approach that is being applied is to move from technical rationality to reflection in action as suggested by Donald A. Schon (1983). Thus, such action-based research advancement could foster sharper team member alignment that would also become fully functional and measureable as a goal in further assessing human capital outcomes regarding performance capacity. A key result would be more vibrant teamwork inside the HR unit to be able to meet new challenges and opportunities for staffing and supports for the larger organization to gain advantage in its competitive marketplace. A key to unlocking already recognizable teamwork potential is the present malleable culture in the organization.

Dialogue for Change: Crucial Conversations/ Deeper Conversations – Sequence Three

Each 90-minute crucial conversations team session of going deeper with HR team members was an interactive exchange environment in which specific information related to a range of possibility for team members to open up personally, and together, about their present and desired approach to communication to consider rooting and establishing dialogue in the HR unit workplace. By seeding and adding in reflective practice with dialogue practice there is a link to William Isaacs again who suggests that "reflective dialogue can then give rise to generative dialogue, in which we begin to create entirely new possibilities and create new levels of interaction" (Isaacs, 2017, p. 38). Over several months the generative dialogue approach was implemented and fully expanded across the entire HR unit. This author facilitated communication between team members that sought to achieve open and honest communication exchanges that embodied safety, respect, and the willingness of team members to operate from trust that embodied authentic exchange while staying on a journey together that is a path of transformation to get to a new place while on a shared journey. See the onsite team conversation matrix that was applied in team based crucial conversations/deeper conversations in the HR unit. Specifically, the team conversation and inquiry matrix format that has been facilitated conversation is presented as a component of the developing communication matrices for managing dialogue change model (CMMDCM) that was applied as a conversational framework. The question matrix included five inter-linked inquiries or questions so that each team member would give a reply or response to each inquiry.

HQ Team Inquiry and Crucial Conversations Matrix

1. As a team member, how do you currently communicate with fellow group or team members and do you willingly operate from openness as well as do you promote openness (both experienced by you and also extended to you by others). Do you value trust on your team, and in your group, and/or with another group or groups, or specific colleagues as a part of your function and work in HR?

2. As a team member, what is your personal commitment to team interdependence that is to communicate openly and honestly and to act and interact purposefully together in order to work collaboratively? Are you in step within your team, and also with another group or team member, and/or in groups or matrix of groups or units elsewhere in HR?

3. How do you recognize and experience "difference" as an approach or way and opportunity for you to engage with HR team members who are on your team or in the group, and beyond your team to other individuals and groups? The context for difference in CCDC were a) personally generating an idea or being a participant in idea generation for problem solving; b) perspective giving, meaning how do you as an HR team member understand an issue or a problem, do you take opportunity to give your perspective? Having a personal view means how do you like or prefer to see a problem, or tend to see and hear an issue or a problem? Do you receive feedback, and do you take and act on the feedback received?

4. Who is in a leadership role in your specific group? Describe how the group communicates and discusses what to do.

5. What is your power in the group and are you able to communicate your power to another team member?

Dialogue for Change: Management Composites – Sequence Four

Throughout the engagement with the HR unit it has been necessary to maintain anonymity in order to build and operate together through trust that is essential to garnering participation and authenticity. As the change process has expanded full participation and the willingness to practice dialogue as a shared and owned process of unit engagement can be sustained, and it will need to be supported and also respected by senior management. There is also recognition that the age-old maxim of "people will at times go along to get along" is a real and credible consideration. In all team cases, the reference barometer in the organization most often mentioned was the HR Employee Engagement Survey and the dialogue construction to drive cohesion in an affirming operating culture and climate where honest dialogue is the currency. In getting to a place of change within the HR unit, there is significant difference in how and why people express themselves when communicating and the selected composites below are meant to tie together and to reflect similar desires and concerns, or representative things of broad to high importance. From the start to the completion of an extended facilitated CCDC as the feature of the, the participating HR team members were in conversations that yielded inputs and observations in a proactive manner and way. While this was the expectation, it is again what was reported as willingness in a structured process to navigate through change dynamics while doing real-time work.

A Group Composite View

- It has been more than two years since the Employee Engagement Survey. I/ we see that unit leaders are doing their best to move things forward as active servant leaders as they interact with us.
- My team leaders are willing to act as a bridge to and from senior leadership and senior management in the unit, and in the larger organization.
- I/we still need to know that ideas offered are acknowledged and can be developed, and then an idea can be communicated and championed by fellow team members and leadership. Is it possible for ideas to move upward or is it only downward?
- I/we are open to suggestions to overcome lack of attention, and felt suppression or dismissal, or rejection leadership and management without explanation. Is it possible for ideas to move upward or is it only downward?
- We need to put in place a standard where the HR team will provide consistently clear communication, information for better alignment. It is important to know that we contribute to decisions and their outcomes for which we are held responsible.
- It will benefit our group to be able to use dialogue to move beyond cognitive dissonance that often results in less effective and ill-timed communication, and at times bad feelings and even holding back. How do we not let fear push us back?

- Change is fast and constant, and I/we do not always understand what is happening and why, let alone be able to manage through it to take advantage of new opportunities.
- Time in employment matters because we have several generations in the group who date from the original company norms and now many post-acquisition organization members in the HR group.
- There are so many new employees that we do not know who they are and it's also the other way around—what are the norms, and what is our culture?
- There is conflict felt and expressed by some—differences are not appreciated enough.
- It is important that we transform our working together from a spaghetti matrix while remaining focused and innovative at times as a cohesive group.
- We have the potential to move away from silos and to begin to function strategically as an interconnected "ecosystem".
- In doing work as contributors in HR we would have stronger relationships throughout our group if openness was practiced along with more intra group transparency. This would aid with achieving greater external transparency.
- We can be more collaborative and intentional. By example, what are we doing it this way as we seek to build? We can get beyond the checklist—there needs to be dialogue. It is taking us a long time to sail together.
- We can be more intentional; what are we doing this for and if it is to build it has taken a long time to sail. It would be better to be proactive and less reactive. The rules here are very gray and they are vague. I/We ought to be able to express ourselves.
- Through better communication more people can begin to understand what I understand and know that is actionable knowledge. We are getting past blockages during change.
- Excellence in teamwork activities should be rewarded more often to establish a tradition and culture of recognition.
- We want to be a part of change management processes as co-founders. My interest and vision can be better aligned with my work contributions.
- Conversation that builds into dialogue makes for honest conversations in our seeking to make a difference. Servant leadership matters to our values.

ACTION RECOMMENDATIONS

Concerning the next steps of ongoing experiential learning and reflective practice activities, the emerging CCDC focus of the CMMDC will benefit from additional shaping and contextualization for organizational fit by HR unit members. The expectation is that it, the CMMDC, is beginning to offer some practical evidence that in application it incorporates communication assessment, design thinking, and new economy planning for build-out as a viable framework. In doing so, this author will continue to review and provide feedback when asked about how the CMMDC dialogic process underway is pointing to results, and can be further modified toward the transforming of a critical unit of the larger organization via a changing communication approach and system. There is also a consideration that a double-looping communication process is critical to build and shape a sustainable dialogue framework for the HR group. It is important to recognize that teaming and teamwork can encounter broad and differing complexity in a given organization. In doing so, such team realities and many interactions that occur often add new complexity in what shared work is and makes possible in teams and larger unit in a given organization. It became clear at the beginning of engagement that the import of technology components and enhancements to spur further innovation would become a factor in meeting performance expectations of the HR unit. In addition, the HR team is continuing to add new members with some members being permanent and others temporary as the team needs to manage inclusion with communication and dialogue being central to meeting the goal.

Consequently, it is important that team members in the HR unit maintain broad and full participation that is accountability for shared learning in the organization to facilitate dialogue generated communication within and across teams in the HR unit more effectively. The envisioned process is learning and doing together that expands into other areas of team member development (Calvin & Igu, 2019). The learning and doing together also accrues with group and team development that again is in line with two previous employee engagement surveys, and can be benchmarked with future employee engagement survey findings.

The author thinks that more applications of CMMDC as a dialogue change model in other organizations will yield key insights to further adapt and strengthen the model as a tool for organizational change. As a change management model that is in use by the HR unit, the CMMDC recommendation is that it is necessary to sustain collective efforts as well as to encourage risk taking and straight talk, in order to find and enable deeper conversations and difficult conversations opportunities for facilitated and self-managed discussion with the full group. Another potential sustaining feature is to encourage team members to practice being brave in their feedback to each other as a supporting mechanism to foster ongoing team communication. Still there is the leadership role inside the HR unit as well as external to the unit in the larger organization. In summary, the inquiry based dialogue process that took place can be further adapted and modified, and altered and shaped as new teaming process inputs are added to the emerging efficacy of CMMDC in the HR unit. It is important to note that ongoing trust building, integrity and openness, is future modeling and adoption of team behaviors for constructive dialogue within and across the HR ecosystem and culture.

The intended culture shift within the HR unit requires buy-in for the integration of new team members to proactively manage team dynamics, and also individual relationships. While a number of unit members have expressed little or no interest in being a formal leader, or to have a leadership role, the stated alignment goal is to become a learning organization that as a unit is a community of commitment (Kofman & Senge, 1993). Toward the goal, there is reference made to Heifetz and Linsky (2002), who suggest that leadership opportunities are commonplace – they happen every day. It does appear so far from the intervention path that getting into effective dialogue does benefit from a crucial conversations process that opens up to shared outcomes. Finally, there will also be future opportunity to correct errant outcomes and gaps in the emerging team and teamwork dialogic process that is representative of active double loop learning and practice together in the HR unit (Argyris, 1977). The starting premise of the case intervention is that new organizational capacity through crucial conversations can enable better team management together by establishing more effective communication matrices as new information technology is rapidly being introduced into the HR unit of the organization.

CONCLUSION

This case chapter is focused sharply on people dynamics in an organization, and the introduction of dialogic processes and practices as actionable data for transformation activity. The case chapter presents a future direction in the organization that emerged through an intervention about dialogue practices to enable the strengthening of information sharing capacity and knowledge sharing across and within teams in the HR unit. The people dynamics referenced follow a merger and intergenerational concerns and transitional impacts. The case chapter also presents a model for discovering communication challenges in organizational settings when a workforce holds different views due to generational knowledge and experiences.

REFERENCES

Argyris, C. (1977). Double loop learning in organizations. *Harvard Business Review*, *55*(5), 115–124. https://hbr.org/1977/09/double-loop-learning-inorganizations

Bohm, D. (1996). *On Dialogue*. New York: Routledge.

Buckingham, M. (2007). *Go Put Your Strengths to Work*. New York: Free Press.

Callon, M., & Latour, B. (1992). Don't throw the baby out with the Bath School! A reply to Collins and Yearley. In A. Pickering (Ed.), *Science as Practice and Culture*. Chicago, IL: University of Chicago Press.

Calvin, J. R., & Igu, J. (2019). Culture, conflict and team management in I4H: Experiential learning in business practice to support community development entrepreneurship. *Journal of Organizational Culture. Communications and Conflicts*, *23*(1), 1.

Cialdini, R. B. (2007). *Influence: The psychology of persuasion*. New York: Collins Business.

Cooperrider, D. L. (2013). Advances in Appreciative Inquiry: Vol. 4. *A contemporary commentary on appreciative inquiry in organizational life*. doi:10.1108/S1475-9152(2013)0000004001

Cummings, S., Bridgman, T., & Brown, K. (2016). Unfreezing change as three steps: Rethinking Kurt Lewin's legacy for change management. *Human Relations*, *69*(1), 33–60. doi:10.1177/0018726715577707

Endicott, D., & Sviola, J. (2019, Summer). Facing up to a four-generation society. *Strategy+Business*, 95.

Foucault, M. (1972). *The Archaeology of Knowledge and the Discourse of Language*. New York: Pantheon.

Foucault, M. (1977). *Truth and Power*. New York: Pantheon.

Fry, R. (2018). *Millennials are the Largest Generation in the U.S. Labor Force*. Pew Research Center. https://www.pewresearch.org/fact-tank/2018/04/11/millennials-largest-generation-us-labor-force

Heifetz, R. A., & Linsky, M. (2002). *Leadership on the Line*. Boston, MA: Harvard Business School Press.

Hofstede, G. (1997). *Cultures and Organisations: Software of the mind*. London, UK: McGraw-Hill.

Isaacs, W. (1999). *Dialogue: The art of thinking together*. New York: Crown Publishing.

Isaacs, W. (2017, Feb. 8). Conversations that change the world. *Strategy+Business*.

Kofman, F., & Senge, P. M. (1993). Communities of commitment: The heart of learning organizations. *Organizational Dynamics*, *22*(2), 5–23. doi:10.1016/0090-2616(93)90050-B

Kotter, J. P. (2012). *Leading Change*. Boston, MA: Harvard Business Review Press.

Kotter, J. P. (2014). *Accelerate: Building strategic agility for a faster-moving world*. Boston, MA: Harvard Business Review Press.

Law, J. (1999). After ANT: Complexity, naming and topology. In J. Hassard & J. Law (Eds.), *Actor Network Theory and After*. Oxford, UK: Blackwell Publishers. doi:10.1111/j.1467-954X.1999.tb03479.x

Law, J. (2007). *Actor Network Theory and Material Semiotics*. http://www.heterogeneities.net/publications/LawANTandMaterialSemiotics.pdf

Lencioni, P. (2002). *The Five Dysfunctions of a Team*. San Francisco, CA: Jossey-Bass.

Lewin, K. (1947). Frontiers in group dynamics: Concept, method and reality in social science; social equilibria and social change. *Human Relations*, *1*(1), 5–40. doi:10.1177/001872674700100103

O'Sullivan, P. B., & Carr, C. T. (2018). Masspersonal communication: A model bridging the mass-interpersonal divide. *New Media & Society*, *20*(3), 1161–1180. doi:10.1177/1461444816686104

Robbins, S. P. (2003). *Organizational Behavior* (10th ed.). Prentice Hall.

Schein, E. H. (1990). Organizational Culture. *The American Psychologist*, *45*(2), 109–119. doi:10.1037/0003-066X.45.2.109

Schon, D. A. (1983). *The Reflective Practitioner*. New York: Basic Books.

Schwab, K. (2018). *Shaping the Fourth Industrial Revolution*. World Economic Forum.

Segars, A. H. (2018). *Seven Technologies Remaking the World*. Boston, MA: MIT Sloan Management Review.

KEY TERMS AND DEFINITIONS

Action Research: The use of techniques from social and psychological research to identify group problems regarding active participation involving group efforts to problem solve.

Appreciative Inquiry: Action-oriented models that seek to engage stakeholders in self-determined or other motivation toward navigating change; it features strengths-based approaches in American management.

Change Management: Is the management of change and development in an organization, community or group, or changes within a computer system.

Crucial Conversations: A discussion between two or more people where perceptions and opinions matter, emotions may run strong and impressions and opinions differ.

Organizational Capacity Building: Is multi-level and multi-tiered at individual, organizational and system levels.

Process Intervention: A focused or deliberate process or procedure designed and intended to assist, move or guide people through a situation involving difficulty in a shared system.

Sustainable Dialogue Framework: A developed dialogue vehicle to both engage and sustain diversity of misunderstanding, understanding, and meaning that can help manage conflicts of complexity.

Technology and Organizational Culture: With four generations in many workplaces, technology tools have impact on/in workplace culture and social and group behaviors, rituals and dynamics.

Chapter 6

Using Big Data to Understand Chinese Users' Intentions to Tap Through Mobile Advertisements

Jing Quan

https://orcid.org/0000-0002-5318-809X
Salisbury University, USA

ABSTRACT

This study examines influencing factors for users' intentions to tap through mobile advertisements. This chapter uses a data set with 115,899 records of ad tap-through from a mobile advertising company in China to fit a logit model to examine how the probability of advertisement tap-through is related to the identified factors. The results show that the influencing variables are application type, mobile operators, scrolling frequency, and the regional income level as they are positively correlated with the likelihood whether users would tap on certain types of advertising. Moreover, a Bayesian network model is used to estimate the conditional probability for a user to tap on an advertisement in an application after the user already taps on another advertisement in the same application. Based on the findings, strategies for mobile advertisers to engage in effective and targeted mobile advertising are proposed.

DOI: 10.4018/978-1-7998-2235-6.ch006

INTRODUCTION

The fastest growing form of marketing is digital advertising, within which, mobile is the fastest growing medium as people feel increasingly comfortable viewing mobile advertising and making purchases (Smith, 2019). The rapid development of mobile technology makes it possible for mobile advertisers to use various applications to dynamically push advertisements onto smartphones and tablets (Wong, Tan, Tan, & Ooi, 2015). The traditional advertising formats of short message service (SMS) and multimedia messaging service (MMS) (Park, Shenoya, & Salvendy, 2008; Samanta, Woods, & Ghanbari, 2009) are gradually being replaced by mobile interactive advertising (Laszlo, 2009). More advantageous than the traditional advertising, this new form of mobile advertising possesses properties of real-time, mobility, higher rates of user reachability, and instantaneous interactions. Because of the unique match between a smartphone and its user identification, mobile advertisers can analyze user behavior and preferences to achieve more accurate advertising content delivery. The mobile advertising service industry, resulting from the popularity of mobile advertising, sets its core business as pushing advertisements to mobile users. They not only organize a large number of mobile application developers to provide application services to mobile customers, but also promote the development and practice of personalized advertising service market.

Since 2007 when Apple marketed the first generation of smartphones the mobile Internet industry has flourished. The emergence of Android, Windows, and other smartphone operating systems, along with iPhone, has provided strong support to smartphone handset manufacturers. The model of mobile applications (app), third-party developers and application stores quickly became the most popular and opportunistic business model in the market. This model calls for sharing smartphone operating system interfaces (API) or the source codes, allowing non-platform developers and third-party operators to develop apps, and then uploading the apps to the app store for global users to download either for free or for a fee. The developers and platform operators share the revenue. Apple and Google are well-known examples of this business model. Because this model allows any developer to upload apps, the number of applications on the platform can increase rapidly to meet users' demand for a variety of applications. Apple's iOS platform has become a mature fee-based model, and its rigorous audit ensures the quality of apps. Because most of the apps in the Apple store are for fee-based downloads and iOS users have been accustomed to paying, iOS developers can earn a decent income. As a result, this business model has created many entrepreneurs.

In contrast to iOS, the Android platform is an open platform. Because most of the apps are free to download, developers on the Android platform develop and upload apps for free. Such an open platform leads to uneven application quality and results in the current situation where the majority of users do not want to pay for downloading apps. For example, Viennot, Garcia, and Nieh (2014) find that about 80% of apps in the Google Play Store are free. In general, developers on the Android platform cannot make money by relying on basic app downloads, although many commercial apps are paid and an important source of revenue for their developers is the price of the app. To overcome this shortcoming, a new kind of profit model of "free apps + advertising" has gained market popularity in recent years. Taking advantage of this trend, a number of mobile advertising companies emerged. Successful examples include Millennial Media, StrikeAd, and AirPush in the U.S., and Cellphone Ads Serving E-Exchange (CASEE), WOOBO, and Youmi in China. In 2012, Millennial Media saw its initial public offering (IPO) price rise more than 90% on its first day listed on the NASDAQ, showing market confidence and expectation for this emerging industry. Among all forms of advertising, mobile advertising is expected to grow the fastest; it is the new frontier of advertising. Social media companies such as Google and Facebook race to gain shares of this form of advertising. According to the U.S. market research firm eMarketer, U.S. and China mobile advertising revenues in 2015 reached $28 and $13 billion, respectively, and in 2018 are expected to reach $57 and $40 billion, respectively (Dogtiev, 2016).

Tsang, Ho, and Liang (2004) summarize the nature of mobile advertising as follows: 1) rapid growth of mobile Internet has made effective one-to-one marketing possible; 2) user attitudes toward mobile advertising are generally passive unless the content is specifically customized; and 3) user attitudes have a direct impact on their behaviors. Xu and Gutierrez (2006) also suggest that the widespread use of mobile phones has resulted in the rapid growth of mobile commerce (m-commerce), and that mobile advertising is one of most important m-commerce applications, as well as one of the highest potential direct marketing channels. To understand the effectiveness of smartphone advertisements and stimulating factors for customers' decision to purchase, Martins, Costa, Oliveira, Gonçalves, and Branco (2019) analyze the data collected from 303 Portuguese respondents. The researchers find that purchase intention is closely related to advertising value, flow experience, web design quality, and brand awareness.

The mobile advertising business model consists of mobile advertising companies, advertisers and app developers. Mobile advertising companies are responsible for contacting advertisers, making advertising banners, and pushing advertising content to a variety of apps. They also provide advertising placement software development kits (SDK) to third party developers who have registered with the companies. Developers embed the SDK in their developed apps and publish them on the web. Mobile phone users can download apps and install them on their phones. When users open an app, the embedded SDK application will request data from the back-end service for specific advertisement banners to display on mobile terminals. The advertisements will scroll in a specific position on the smartphone. When interested in the content of a scrolling banner, a user can tap on it. Then the specific content of the advertisement is shown in appropriate forms on the phone screen. This completes the publication cycle of an advertisement. The mobile advertising company records the number of taps and advertisers pay an appropriate fee based on the hits. The mobile advertising company then shares part of the revenue with developers.

Because this advertising model is the combination of ad push by mobile advertising companies and ad tap by mobile users, many factors are involved. Tap-through on mobile devices is similar to click-through on desktop/laptop computers. The tap-through rates (TTR) are usually low. One online experiment measured TTR as low as 0.18 percent (MetaRain Blog, 2014). The low TTR may be attributed to the poor effectiveness of the mobile application advertising. In addition, too many ineffective ad displays can make mobile users unhappy because of unwanted interferences. Huang and Wang (2010) argue that mobile media companies should respect users by highlighting the core advertising value of displaying accurate advertising for targeted customers. How to increase the accuracy of advertising placements and reduce user irritation is a very challenging proposition for mobile advertising companies.

This chapter answers the challenge of personalized marketing "at the right time, sent to the right person" (Chen & Hsieh, 2012) using an empirical model based on 115,899 records from a local mobile advertising company to discern the relationships between tap-through of an advertisement by a user, type of apps, mobile carriers, and the number of scrolls. The local mobile advertising company was located in one of the largest metropolitan areas in China. The data should be representative of urban areas in China. In addition, a Bayesian network model to estimate the conditional probability of a particular ad tapping through on an ad already being tapped was constructed and provided the basis for more precise advertisement delivery.

BACKGROUND

Mobile advertising is a type of advertising that appears on mobile devices. Those devices typically are smartphones and tablets with wireless connections. Mobile advertising is often regarded as a subset of mobile marketing. The various forms of mobile advertising include text ads via SMS, or banner advertisements that appear embedded in a mobile web site, in downloaded apps, or mobile games. Big mobile advertising integrators such as Google and Facebook tailor mobile advertisements toward an individual's web browsing history, geographic location, and with data collected by shopping habits. Due to the fact that mobile devices typically have smaller screens than the traditional devices like computers or laptops, this form of emerging advertising must be optimized for small displays using more concise and short formats. For example, mobile versions of websites with advertisements are typically optimized for the smaller mobile displays than the full version of the same website tailored for computers or laptops.

The most recent development in mobile advertising is that targeted advertisements can be displayed when a user is in close proximity to a service provider or certain store. Mobile ad placement is determined by way of a programmatic bidding process for ad placement. In such a format, advertisers bid in real-time for the right to display an ad on a mobile device. A demand-side platform (DSP) is the infrastructure that enables this process. Mobile advertising platforms can help advertisers optimize their performance as measured by a number of key performance indicators (KPI), such as effective cost per click (eCPC) and effective cost per action (eCPA).

As the number of mobile devices grow, the chances of a potential customer seeing a mobile ad are greater than that of most other forms of advertising. Cost per install (CPI) is one popular model in mobile advertising, where payment is based on the user installing an app on their mobile device. CPI mobile advertising models can be classified either as incent or non-incent. In the incent model, the user is given some form of payments such as virtual points or rewards to install the game or app. In the non-incent model, the user is not given any form of payment such as virtual points or rewards to install the game or app. The early form of mobile advertising took place via SMS text messages. But due to its ineffectiveness, the form has quickly evolved to mobile web and in-app advertisements. Although many apps offer a free version that can be downloaded at no cost, it is paid for by placement of advertisements within the app. If a user does not want to see the advertisements, they can purchase a full or premium version of the app.

Effectiveness of Mobile Advertising

Mobile advertising is an emerging area of research with many researchers attempting to identify adoption factors or effectiveness (Ma, Suntornpithug, & Karaatli, 2009; Park et al. 2008; Vatanparast & Butt, 2010). Identified factors include time, location, information, and personalization (Bauer, Barnes, Reichardt, & Neumann, 2005), as well as social norms, users' motives, mode, and personal characteristics (Barwise & Strong, 2002). Studies also propose other key variables including perceived information, entertainment, and social utility (Bauer et al., 2005) as well as entertainment, irritation, informativeness, credibility, and personalization (Xu & Gutierrez, 2006). Similarly, Cheng, Blankson, Wang, and Chen (2009) analyze four strategies of digital advertising placements on mobile devices and discover that three elements – informativeness, entertainment, and irritation – have an impact on the effectiveness of mobile advertising. Jun and Lee (2007) find that convenience and multimedia service are statistically related to users' acceptance of mobile advertising. Ozcelik and Varnali (2019) focus on the psychology of the recipient in explaining the effectiveness of online ads and find that the promotion focus level of a consumer has is significantly related to perceptions regarding informativeness and entertainment of a customized online ad, whereas perceived security risk associated with clicking customized online ads has a directly inverse effect of irritation. In addition, the attitude toward the ad and brand attitude mediates the effect of ad value dimensions on behavioral ad responses.

de Castro and Shimakawa (2006) introduce customer location information and user interest in mobile advertising push research. The authors use decision keywords to filter the neighborhood list to find the similarity between user locations and interests and make recommendation for advertisements. The experiment shows good results with almost 100% of the users expressing a certain level of interest in the received advertisement recommended by the system. Kim, Lee, Park, and Choi (2009) design a system that not only provides recommendations based on users' interest, but also improves the efficiency of advertising by mining user preferences based on text messages. The simulation of the system achieved good experimental results. A qualitative study by Peters and Amato (2007) finds that user adoption of wireless advertising depends on process motives, social needs, and content needs.

From the marketing perspective, some mobile advertising research focuses on how to provide users with valuable information and accurate marketing services based on market segmentations and user preferences. Tsang et al. (2004) propose that entertainment, credibility, irritation, and informativeness are important influencing factors for users' acceptance of mobile advertising. In a study of young African consumers, Waldt, Rebbello, and Brown (2009) find that users generally have negative attitudes toward mobile ads due to entertainment, credibility, and irritation. Similarly, Chowdhury et al. (2006) discover that among credibility, irritation, entertainment, and information, only credibility is a significant factor influencing users' attitude toward mobile advertising.

In a comparative study, Cheng et al. (2009) offer some interesting insights into the old and new advertising push methods. Traditional forms of mobile advertising generally use SMS and telephone calls to push advertising content. However, this type of advertising is often treated as spam messages or spam calls. In the 3G era, the widespread use of smartphones made the new advertising push mode more appealing, because users have the freedom to view or not view the advertising content. This leads to the decreased psychological resistance for mobile advertising.

Another popular mode of mobile advertising is advertiser-sponsored services offered by mobile operators. Relative to banner advertisements, sponsored advertising is more reliable at consumer targeting because it can be customized based on a user's web search history on such social network sites as Facebook (Barreto, 2013). Dehghani and Tumer (2015) state that sponsored mobile advertising is an effective way of marketing message dissemination because of direct connections among advertising consumers, producers, and brands. A specific process may involve a sponsor presenting an advertisement as a story with a user's real time experience with a product. Once followers start to repeat story-telling and additional information sharing and exchanges about the product, more intensive brand experiences are created (Dyrud, 2011). Lin and Kim (2016) frame their study based on the technology acceptance model (TAM) and find that both privacy and intrusiveness concerns are impactful variables for perceived usefulness but not for perceived ease of use of sponsored advertising. In addition, consumer attitudes toward sponsored advertising are impacted by concerns of both privacy and intrusiveness, but product purchase intentions are only influenced by privacy concerns. Park, Kim, and Lee (2018) study the interaction effects of ad nativity and thinking styles and find that non-native ads are more effective for analytic thinkers, while native ads are more effective for holistic thinkers. In addition, the absence of brand-app congruency lowers non-native ad irritation.

Although current research on mobile advertising enhances the understanding of this new form of advertising and its effectiveness, two gaps between theory and practice still exist. First, theoretical frameworks proposed in the extant literature are mostly abstract in nature. This makes their applications to reality difficult. Second, most research is focused on the sender (seller) side of advertising instead of on the recipient (user) side. This leads to the need to examine advertising effectiveness from the users' perspective (Ahn, Kim, & Han, 2006). The rapid growth of mobile phone users has attracted a large number of mobile advertisers to enter the market. To minimize irritations with mobile user experience, it is crucial for advertisers to find an innovative and non-invasive method of advertising placements. Topsümer and Yarkin (2015) argue that customers will view unwanted mobile advertising as "time loss". Tripathi and Nair (2006) argue that the precise advertising and targeting face challenges because of the increasingly large demand for mobile advertising and the uncertainty of user behavior. Kim and Lee (2015) propose a new theoretical framework based on customer psychological typologies in smart mobile advertising industries by departing from previous demographical criteria or researcher-oriented empirical research.

PURPOSE OF THE STUDY

This study aims to close these gaps by proposing an empirical and testable model for the likelihood that a user would tap through a particular advertisement. Moreover, this study introduces four key explanatory variables directly related to users: app type, income level of the user location, mobile operators, and the number of scrolling advertisements as described below. First, app type is used as a proxy for user interests, which are the most decisive factor for a successful advertisement (Zhu & Chen, 2015). For example, when users open a game app, it is an indication of their interest in playing games. This variable is similar to the informativeness and relevancy dimensions of mobile advertising in literature (Barwise & Strong, 2002; Bauer et al., 2005; Cheng et al. 2009; Topsümer & Yarkin, 2015; Xu & Gutierrez, 2006).

Second, the study suggests that the level of regional income is related to the popularity of certain types of advertising. For example, users in a relatively low-income region may be more interested in downloading coupons from their cell phones, whereas users in more affluent regions can obtain coupons in a variety of ways. This is similar to the user location concept in literature (Bauer et al., 2005; de Castro & Shimakawa, 2006; Gana & Thomas, 2016).

Third, the mobile operator situation in China is unique. Among the three major mobile operators (China Mobile, China Unicom, China Telecom), China Mobile is much larger than its two smaller rivals. Because the big operator can offer more megabytes per month to their users and provide offers for smartphones with more capabilities than the smaller rivals, users are less worried about data usage when viewing and tapping on ads. As a result, users of different mobile operators may exhibit a different level of preference to certain types of advertising.

Finally, the study is focused on the number of scrolling advertisements. When users open an application on their phone, a mobile advertising company starts to send advertisements to scroll in the application. This number is cleared to zero when one advertisement is tapped on. This variable represents the irritation factor identified in the literature (Le & Nguyen, 2014; Lin, Zhou, & Cen, 2014; Topsümer & Yarkin, 2015; Tsang et al. 2004; Waldt et al., 2009). In addition, a Bayesian network model was created to predict the conditional probability for a user to tap through one particular ad after the user tapped through an ad. Bayesians believe that events that have occurred in the past are capable of providing relevant information for the prediction of future behavior. Researchers widely use Bayesian networks to estimate conditional probabilities based on users' past behavior (Cui, Wong, & Lui, 2006; Zhu, 2013).

RESEARCH METHODOLOGY

The study was conducted in three steps. First, user data from a mobile advertising company in Guangzhou, China was collected over a period of three months, including the number of ad displays, tap-through, the number of scrollings, and mobile carriers from the mobile advertising company. Second, data for the variables used in this study was extracted. Finally, data analysis using logistic regression to calculate the probability of user tap-through based on app types, mobile carriers, the number of scrolling advertisements, and local GDP (collected from the China Statistics Book) was conducted.

The data were randomly selected from the company's back-end servers. The volume of the dataset was 80 gigabytes. The back-end data was stored as text-based on a predefined structure specifying the length of each variable. The value of the variables used in this study was calculated according to the specification of the defined format. Given the variables were measured in raw numbers, no classification was performed. Additionally, a Java program to segment and extract the raw data and saved the results in a database for forthcoming analysis was created. To overcome the large amount of data and limited computing capacity, the records were filtered for the time period 17:00-20:00 each day. This time period was selected mainly because this was when people got off work and had the leisure to use apps on their phones; this was confirmed by the higher tap-through rates during this time interval compared to any other time of the day. The filtering procedure reduced the number of records to 60 million, among which 115,899 were tap-through, representing a rate of about 1.9%, consistent with findings in the current literature (MetaRain Blog, 2014). The 115,899 records constituted the working dataset for this study.

The classifications for advertisements and apps as defined by the company were used for this study. The classification system is based on the specific form of advertising and promotional content. There are four categories for advertisements. The first category is website promotion advertising, mostly the promotions of e-commerce, portals and other websites. This type of advertising is mainly pushed to smartphones in the form of text. The second category of advertising is promotional sales of goods and services by merchants in the form of GIF images. The third class of advertising is for group shopping cards, coupons, as well as application software downloads. And the last category is the direct introduction and showcase of new products using rich media of audio, video, and animation.

QUANTITATIVE ANALYSIS

Using the 115,899 tap-through records, descriptive statistics and correlation analysis were computed and are presented in Tables 1 and 2.

Table 1. Descriptive statistics

Type	Description	Ad1 (Website Promotions)	Product recommendations)	Ad3 (Coupons and Promotions)	Ad4 (Rich Media Promotions)	Total	%
App0	Application Software	3375	2232	9021	30	14658	12.647
App1	Communication Aids	10	0	335	0	345	0.298
App2	Casual Games	4657	2212	39446	1676	47991	41.408
App3	Chess Puzzle	472	290	6736	1	7499	6.470
App4	Other	10279	9001	8941	805	29026	25.044
App5	Multimedia Software	264	800	2912	90	4066	3.508
App6	Strategy Games	57	18	625	4	704	0.607
App7	Network Application	124	6	1072	0	1202	1.037
App8	System Software	29	0	1120	2	1151	0.993
App9	Role-playing	94	1	1854	4	1953	1.685
App10	Shooting & flight	310	0	3754	0	4064	3.507
App11	Adventure Simulation	9	2	716	12	739	0.638
App12	Security Software	10	0	94	0	104	0.090
App13	Sports Competition	32	5	1144	0	1181	1.019
App14	Action Fighting	34	189	992	1	1216	1.049
Total		19756	14756	78762	2625	115899	
%		17.046	12.732	67.957	2.265		100

Table 1 offers a few insights into the relationships between apps and ads. First, the tap-through on three apps, Application Software (App0), Casual Games (App2), and Other (App4) account for 67.96% of all tap-through, with Casual Games accounting for more than 41%. Second, four apps, Security Software (App12), Communication Aids (App1), Strategy Games (App6), and Adventure Simulation (App11), account for only 1.03% of the total tap-through. Third, ad type Coupons and Promotions (Ad3) is the most popular, accounting for 67.96% of the total tap-through. Fourth, ad type Rich Media Promotion (Ad4) were tapped through the least for only 2.27%, of which 63.84% were opened in Casual Games (App2).

Correlation analysis in Table 2 shows that the correlations between app and ad are significant in most of the cases. The positive correlation implies that ad type is more likely to be opened in that particular app. The negative correlation implies that ad type is less likely to be opened in that particular app. The results in Table 2 suggest that Other apps (App4) are highly correlated with Website Promotions (Ad1) and Product Recommendations (Ad2), but negatively with Coupons and Promotions (Ad3). Moreover, Website Promotions (Ad1) is least likely and Coupons and Promotions (Ad3) is most likely to be tapped by China Mobile users. Finally, users in more affluent regions are more like to tap Website Promotions (Ad1) but least likely to tap Coupons and Promotions (Ad3).

Table 2. Correlation analysis

	Ad1	Ad2	Ad3	Ad4
app0	.061**	.028**	-.052**	-.053**
App1	-.021**	-.021**	.034**	-.008**
App2	-.164**	-.205**	.256**	.069**
App3	-.075**	-.070**	.123**	-.040**
App4	.282**	.317**	-.460**	.020**
App5	-.054**	.040**	.015**	-.001
App6	-.019**	-.024**	.035**	-.009**
App7	-.018**	-.038**	.047**	-.016**
App8	-.039**	-.038**	.063**	-.014**
App9	-.043**	-.050**	.076**	-.018**
App10	-.048**	-.073**	.100**	-.029**
App11	-.034**	-.030**	.050**	-.003
App12	-.006*	-.011**	.014**	-.005
App13	-.039**	-.037**	.063**	-.015**
App14	-.039**	.009**	.030**	-.015**
Tc1	-.274**	-.109**	.292**	.021**
Tc2	.022**	.031**	-.034**	-.017**
Tc3	.208**	.064**	-.214**	-.001
Tc4	.174**	.066**	-.182**	-.017**
GDP	.143**	.082**	-.173**	-.003
Scrolling Freq	.005	.018**	-.011**	-.019**

**significant at the 0.01 level.
*significant at the 0.05 level.
Tc1 = China Mobile, Tc2 = China Unicom, Tc3 = China Telecom, Tc4 = other

Logistic Regression

A logistic regression model was created to estimate the factors affecting the probability of a user tapping through an advertisement. This technique is the appropriate regression analysis to use when the dependent variable is binary (e.g., buy vs. not to buy or presence vs. absent). Similar to other regression analyses, the logistic regression is predictive in nature. Logistic regression is deployed to describe data and to explain the relationship between one dependent dichotomous variable and one or more independent variables.

The dependent variable of the logical model is defined as:

y = 1 if an ad was tapped

0 otherwise

The independent variables are app type, mobile operators, GDP and the number of scrolls of an advertisement. Specifically, the logit model is as follows:

$$\ln \frac{P}{1-P} = \sum_{i}^{14} \alpha_i app_i + \sum_{j}^{3} \gamma_j tc_j + \tau GDP + \sigma RC + \rho \tag{1}$$

where P is the prob(y=1); app is the app type, for i = 1,2,3,4; GDP is the local income level of the area where the users resided; RC is the number of scrolls after the app was turned on; and tc is the mobile operator, defined as:

tc1 = 1 if China Mobile,
    0 otherwise

tc2 = 1 if China Unicom,
    0 otherwise

tc3 = 1 if China Telecom,
    0 otherwise

Bayesian Network Model

The logistic model estimates the probability that a user taps through an ad based on a set of factors including the types of app, mobile operators, GDP and the number of scrolls of an advertisement. It does not, however, take into consideration users' past behavior. It is important for advertisers to know the probability the person would tap through another ad, after a user tapped through a certain ad. To this end, a Bayesian network model was created based on the existing behavior of the user to calculate the probability of subsequent behavior of the user. In general, Bayesian networks are graphical models for probabilistic relationships between a set of random variables and their conditional dependencies. They capture the conditional probabilities between variables. Bayesian network models are a type of probabilistic graphical model that uses Bayesian inference for probability computations. In fact, a Bayesian network can be best represented in a directed acyclic graph. The goal of Bayesian networks is to model conditional dependence, and therefore causation, by representing conditional dependence by edges in a directed graph. These relationships can be helpful for efficiently conducting inference on the random variables in the graph through the use of factors.

In its simplest form, a Bayesian network has two nodes (A and B) and an edge between them. An edge from A to B represents causality with A being the cause and B the effect (Cui, Wong, & Lui, 2006). In this case, the first level domain variables (node A) are the ads being tapped, and second level variables (node B) are the ads to be tapped. Bayesian networks can quantify the conditional probabilities of B given A as shown in Figure 1.

Figure 1. Bayesian network model

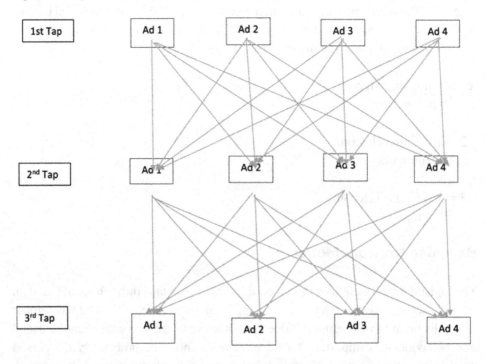

In the personalized advertising recommendation system, users' previous selections of ads can be seen as a priori knowledge for the Bayesian network. Users' uncertain future behaviors and preferences can be regarded as the posterior probabilities verified by a Bayesian network model. In order to facilitate the parameter estimation of the Bayesian network model, the 15 types of mobile applications were reclassified into three categories according to the characteristics of the applications. They are Games, Applications, and Others.

Results

The logit model was run separately for the four different ad types. The estimation results using SPSS are reported in Table 3. The estimated coefficients of a logistic regression reflect the change in the logarithm odds of the dependent variable for a one-unit increase in the predictor variable. Overall, the probability of a tap-through of a certain type of ad is related to app type, mobile operators, the income level of the area where a user resided, and the number of scrolling advertisements.

Table 3. Logit estimation

	Ad1	Ad2	Ad3	Ad4
App0	2.067**	-.092	-.770**	.963
App1	.133	-19.457	2.007**	-14.137
App2	1.314**	-1.336**	.074	3.809**
App3	.835**	-1.551**	.777**	-1.596
App4	2.622**	.818**	-2.112**	3.525**
App5	.631**	.244**	-.405**	3.351**
App6	.957**	-1.986**	.784**	1.889
App7	1.342**	-4.016**	.746**	-14.046
App8	-.324	-19.513	2.346**	.634
App9	.673**	-5.847**	1.419**	.871
App10	1.070**	-19.501	1.069**	-13.968
App11	-.941*	-4.217**	2.093**	3.361**
App12	1.457**	-19.499	.714*	-14.191
App13	-.123	-3.763**	2.086**	-14.044
tc1	-2.303**	-.433**	2.363**	.972**
tc2	-1.199**	-.121**	1.557**	.568**
tc3	-.689**	-.206**	1.105**	.790**
GDP	.276**	.136**	-.325**	.015
RC	.030**	.071**	-.076**	-4.594**
ρ	-2.104**	-1.393**	-.300**	-8.431**

**significant at the 0.01 level.
*significant at the 0.05 level.

Among the four types of advertisements, the first type is text based website promotion advertising, mostly for the promotions of e-commerce, portals and other websites. The probability of tap-through of this type of ads is correlated with the types of apps. The likelihood of tap-through is largest in the apps in the Other category (App4), while smallest in the Adventure Simulation category (App11). This suggests that adventure simulation gamers most likely do not want to be interfered by this type of ad in the form of text. The second category of advertising is GIF images based promotional sales of goods and services by merchants. They are more likely to be opened in App4 (Other) and App5 (Multimedia Software). The third category of advertising (Coupons and Promotions) is for group shopping cards, coupons and application software downloads. They are most likely to be tapped through in App8 (System Software), while least likely in App4 (Other). For the fourth ad category (Rich Media Promotions), it is most likely to be opened in App2 (Casual Games), App4 (Other), App11 (Adventure Simulation), and App5 (Multimedia Software). Because this category of ad relies on audio, video and animation for deliveries, users who open multimedia related apps should be more interested in this type of advertisement.

The probability of tap-through is also correlated with mobile carriers. On one hand, the results show users on the big three networks (China Mobile, China Unicom, and China Telecom) were more likely to tap on Ad3 (Coupons and Promotions) and Ad4 (Rich Media Promotions) than those on the other smaller operators. On the other hand, users on the smaller operators were more likely to open Ad1 (Website Promotions) and Ad2 (Product Recommendations) than those on the big three network.

The income level of geographical locations of users has different effects on the ad tap-through probability. The higher GDP was correlated with the likelihood of Ad1 (Website Promotions) and Ad2 (Product Recommendations) being tapped on. That is, Website Promotions and Product Recommendations were more acceptable to users in areas with high income. On the contrary, Ad3 (Coupons and Promotions) was more acceptable for users in regions with a lower income level. This phenomenon can be attributed to the fact that coupons and group shopping cards are relatively more valuable to users in the lower income areas and smartphones may be one of few ways of getting them. However, users in more affluent and developed areas, such as big urban centers, can obtain coupons and group shopping cards through a variety of ways because discount delivery terminals are relatively common. This resulted in the weakened use of mobile phones to download coupons or group shopping cards.

The results on the scrolling frequency are mixed. On one hand, the number of scrolling has a negative effect on the tap-through for Ad3 (Coupons and Promotions) and Ad4 (Rich Media Promotions). That is, the increased number of scrolling reduces the likelihood of tap-through for these types of advertisement. This is consistent with previous studies that have found that the scrolling irritates users for their normal use of apps and would reduce the probability of tap-through (Cheng et al., 2009; Xu & Gutierrez, 2006). On the other hand, the number of scrolling has a positive impact on the probability of tap-through of Ad1 (Website Promotions) and Ad2 (Product Recommendations). That is, a positive correlation is found to be between the number of scrolling of such advertising and their tap-through probability.

DISCUSSION

This research extends the current understanding of mobile advertising effectiveness. The research framework makes theoretical contribution by identifying four variables – app type, income level, mobile operators, and the number of scrolling advertisements – that are related to better mobile advertising customization. The logistic model identifies the probability of each of four different ads being tapped given the four independent variables. In addition, the Bayesian network model outlines the conditional probability of a certain type of ad being tapped given one type of ad is already tapped.

Specifically, the findings show a close relationship between apps and ad type. The type of apps used by a user may help reveal a part of personal preference. For example, adventure simulation gamers do not want to be interfered by the type of ad in the form of text. This extends the current literature on informativeness and relevancy of mobile ads (Barwise & Strong, 2002; Bauer et al., 2005; Cheng et al. 2009; Topsümer & Yarkin, 2015; Xu & Gutierrez, 2006) or customer sensitivity (Martín-Consuegra, Gómez, & Molina, 2015). This study enriched the user location variable in literature (Bauer et al., 2005; Castro, 2006) with the levels of income in user locations. The findings suggest that the probability of ad tapping is related to local GDP and that users exhibit different levels of preference for certain types of advertising based on their mobile operators in China. This represents a new construct in mobile advertising study. Finally, the number of scrolling advertisements is also significant. This is consistent with the irritation factor identified in Peng, Qu, Peng, and Quan (2017), Topsümer and Yarkin (2015), Tsang et al. (2004), and Waldt, (2009).

The results provide helpful guideline for the mobile advertising company to determine the best possible strategy for ad placement based on user characteristics. By knowing the probability of tap-through of a particular ad given app type, mobile carrier, scrolling frequency, and the income level of the region, the company can push the ads to users who are most likely to tap-through.

Table 4. Order of ad pushing by app

Order from highest to lowest	Ad1	Ad2	Ad3	Ad4
1	App4	App4	App8	App2
2	app0	App5	App11	App4
3	App12	App14	App13	App11
4	App7	App2	App1	App5
5	App2	App3	App9	App6
6	App10	App6	App10	App14
7	App6	App13	App6	
8	App3	App7	App3	
9	App9	App11	App7	
10	App5	App9	App12	
11	App14	App1	App5	
12	App11		app0	
13			App4	
14			App14	

Table 4 lists the apps by the advertising type in descending order based on the probabilities of ad tap-through predicted by the model. It omits the insignificant coefficients in Table 4. Based on the probabilities, the mobile advertising company can select the advertising type with the highest probabilities to push to users based on the opened apps. For example, for users who open App4 (Other) and are in high-income areas, the company should give a high priority to push Ad1 (Website Promotions) and Ad2 (Product Recommendations). Similarly, for users who open App8 (System Software) and App2 (Causal Games) and live in moderate-income regions, the company may select first Ad3 (Coupons and Promotions) to push to App8 (System Software) and Ad4 (Rich Media Promotions) to push to App2 (Casual Games). If a user opens App5 (Multimedia Software), the company should push Ad2 (Product Recommendations) first.

CURRENT RESEARCH TRENDS

Through analysis of a large data set of 115,899 records, variables that have significant relationships with the likelihood of ad tap-through are identified. The findings provide a theoretical basis for mobile advertising companies to switch from random ad placements to more personalized ad deliveries based on users' individual characteristics. This consequently can increase the probability for mobile phone users to tap through advertisements, resulting in enhanced efficiency of mobile advertising.

This exploratory study offers many avenues for future research. First, more sophisticated modeling techniques can be used. For example, one can build a Bayesian network to reveal the conditional probability for tapping through a mobile ad after a particular ad is tapped. Second, individual personal characteristics, such as age, gender, education, etc., of mobile phone users could be directly related to their preference to certain types of advertising. Future research can consider collecting this type of data by surveying mobile users through a questionnaire. Analysis of both data collected by mobile advertising company and from the survey can provide more insights for the effectiveness of personalized mobile advertising (Varshney & Joy, 2015). Finally, the fact that this research filters the data to a specific time period may limit the generalization of the findings. Future research can expand the time period or focus on a certain type of event such as the search for a night club during the evening hours or meal carry-out during the lunch hours.

ACKNOWLEDGMENT

A prior version of this manuscript appeared in the *Information Resources Management Journal.*

REFERENCES

Ahn, H., Kim, K., & Han, I. (2006). Mobile advertisement recommender system using collaborative filtering: MAR-CF. *Proceedings from the KGSF-Conference 2006*, 709-715.

Barreto, A. M. (2013). Do users look at banner ads on Facebook? *Journal of Research in Interactive Marketing*, 7(2), 119–139. doi:10.1108/JRIM-Mar-2012-0013

Barwise, P., & Strong, C. (2002). Permission-based mobile advertising. *Journal of Interactive Marketing*, 16(1), 14–24. doi:10.1002/dir.10000

Bauer, H. H., Barnes, S. J., Reichardt, T., & Neumann, M. M. (2005). Driving consumer acceptance of mobile marketing: A theoretical framework and empirical study. *Journal of Electronic Commerce Research*, 6(3), 181–192.

Chen, P. T., & Hsieh, H. P. (2012). Personalized mobile advertising: Its key attributes, trends, and social impact. *Technological Forecasting and Social Change*, 9(3), 543–557. doi:10.1016/j.techfore.2011.08.011

Cheng, J. M. S., Blankson, C., Wang, E. S. T., & Chen, L. S. L. (2009). Consumer attitudes and interactive digital advertising. *International Journal of Advertising*, *28*(3), 501–525. doi:10.2501/S0265048709200710

Chowdhury, H. K., Parvin, N., Weitenberner, C., & Becker, M. (2006). Consumer attitude toward mobile advertising in an emerging market: An empirical study. *International Journal of Mobile Marketing*, *1*(2), 33–42.

Cui, G., Wong, M. K., & Lui, H. K. (2006). Machine learning for direct marketing response models: Bayesian networks with evolutionary programming. *Management Science*, *52*(4), 597–612. doi:10.1287/mnsc.1060.0514

de Castro, J. E., & Shimakawa, H. (2006). Mobile advertisement system utilizing users contextual information. *Proceedings from the 7th International Conference on Mobile Data Management*, 91. doi: 10.1109/MDM.2006.105

Dehghani, M., & Tumer, M. (2015). A research on effectiveness of Facebook advertising on enhancing purchase intention of consumers. *Computers in Human Behavior*, *49*, 597–600. doi:10.1016/j.chb.2015.03.051

Dogtiev, A. (2016). *Mobile Advertising Revenue Forecasts Roundup*. http://www.mobyaffiliates.com/blog/mobile-advertising-blog/mobile-advertising-revenue-forecasts-roundup/

Dyrud, M. A. (2011). Social networking and business communication pedagogy: Plugging into the Facebook generation. *Business Communication Quarterly*, *74*(4), 475–478. doi:10.1177/1080569911423964

Gana, M. A., & Thomas, T. K. (2016). Consumers attitude towards location-based advertising: An exploratory study. *Journal of Research in Marketing*, *6*(1), 390–396. doi:10.17722/jorm.v6i1.130

Huang, W., & Wang, H. (2010). *Credibility of the mobile phone advertising media. Journalism & Media Research, (9)*, 24-26.

Jun, J. W., & Lee, S. (2007). Mobile media use and its impact on consumer attitudes toward mobile advertising. *International Journal of Mobile Marketing*, *2*(1), 50–58.

Kim, K. Y., & Lee, B. G. (2015). Marketing insights for mobile advertising and consumer segmentation in the cloud era: A Q-R hybrid methodology and practices. *Technological Forecasting and Social Change*, *91*, 78–92. doi:10.1016/j.techfore.2014.01.011

Kim, Y., Lee, J. W., Park, S. R., & Choi, B. C. (2009). Mobile advertisement system using data push scheduling based on user preference. *Proceedings of the 2009 Wireless Telecommunications Symposium*, 1-5.

Laszlo, J. (2009). The new unwired world: An IAB status report on mobile advertising. *Journal of Advertising Research*, *49*(1), 27–43. doi:10.2501/S0021849909090035

Le, T. D., & Nguyen, B. H. (2014). Attitudes toward mobile advertising: A study of mobile web display and mobile app display advertising. *Asian Academy of Management Journal*, *19*(2), 87–103.

Lin, C. A., & Kim, T. (2016). Predicting user response to sponsored advertising on social media via the technology acceptance model. *Computers in Human Behavior*, *64*, 710–718. doi:10.1016/j.chb.2016.07.027

Lin, H., Zhou, X., & Cen, Z. (2014). Impact of the content characteristic of short message service advertising on consumer attitudes. *Social Behavior and Personality*, *42*(9), 1409–1420. doi:10.2224bp.2014.42.9.1409

Ma, J., Suntornpithug, N., & Karaatli, G. (2009). Mobile advertising: Does it work for everyone? *International Journal of Mobile Marketing*, *4*(2), 28–35.

Martín-Consuegra, D., Gómez, M., & Molina, A. (2015). Consumer sensitivity analysis in mobile commerce advertising. *Social Behavior and Personality*, *43*(6), 883–897. doi:10.2224bp.2015.43.6.883

Martins, J., Costa, C., Oliveira, T., Gonçalves, R., & Branco, F. (2019). How smartphone advertising influences consumers' purchase intention. *Journal of Business Research*, *94*, 378–387. doi:10.1016/j.jbusres.2017.12.047

MetaRain Blog. (2014). *An Experiment in iAd*. http://blog.metarain.com/post/83086723160/an-experiment-in-iad

Ozcelik, A. B., & Varnali, K. (2019). Effectiveness of online behavioral targeting: A psychological perspective. *Electronic Commerce Research and Applications*, *33*, 100819. doi:10.1016/j.elerap.2018.11.006

Park, H., Kim, S., & Lee, J. (2018). Native advertising in mobile applications: Thinking styles and congruency as moderators. *Journal of Marketing Communications*, *24*(1), 1–21. doi:10.1080/13527266.2018.1547918

Park, T., & Salvendy, G. (2012). Emotional factors in advertising via mobile phones. *International Journal of Human-Computer Interaction*, *28*(9), 597–612. doi:10.1080/10447318.2011.641899

Park, T., Shenoya, R., & Salvendy, G. (2008). Effective advertising on mobile phones: A literature review and presentation of results from 53 case studies. *Behaviour & Information Technology*, *27*(5), 355–373. doi:10.1080/01449290600958882

Peng, J., Qu, J., Peng, L., & Quan, J. (2017). An exploratory study of the effectiveness of mobile advertising. *Information Resources Management Journal*, *30*(4), 24–38. doi:10.4018/IRMJ.2017100102

Peters, C., Amato, C. H., & Hollenbeck, C. R. (2007). An exploratory investigation of consumers' perceptions of wireless advertising. *Journal of Advertising*, *36*(4), 129–145. doi:10.2753/JOA0091-3367360410

Samanta, S. K., Woods, J., & Ghanbari, M. (2009). MMS to improve mobile advertising acceptance and replace billboards. *International Journal of Mobile Marketing*, *4*(2), 61–67.

Smith, K. T. (2019). Mobile advertising to digital natives: Preferences on content, style, personalization, and functionality. *Journal of Strategic Marketing*, *27*(1), 67–80. doi:10.1080/0965254X.2017.1384043

Topsümer, F., & Yarkin, D. (2015). Social media as an advertisement tool: Strategical need of being more experiential. In N. Ö. Taşkıran & R. Yılmaz (Eds.), *Handbook of Research on Effective Advertising Strategies in the Social Media Age*. Hershey, PA: IGI Global. doi:10.4018/978-1-4666-8125-5.ch003

Tripathi, A. K., & Nair, S. K. (2006). Mobile advertising in capacitated wireless networks. *IEEE Transactions on Knowledge and Data Engineering*, *18*(9), 1284–1296. doi:10.1109/TKDE.2006.144

Tsang, M. M., Ho, S.-C., & Liang, T.-P. (2004). Consumer attitudes toward mobile advertising: An empirical study. *International Journal of Electronic Commerce*, *8*(3), 65–78. doi:10.1080/10864415.2004.11044301

Varshney, S., & Joy, J. (2015). Consumer attitudes toward mobile marketing and its impact on customers. *International Journal of Information, Business and Management*, *7*(2), 44–62.

Vatanparast, R., & Butt, A. H. (2010). An empirical study of factors affecting use of mobile advertising. *International Journal of Mobile Marketing*, *5*(1), 28–40.

Viennot, N., Garcia, E., & Nieh, J. (2014). A measurement study of Google play. SIGMETRICS '14: The 2014 ACM International Conference on Measurement and Modeling of Computer Systems, 221-233. 10.1145/2591971.2592003

Waldt, D., Rebbello, T. M., & Brown, W. J. (2009). Attitudes of young consumers towards SMS advertising. *African Journal of Business Management*, *3*(9), 444–452.

Wong, C. H., Tan, G. W. H., Tan, B. I., & Ooi, K. B. (2015). Mobile advertising: The changing landscape of the advertising industry. *Telematics and Informatics*, *32*(4), 720–734. doi:10.1016/j.tele.2015.03.003

Xu, D. J. J. (2006). The influence of personalization in affecting consumer attitudes toward mobile advertising in China. *Journal of Computer Information Systems*, *47*(2), 9–19.

Xu, G., & Gutierrez, J. A. (2006). An exploratory study of killer applications and critical success factors in m-commerce. *Journal of Electronic Commerce in Organizations*, *4*(3), 63–79. doi:10.4018/jeco.2006070104

Zhu, X. (2013). Machine teaching for Bayesian learners in the exponential family. Advances in Neural Information Processing Systems, 26, 1905-1913.

Zhu, Y.-Q., & Chen, H.-G. (2015). Social media and human need satisfaction: Implications for social media marketing. *Business Horizons*, *58*(3), 335–345. doi:10.1016/j.bushor.2015.01.006

KEY TERMS AND DEFINITIONS

Bayesian Network Model: Statistical model utilizing past user behavior to predict the probability of future behavior.

Mobile Advertising: A form of mobile commerce that includes text ads, banner advertisements, and downloadable apps.

Mobile Commerce (M-Commerce): Buying and selling products on wireless devices such as smartphones.

Tap: When a user clicks on a digital advertisement.

Tap-Through/Tap Through Rate (TTR): Measure of conversion from an advertisement that is shown to an advertisement that the user interacts with by tapping.

Chapter 7

Big Data Adoption:
A Comparative Study of the Indian Manufacturing and Services Sectors

Hemlata Gangwar
Pune Institute of Business Management, India

ABSTRACT

This study inspects how big data is comprehended by IT experts and the difficulties that they have in respect to the reception of big data examination. The study also looks into the contributing factors of big data adoption within the manufacturing and services sectors in India. The data were analyzed using exploratory and confirmatory factor analyses, and relevant hypotheses were derived and tested by SEM analysis. The findings revealed that relative advantage, compatibility, complexity, organizational size, top management support, competitive pressure, vendor support, data management, and data privacy are the factors that are important for both industries. Through a comparison of the industries, statistically significant differences between the service and the manufacturing sectors were found; in other words, it has been noted that the relative importance of all factors for big data adoption differs between the industries, with the only exception being its complexity – it was found to be insignificant for the manufacturing sector.

INTRODUCTION

The development of Big Data has changed the manner in which organizations work and contend. The approach of Big Data has as of now and will further modernize numerous fields, including organizations, logical research, open organization,

DOI: 10.4018/978-1-7998-2235-6.ch007

genomics, social insurance, operations management, the industrial internet, finance, etc. Big Data may be defined as a collection of massive and diverse data sets requiring advanced techniques and technologies to enable the capture, storage, distribution, management, and analysis of the information (Gandomi & Haider, 2015). In other words, it is a collection of huge and complex amalgamation of data sets that make it difficult to process using traditional data processing platforms. Big Data analytics (BDA) refers to the process and techniques used to analyze massive data in order to obtain value from that data.

Pragmatically, Big Data brings many attractive opportunities, such as increasing operational efficiency, enhanced strategic directions, developing better customer service, identifying and developing new products, services, new customers and markets. Use of BDA examines geospatial information and stock use on distributions, which gives bits of knowledge to manufacturing and service firms. These experiences could empower firm leaders to get request gauge continuously, mechanize substitution choices and distinguish main drivers of cost wastefulness (Dubey et al., 2016; Verma, Bhattacharyya, & Kumar, 2018). These measures could lessen lead times, costs, deferrals and procedure interferences, along these lines at last making worth. Besides, from the provider side, the quality or value aggressiveness can be improved by examining the provider's information to screen execution (Ren et al., 2017).

BDA can likewise limit execution fluctuation and avert quality issues by diminishing piece rates and diminishing an opportunity to advertise. In social insurance, BDA can make an incentive by improving quality and proficiency of administrations, and by coordinating patient information crosswise over various divisions and establishments (Gandomi & Haider, 2015). BDA can likewise give different constant data on perspectives, for example, traffic and climate. BDA can make an incentive for the financial area by empowering measurement of different operational dangers. BDA can even be utilized to recognize systems of teaming up fraudsters, or find proof of deceitful protection or advantages claims. This may at last lead to the revelations of until now unnoticed fake exercises (Elgendy & Elragal, 2014). However, despite these advantages of Big Data, evidence suggests that not all companies are rushing to adopt Big Data, or for that matter, Big Data analytics (Kwon, Lee, & Shin, 2014).

The purpose of this study is to understand the factors of the adoption of Big Data and its relative advantage to organizations. Most of the earlier studies on Big Data have focused solely on the technical and operational issues (Chen & Zhang, 2014; Lee, Kao, & Yang, 2014). Only a few studies have addressed the quintessence of adopting Big Data from an organizational perspective. As a matter of fact, no study has conducted a comprehensive evaluation of the factors on Big Data adoption. This study thereby looks to develop a research model based on technological, organizational and environmental framework in an attempt to lend more clarity. Further, two new constructs specific to Big Data have been added: data management and addressing privacy concerns. This study presents therefore, a more holistic assessment of the factors of Big Data by splitting them in two sectors – the manufacturing and the service sectors; in the process, this study contributes to a wider body of scientific knowledge that has so far not been studied. Further, this study highlights the importance of systematically evaluating the factors of Big Data at the industry level; and through the literature review provides the background on Big Data and related research. Further the study discusses the theoretical foundations for the research model and proposes hypotheses. The research methodology and the results are then presented, followed by a discussion of the major findings. The study concludes with implications of the findings and the scope for future study.

BACKGROUND

The term Big Data is used to describe unstructured enormous data that require more real-time analysis. Manyika et al. (2011) defined Big Data as "datasets whose size is beyond the ability of typical database software tools to capture, store, manage, and analyze" (p. 1). According to Hashem et al. (2015), Big Data is "a set of techniques and technologies that require new forms of integration to uncover large hidden values from large datasets that are diverse, complex, and of a massive scale" (p. 100). Thus, Big Data develops new methods or technologies for massive data that are difficult to store, process, and analyze through traditional database technologies (Tao et al., 2017; Zhong et al., 2016). This study regards Big Data as the infrastructure and technologies of the organization to collect store and analyze various types of data. Thus, Big Data can create value using advanced analytical techniques that could not be processed using a traditional database.

Big Data and "regular-sized" data can be distinguished based on the characteristics commonly referred to as the four 'Vs': i.e., volume, variety, velocity, and veracity (Abbasi, Sarker, & Chiang, 2016; Gandomi & Haider, 2015; Goes, 2014; Wang, Gunasekaran, Ngai, & Papadopoulos, 2016). There's no universal benchmark for volume, variety, velocity, veracity for defining Big Data; it depends upon the size, sector and location of the firm. Big Data and its four Vs clearly change how organizations store and manage data. Definitely Big Data and its four V characteristics have had a huge impact on the people, processes, and technologies related to the information value chain.

Big Data Analytics

Over the past two decades Big Data analytics has increased in importance in both academic and business communities alike. Big Data analytics could be referred as the techniques, technologies, systems, methodologies, tools and applications that analyze excessive variety of critical business data to make timely efficient and effective decision making (Gandomi & Haider, 2015; McAfee & Brynjolfsson, 2012). Some of the Big Data techniques include text analysis, audio analysis, video analytics, social media analytics, and predictive analytics. Even though some leading companies are actively adopting Big Data analytics to enhance decision making, understanding process optimization, strengthening market competition and thereby opening up new business opportunities, many companies are still at a nascent stage as regards the adoption of Big Data due to their lack of understanding and experience as regards this disruptive technology.

Big Data Adoption

Even though some leading companies have actively adopted Big Data analytics to enhance decision making and reducing business costs, many companies are still at an early stage regarding the ad option of big data due to their lack of understanding and experience regarding this disruptive technology (Verma, 2018). Many studies have addressed the technical and operational issues related to Big Data, including issues such as creating value from Big Data (Chen, Chiang, & Storey, 2012; Chen & Zhang, 2014; Jagadish et al., 2014), data processing framework for data storage and analysis (Chen et al., 2012), issue related to data transformation, data quality/ heterogeneity, security, privacy and legal/regulatory issues (Hashem et al., 2015; Hu & Vasilakos, 2016). Only few study evaluated big data adoption from organizational perspective. Sun, Cegielski, Jia, and Hall (2016) developed a conceptual framework to identify the factors affecting organizational adoption of Big Data. Their framework is not extensive as the factors are explored from a theoretical perspective based on content analysis of IT adoption literature. Thus empirical research is needed for a better explanation of the adoption of Big Data at an organizational level.

Kwon et al. (2014) developed a research model using the resource view and isomorphism theories to explain the adoption intention of big data analytics. The result concluded that data quality and data usage benefits as the important indicator for Big Data adoption. Chaurasia and Rosin (2017) examined the applicability of Big Data in higher education institutions. Using qualitative methodology four major application areas that is reporting and compliance; analysis and visualization; security and risk mitigation; and predictive analytics were identified in their study. Verma and Bhattacharyya (2017) identified the factors that influence Big Data usage and adoption in the context of emerging economies. They used a qualitative exploratory study using face-to-face semi-structured interviews to collect data from 22 enterprises in India. Also they have not considered key factors such as data management and privacy concerns that are critical to the firm's adoption of Big Data.

Verma et al. (2018) investigated the effects of system characteristics on the attitude of managers toward the usage of Big Data analytics. The finding shows that Big Data characteristics have significant direct and indirect effects on the benefits of Big Data and perceived usefulness, attitude, and adoption. No study has taken a holistic approach to empirically validate the technology context, organization context, and environment context perspective for effective usage of Big Data. This study extended Technology Organization Environment (TOE) framework to study the effect of technology context, organization context, environment context, and security context on big data adoption. Also this study compares result in manufacturing and service industry. Big Data solutions are able to help organizations in every industry. Big Data in manufacturing can decrease product development and assembly costs by and can cause a reduction in working capital (Mourtzis, Vlachou, & Milas, 2016).

Adoption Models

There are many adoption behavior models/theories being developed in the information system to study technological adoption both at an organizational and an individual level. Some prominent theories used to understand technology adoption at an individual level include innovation diffusion theory (IDT) (Rogers, 1962), theory of reasoned action (TRA) (Fishbein & Ajzen, 1975), the technology acceptance model (TAM) (Davis, 1989), theory of planned behavior (TPB) (Ajzen, 1991), and the unified theory of acceptance and use of technology (UTAUT) (Venkatesh, Morris, Davis, & Davis, 2003). At an organizational level, theories such as diffusion of innovation (Rogers, 2003) and technology organization environment framework (TOE) have been widely applied to studies considering how innovations are actually adopted and diffused. Although Rogers' (2003) diffusion of innovation has solid theoretical foundation, is found to have consistent empirical support, and appears to be most applicable to study the innovation process, researchers are still searching for other contexts influencing the adoption process for better and smoother adoption (Moore & Benbasat, 1991; Zhu, Dong, Xu, & Kraemer, 2006; Zhu, Kraemer, & Xu, 2006).

Technology Organization Environment (TOE) Framework

Tornatzky and Fleischer (1990) proposed the Technology Organization Environment (TOE) framework, where technology and organization contexts are identical to the IDT construct. In fact, compared to the IDT framework, the TOE framework includes an environmental context, which offers both constraints and opportunities for technological innovation. According to Zhu, Kraemer, and Xu (2003), the TOE framework is more significant than IDT as it includes new constructs as well. Moreover, the TOE framework has been used to examine various technology adoption issues in order to distinguish adopters from non-adopters (Low, Chen, & Wu, 2011). Further Rui (2007) and Maduku, Mpingamjira, and Duh (2016) advocated that the TOE framework coasts up the inherent limitation of the dominant technical perspective, and suggests a useful analytical tool to differentiate between the intrinsic characteristics of innovation and drivers, capabilities, along with wider environmental circumstances of the adopting organization. Thus in order to better understand the Big Data adoption process, a conceptual model for BDA was developed based on the technology–organization–environment framework from the technology innovation and information systems (IS) literature (Tornatzky & Fleischer, 1990).

The TOE framework states that adoption to the technology innovation process is influenced by three contexts in an organization: technological context, organizational context and environmental context (Tornatzky & Fleischer, 1990). Technological context refers to the internal and external technologies relevant to the organization, both for technologies that are already in use, as well as those that are available in the market but not currently in use (Oliveira, Fürlinger, & Kranzlmüller, 2012). Organizational context refers to descriptive measures such as firm size, managerial structure, organizational structure etc. (Alsaad, Mohamad, & Ismail, 2017; Tornatzky & Fleischer, 1990). Environmental context refers to arenas in which firms conduct their businesses, typically in the context of market elements, competitors the regulatory environment etc. (Alshamaila, Papagiannidis, & Li, 2013; Oliveira & Martins, 2010a; Tornatzky & Fleischer 1990).

The technological context of the TOE framework will determine whether the technological readiness of the firm will restrain or facilitate the adoption of Big Data. It includes five innovation attributes including relative advantage, compatibility, complexity, triability, and observability, which put together influence the likelihood of adoption (Alsaad et al., 2017; Rogers, 2003). Relative advantage, compatibility, and complexity have been consistently reported to be the most important factors and therefore they've been considered in this study (Alsaad et al., 2017; Alshamaila et al., 2012; Gangwar, Date, & Ramaswamy, 2015; Hung, Hung, Tsai, & Jiang, 2010; Tornatzky & Klein, 1982).

Relative Advantage

The relative advantage of an innovation over its existing technologies and other alternatives shows imperative role in its adoption. Rogers (2003) defines relative advantage as "the degree to which a technology perceived as providing greater benefit for organizations" (p. 229). The valid role of relative advantage is well recognized in IT adoption literature (Alshamaila et al., 2013; Low et al., 2011; Ramdani, Kawalek, & Lorenzo, 2009; Tornatzky & Klein, 1982; Wang & Wang, 2016). Thus it is perceived that the likelihood of adoption will increase when organizations perceive a relative advantage in an innovation. Big Data allows organizations to reduce cost, improve decision making and have competitive offerings, implementing new strategies business models along with higher transparency of information. Although Big Data Analytics tools are expensive at the outset, but eventually it saves a lot of money, as it accesses massive amount of data at incomparable speeds and thereby results in a cost-effective strategy in the long run (Murdoch & Detsky, 2013). BDA offers organizations a data-driven decision making process based on data and analysis, rather than experience and intuition for a more informed decision making process, improved profitability and efficiency (Waller & Fawcett, 2013). It also delivers greater opportunities for having a competitive advantage by collating and analyzing information across organizations and industries in order to improve the overall operational efficiency, develop marketing strategies, support business growth and, create the "distinguishing factor". Further, BDA helps organizations to understand how others perceive their products, by analyzing the market and its customers, which in turn goes on to provide crucial insights to develop and improve new versions of the product; it allows higher transparency of information within organizations. These findings contribute to the development of H1.

H1: Relative advantage has positive effect on Big Data adoption.

Compatibility

According to Rogers (2003), compatibility means "the degree to which an innovation is perceived as consistent with the existing values, past experiences, and needs of potential adopters" (p. 170). The role of compatibility is widely recognized in IT adoption literature (Alsaad et al., 2017; Gangwar et al., 2015; Low et al., 2011; Peng, Xiong, & Yang, 2012; Ramdani et al., 2009; Wang, Wang, & Yang, 2010). Compatibility takes into account organizational environment, considers business structures, business strategy, existing values, experience, work practice, organizational needs, information systems' environment and finally the employee, who are all in the reconcilability of a new technology. Further, Big Data adoption may require change in existing technological infrastructure, data environment, organizational process and culture, capabilities and skills. Building and supporting technology infrastructure for Big Data adoption requires infrastructure for storage, analytics software, processing and networking capacity. In addition to technological infrastructure, new data environment must accommodate existing methods to extract

Figure 1. TOE framework for big data adoption

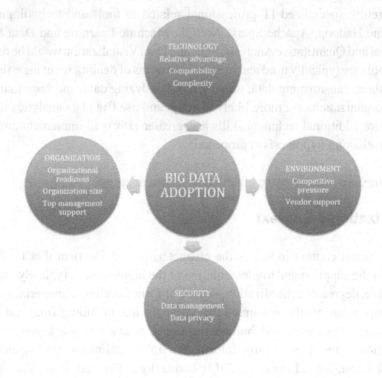

data from multiple sources. It is important to note that Big Data strategy should also be compatible with the existing organizational processes and culture, which in turn is ensured by inculcating changes in business processes, having managerial support and commitment, encourage a knowledge-sharing culture including a drive for innovation, experimentation and integration. Big Data adoption may also require special knowledge and skills, such as analytical and statistical skills in order to manage Big Data projects or assess how Big Data tools might help the organizations. The more compatible is the Big Data strategy with the existing development environment, the less effort would be required in actually adopting it, leading to H2.

H2: Compatibility has positive effect on Big Data adoption.

Complexity

Rogers (2003) describes complexity as the extent to which an innovation is difficult to use or understand. It is believed that easier to integrate and using the technology into business environment, the more the chance of its adoption (Alshamaila et al., 2013; Chaudhury & Bharati, 2008; Igbaria, Guimaraes, & Davis, 1995). However,

Big Data strategy can be challenging to companies that lack technological expertise, and therefore specialized IT professional related to tools and technologies such as Apache Hadoop, Apache Spark, NoSQL, Machine Learning and Data Mining, Statistical and Quantitative Analysis, SQL and Data Visualization would be required. These tools are typically used and measured in terms of dealing with: ingesting data, storing data, transforming data, moving data, analyzing data, and visualizing data. Hence, organizations are more likely to adopt and use Big Data analytics if it does not require additional technical skills and greater efforts to implement and use it. So, the following hypothesis is proposed:

H3: Complexity has negative effect on Big Data adoption.

Organizational Context

Organizational context indicates the characteristics of the firm that facilitate or constrain the adoption and implementation of the innovation. It typically includes a firm's size, degree of centralization, degree of formalization, managerial structure, leadership behavior, the resources that the firm has including financial capital, technological resources and human resources, amount of slack resources, the distribution of power and control, information links, and linkages among employees (Kuan & Chau, 2001, Low et al., 2011; Tornatzky & Fleisher, 1990; Zhu, Dong et al., 2006). Of these, organizational readiness, management support, and the firm size are the most important factors for assessing the adoption of Big Data (Wang et al., 2010).

Organizational Readiness

Organizational readiness can be defined as having technological resources, financial resources and IT human resources (Zhu, Dong et al., 2006). Technological resources refer to possessing the right tools and technologies, platform, databases, architectural standard for storing, analyzing data in the Big Data environment. Financial resources refer to financial readiness to install, maintain, and upgrade the company's information systems and for ongoing expenses during its usage. IT human resources provide the knowledge and skills to implement Big Data-related IT applications. Big Data can become part of the value chain if organizations have sufficient resources and IT personnel. Therefore, firms that have organizational readiness are more prepared for the adoption of Big Data, leading to the following hypothesis:

H4: Organizational readiness has positive effect on Big Data adoption.

Organizational Size

Organizational size defines the number of employees in an organization, is one of the most commonly studied factors of IT adoption (Gangwar et al., 2015; Jeyaraj, Rottman, & Lacity, 2006; Lee & Xia, 2006; Oliveira & Martins, 2010b). However, literature indicates that the effect of organizational size varies and isn't clear yet. Some empirical studies indicate that there is a positive relationship between the two variables (Bose & Luo, 2012; Hsu, Kraemer, & Dunkle, 2006; Low et al., 2011; Pan & Jang, 2008; Premkumar, Ramamurthy, & Crum, 1997; Ramdani et al., 2009; Wang et al., 2010; Zhu, Kraemer et al., 2003); whereas some report a negative correlation (Zhu & Kraemer, 2005; Zhu, Kraemer et al., 2006). Further, it is believed that larger organizations have more ability to absorb risk so they are more innovative; on the other hand, small firms can be more innovative, they are flexible enough to adapt quick changes in their environments (Oliveira & Martins, 2010b; Zhu & Kraemer, 2005). In the case of Big Data adoption, the authors expect that large organizations have more resources and may be better able to take on risk and provided the basis of the following hypothesis.

H5: Organizational size has positive effect on Big Data adoption.

Top Management Support

Top management support refers to the degree to which top management understands the strategic importance of IS innovation and the extent to which it is involved in IS activities (Gangwar & Date, 2016; Miller & Toulouse, 1986). Top management support refers to the extent to which senior executives provide the necessary technological and financial resources, vision, support, authority for the innovative implementation, cultivation of favorable organizational climate, higher assessments of individual self-efficacy, support in overcoming barriers and resistance to change, along with a commitment to create a positive environment for innovation at large (Alsaad et al., 2017; Jang, 2010; Ramdani et al., 2009; Teo, Lin, & Lai, 2009; Wang & Wang, 2016; Wang et al., 2010). Top management support is more critical for Big Data adoption because it not only means integrating an information system but also requires addressing issues of organizational alignment, change management, business process reengineering, coordination, and communication (Wang & Wang, 2016). Accordingly, the following hypothesis is thus proposed:

H6: Top management support has positive effect on Big Data adoption.

Environmental Context

The environmental context in the TOE framework refers to the arena in which an organization conducts its business, wherein it may have a direct effect on organizational decision-making process. It includes factors such as external and internal pressure, trading partner pressure, vendor support, commercial dependencies, environmental uncertainty, information intensity, network intensity and government regulations (Alshamaila et al., 2013; Gangwar et al., 2015; Low et al., 2011; Wang et al., 2010). Of these, the factors that have an impact on Big Data are the organization's competition/competitors and vendor support (Alsaad et al., 2017; Alshamaila et al., 2013; Gangwar et al., 2015).

Competitive Pressure

The role of competitive pressure is widely recognized in IT adoption literature (Lian, Yen, & Wang, 2014; Low et al., 2011; Oliveira & Martins, 2010a; Ramdani et al., 2009; Zhu, Dong et al., 2006). Competitive pressure can be described as the amount of pressure a company experiences from competitors (Zhu & Kraemer, 2005). Ramdani et al. (2009) reported that when technology affects competition, it exerts pressure on an organization's ability to adopt new technologies to compete in the market. Adoption of Big Data can therefore lead to greater capacity utilization, accurate forecasting, operational efficiency, better market visibility, decision making and more accurate access to real-time data (Gandomi & Haider, 2015). Accordingly, the following hypothesis is proposed:

H7: Competitive pressure has positively effect on Big Data adoption.

Vendor Support

Vendor support is very important because most of the Big Data tools and technologies are open source and organizations want to make sure about support and availability at the time when they need it (Alshamaila et al., 2013). Organizations can develop innovation-related capabilities by tapping into the experiential learning of its supplier and may influence the firm's innovation adoption. Further, support is the key demand for problem resolution, offering technical solutions, customizing various apps, swift response to patches, fixes and bug detection in Big Data; it can thereby be inferred that support from the vendor can affect adoption as it ensures data availability, reliability and completeness. This contributes to the following hypothesis:

H8: Vendor support has positive effect on Big Data adoption.

Security Concern

The five 'Vs' of data changed the landscape including capturing and storing data, data storage devices, data storage architecture, and data access mechanism (Chen & Zhang, 2014; Oliveira et al., 2012). Big Data phenomenon arises from collecting and processing massive amounts of information from various sources including the internet. Thus ensuring security is more vital in the case of Big Data, as it deals with innumerable and limitless data. Risk areas that need to be considered include data ownership and classification, data creation and the collection process, data security protection, protection of intellectual property, personal privacy, commercial secrets and protection of financial information. These security challenges could be broadly categorized under two aspects of security – data management and data privacy.

Data Management

Big Data management is the process of ensuring accuracy, availability, accessibility, and quality of large stores of data by allocating right people, policies and technologies in place. It is an assortment of old and new best practices for administration, management and governance of large volumes of data. Al Nuaimi, Al Neyadi, Mohamed, and Al-Jaroodi (2015) define Big Data management as the development and execution of architectures, policies, practices and procedures for ensuring the availability, usability, integrity and security of data. Data availability issue arises when data is accessed by a large number of users from a huge pool of applications, wherein the user wants information available all the time or at the time when they need it. Reliability of data for decision making can be attained through high data quality. Appropriate data management allows an organization to improve availability, efficiency, accuracy and quality based on thorough cleansing of data regularly, integrating data across departments, normalizing user-specific data and have built-in high availability features. Moving to the Big Data adds new layers of complexity for managing data and thus influences an organization's decision to adopt the innovative tool. Thus proper Big Data management can result in higher availability, reliability and accessibility of data. Based on this argument, the following hypothesis is proposed:

H9: Data management has positive effect on Big Data adoption.

Data Privacy

Data privacy is related to an issue of data storage from various human studies as well as hosting of data sets on publicly accessible servers (Schadt, 2012). Big Data privacy includes protection of personal privacy during data acquisition and protection of personal privacy data during storage, transmission, and usage. The challenge here is ensuring citizens' rights of privacy while collecting and using Big Data. The objective of data privacy is on the use and governance of individual data such as setting up policies in place to ensure that consumers' personal information is being collected, shared and utilized in appropriate ways. The existing non-Big Data security solutions are not designed to handle the scale, speed, variety and complexity of Big Data. So, organizations need to embed specific data privacy and data protection measures into their processes and systems. Ensuring privacy through efficient protection mechanism will result in greater security, leading to the next hypothesis:

H10: Data privacy has positive effect on Big Data adoption.

RESEARCH METHODOLOGY

A survey was conducted in India from the manufacturing and service industries in order to evaluate the theoretical constructs of Big Data and Big Data analytics. A questionnaire was developed based on the literature. The questionnaire went through an evaluation process before it was administered. At first, pre-testing was carried out with an expert panel including two researchers, two local professors, and one external professor. The questionnaire was refined according to the comments/ suggestions made by this panel for survey pre-testing and feedback from three well-known exponents of Big Data. Since there were no major comments received, the questionnaire was considered ready for data collection. The questionnaire had two parts including a cover letter, which explained the objective of this study and briefly described the concept of Big Data. The first part contained questions about business background information. The second part included items that assessed the ten factors affecting Big Data adoption. To be consistent with the sources, the constructs (relative advantage, compatibility, complexity, organizational readiness, top management support, competitive pressure, vendor support, data management data privacy) were measured using a five-point Likert scale from "strongly disagree" to "strongly agree". Further, responses on the questionnaire were collected from the top and middle-level IT professionals of companies who were in the process of adopting Big Data (potential adopters).

Survey Administration

An online version of the questionnaire was emailed to qualified individuals (IS managers) at 1500 manufacturing and service companies in India. The company and contact data were accessed from the Bombay Chamber of Commerce and of Industry of India. Data were collected using an online questionnaire between November 2016 and July 2017. The survey was completed by IT staff or managers in the organization because they were in a better position to understand the current IT operations and future trends of the firms. This should contribute to content validity. The responses were collected from organizations that were in the process of adopting Big Data (potential adopters). In the first stage, 379 valid responses were received. A follow-up email was sent in the second stage to those who did not respond in the first stage. In this second stage, 99 valid responses were obtained, for a combined total of 478 usable responses. The overall response rate was 31.86%, which is comparable to other studies of similar scale in technology adoption (McCole & Ramsey, 2005). Of these valid responses 43.9 percent were received from manufacturing sector whereas 56.1 were received from service sector. Table 1 displays the categorization of firms with respect to size and Table 2 displays the categorization of firms by industry type.

Table 1. Categorization of firms with respect to size

Size	Number of Employees	n
Small	< 400	164
Medium	400 - 800	137
Large	> 800	177
Total		478

A series of statistical tests for nonresponse bias were computed by comparing early responses with late responses in terms of item responses. The sample distributions of the two groups did not differ statistically, indicating an absence of nonresponse bias. Therefore, nonresponse bias does not appear to be a concern.

Validity and Reliability Assessment

To test the instrument, a pilot study was conducted among 34 firms, which were not included in the main survey. Reliability analysis revealed Cronbach's α value as 0.821, which is comparable with the reliabilities reported in earlier studies. Construct validity was evaluated using principal component analysis and Varimax rotation. The result for Bartlett's test of Sphericity was 0.000 and the KMO value 0.686. This value is more than 0.5 that shows high measure of sampling adequacy and ensures factorability of data. Items were retained based on the following criteria: (i) items with loading of 0.50 or more; (ii) items with loading of less than 0.50 were

Table 2. Categorization of firms by industry type

Manufacturing	n
Electrical machinery	44
Food and beverages	53
Motor vehicles	37
Base Metals	19
Chemicals	23
Textiles and apparel	34
Total Manufacturing	210
Service	n
Hotel, Banking, Real estate	89
Health	76
Commerce	64
Information and communication	39
Total Service	268

removed; and (iii) items with loading beyond 0.50 on two or more components were removed. From a total of 47 items, 3 of the items were dropped in the exploratory factor analysis. The reliabilities of sub-scales varied between 0.620 and 0.947; which exceeded the recommended level of 0.6. The variables were grouped in ten factors and all together accounted for 76.23% of the total variance. This value of total variance explained that the set of factors extracted from the data explain the adoption intention to a very high extent, and a lesser part of the adoption remains unexplained.

Confirmatory Factor Analysis

To test the stability of the scale, confirmatory factor analysis was employed on the sample using structural equation modeling (SEM). A measurement model was developed using of partial least squares (PLS); PLS can be used when data is distributed normally. The Kolmogorov–Smirnov test showed that none of the items were distributed normally ($p < 0.001$). The minimum sample size for using is obtained from the following formula: (1) ten times the largest number of formative indicators used to measure one construct or (2) ten times the largest number of structural paths directed at a particular latent construct in the structural model. The sample consisted of 478 firms, which fulfill the necessary conditions for using PLS. Smart PLS software was used for confirmatory factor analysis and hypothesis testing.

Analyses were conducted utilizing the full sample for identifying the key factors of Big Data adoption and then sub-samples of the data for the manufacturing and services sectors to examine how the factors vary across different industries. The composite reliability for each construct ranged higher than 0.7 for the full sample, and the industry specific samples suggesting acceptable levels of reliability. The average variances extracted (AVEs), were greater than 0.50 for the full sample and the industry specific samples. All the indicators had significant loading greater than .50 for both full and industry specific value. Thus, measurement models for both industries ensure convergent validity. Discriminant validity was assessed by comparing the correlation between factors with average variance, which was extracted from the individual factors. Analyses showed that the square root of AVE is greater than the correlation between each of the pair that supports the discriminant validity of the construct.

HYPOTHESIS TESTING

To test proposed hypotheses, the measurement model was converted to structural model in PLS; results were interpreted using the regression weight table. Relative advantage was found to be significant on adoption for both the full sample and industry specific sample. Therefore, this supports the prior work of Wang and Wang (2016) that found relative advantage to be the most influential determinant of technology adoption. This is also in concurrence with the findings of Maduku et al. (2016) who found a positive relationship of relative advantage for mobile marketing adoption. These findings actually allow users to recognize that Big Data can certainly contribute to the efficiency and effectiveness of organizations, and thereby organizations are more likely to implement and adapt Big Data.

Compatibility is found to be a significant facilitator of Big Data adoption for both the full sample and industry specific sample. This is inconsistent with prior studies by Grandon and Pearson (2004), Lin and Chen (2012), Alshamaila et al. (2012), Gangwar et al. (2015), Wang and Wang (2016), Alsaad et al. (2017), and lastly Maduku et al. (2016). Complexity is also found negatively to affect adoption for full sample and service sector and insignificant for manufacturing sector. This is in consistent with Ramdani et al. (2009), Alshamaila et al. (2012), Tsai et al. (2013), Gangwar et al. (2015), and Wang and Wang (2016). The results show that there is no significant negative relationship between perceived complexity and Big Data adoption intention for the services sector. This finding is consistent with the earlier finding of Low et al. (2011) and Maduku et al. (2016).

Organizational readiness does not have any significant effect on organizations' decision to adopt Big Data for both the full sample and industry specific sample. This finding is consistent with Grandon and Pearson (2004), Wang et al. (2010), and Low et al. (2011). Organizational size is found to have a positive effect on adoption for both full sample and industry specific sample. The results are similar to those of Lee and Xia (2006), Zhu, Kraemer et al. (2003), Teo et al. (2003), Lippert and Govindarajulu (2006), and Hung et al. (2010). In addition, top management support shows a significant positive relationship with Big Data adoption for both full sample as well as industry specific sample. The importance of top management support is consistent with studies of Premkumar and Roberts (1999), Lewis, Agarwal, & Sambamurthy (2003), Teo et al. (2009), Sila (2013), and Alsaad et al. (2017).

Competitive pressure is supported to positively effect on adoption of Big Data for both the full sample and industry specific sample. The results are similar to those of Lin and Lin (2008), Oliveira and Martins (2010a), Low et al. (2011), and Alsaad et al. (2017). Vendor support does have significant effect on organizations' decision to adopt Big Data for both the full sample and industry specific sample. The results are similar to those of Gangwar and Date (2016) and Alshamaila et al. (2013).

Big Data adoption is more influenced by other factors such as data management. It ensures availability, quality and security of data. This finding is consistent with Gustin, Daugherty, and Stank (1995), Alshawi, Farouk, and Irani (2011), and Gangwar et al. (2015). Data Privacy is also found to have an impact on Big Data adoption for both the full sample and industry specific sample; this finding is consistent with Oliveira, Thomas, and Espadanal (2014) and Alsaad et al. (2017). The results are summarized below.

DISCUSSION AND RECOMMENDATIONS

Findings of the study show that relative advantage has a positive impact on Big Data adoption for both the full sample and industry specific sample. Positive relationship between relative advantage and adoption intention indicates that organizations which have an overall positive perception of the benefits of Big Data are likely to have a positive intention to go on to adopt it. Advantages identified by the study include improving the decision making process, cost reduction, competitive offerings, implementing new strategies and new business models, and providing new business opportunities. The relative advantage of Big Data leads to greater result, such as improved customer services, greater operational efficiency, reduced operating costs and improved business strategy and business plans. Advanced understanding of the advantages of Big Data over existing technology helps managers in their management

Figure 2. SEM result

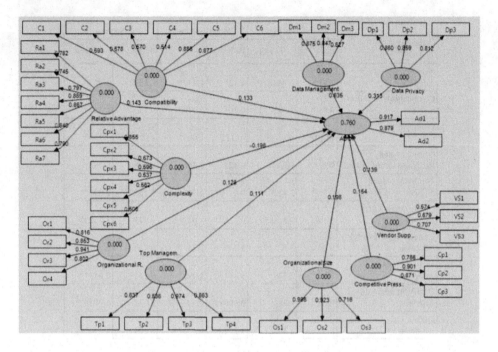

processes to build policies, and also improves relationship with customers. Thus it may be said that more the opportunity, easier would the technology become in terms of its day-to-day use. Moreover, the marginal effects are different between manufacturing and service industries. Relative advantage is more important in the service sector the possible reason might be because in the manufacturing sector the organizations are more informed of the perceived benefits of Big Data.

Compatibility between Big Data and an organization's existing technological architecture, techniques, and preferred work practices was also found to be an influential factor in this study. Organizations have positive attitudes and agreement about technological innovation when there is a good fit between a technological innovation, the people, processes, practices of the organization at large. Big Data should also be compatible with the organization's policies, IT development environment, and business needs (Lin & Chen, 2012). To enhance compatibility, organizations should make necessary contributions to make the Big Data system compatible with the organization's internal processes and policies. On the flip side, providers may customize Big Data services to the needs of individual organizations, wherein they need to understand the existing business processes, IT infrastructures, and organizational cultures in order to meet the compatibility parameters of Big

Table 3. SEM coefficients

Construct	Full Sample		Manufacturing		Service	
	Path Coeff.	T-Value	Path Coeff.	T-Value	Path Coeff.	T-Value
Relative Advantage -> Adoption	0.143	2.1825*	0.125	1.999*	0.134	2.001*
Compatibility -> Adoption	0.133	3.0827**	0.103	2.034*	0.146	2.283*
Complexity -> Adoption	-0.198	2.3509*	-0.122	1.0675	-0.21	3.356**
Organizational Readiness -> Adoption	0.128	1.336	0.121	1.456	0.128	1.088
Top Management Support -> Adoption	0.111	2.421*	0.11	2.345*	0.122	2.872**
Organizational Size -> Adoption	0.198	3.554**	0.123	3.012**	0.213	3.679**
Competitive Pressure -> Adoption	0.154	3.172**	0.145	2.346*	0.163	2.967**
Vendor Support-> Adoption	0.139	2.349*	0.114	1.998*	0.141	2.619**
Data Management-> Adoption	0.635	6.3819**	0.6004	5.867**	0.638	6.9019**
Data Privacy -> Adoption	0.313	4.304**	0.278	3.929**	0.324	4.656**

** Significance at $p < 0.01$

* Significance at $p < 0.05$

Data solutions. Thus, if Big Data functions are consistent with the work styles, data format structural data, business needs, and practices of organizational activities, a positive impression of Big Data is likely to occur and this in turn, can facilitate Big Data implementation at a larger scale and mass.

The service sector reveals a statistically significant higher relative importance of compatibility for Big Data adoption when compared with manufacturing. One possible explanation is that as service sector firms have higher levels of compatibility in terms of existing IT infrastructure, practices and structure of the organization, skill and knowledge required working with Big Data, only these firms can take advantage of Big Data integration to the existing environment, i.e. improving the decision making process, improving customer service, and lowering inventory costs. Managers in the manufacturing industry in particular need to improve compatibility by introducing changes in existing practices and policies in order to customize to avail the Big Data services and thereby take its full advantage.

Organizations did not perceive Big Data technology to be intrinsically more complex in the services sector. They are not more complex for those who have expertise to integrate existing applications to Big Data and the skill set to develop customized solutions. This study has described the complexity in terms of efficiency of data transfer, data analysis, visualizing data etc. Big Data is found to be easy to learn, thereby taking lesser time in performing tasks of employees. The complexity of Big Data by its characteristics of volume, velocity, and variety is eased when service providers offer easy to use development and analytic tools. These tools, developed over a period of time, allow users to mine valuable information from Big Data. It has therefore been identified that lesser the complexity in using Big Data, more is the likelihood of their adoption and usage. Technology complexity is a statistically insignificant facilitator only in the manufacturing sector. One possible explanation is that manufacturing organizations perceive Big Data as complex technology because they don't have the expertise and skills needed to integrate and work with Big Data analysis (Zhong et al., 2015).

Organizational readiness is statistically insignificant factor for Big Data adoption for both full sample and industry specific sample. However, this may be because of organizations adopting Big Data may have already made requisite sophisticated technological changes including hardware, software, and overall expertise. Another possible explanation might be when organizations believe in the benefit of technology, they are able to manage the technological, financial and specialized IT skills better. Thus organizational readiness may not influence the initial part of Big Data adoption, but rather the extent of its usage.

Firm size is statistically significant for Big Data adoption in full sample as well as industry specific sample; this finding is consistent with extant literature suggesting that larger companies have more resources to cover the cost and have higher risk taking capability in terms of changing processes, practices and policies that have emerged because of this technological innovation. The results can help managers to predict the possibility of the adoption of Big Data by assessing the size of their organization. Notably, there is no size-fit relationship between organizational size and Big Data adoption; but managers must recognize the advantages and disadvantages of their size while adopting Big Data.

The study provides empirical evidence that top management support is significant in explaining the adoption of Big Data for full sample and industry specific sample. It demonstrates support of committing financial and organizational resources, development of IS/IT capabilities, reducing resistance, resolving conflicts, improving communications, convincing employees, and lastly overcoming the implementation barriers. Technology adoption should be carried out using a top down approach. First, organizations should realize the strategic importance of technology, it's only then they will take the initiative to adopt a technology per se. Top management support can encourage and motivate people to use Big Data and then influence the decision making process for adopting it by harping on the enhanced efficiency of the organization post implementation. Thus, top managers should take the initiative to convince one and all for the effective and efficient use of new technology.

This study determines that competitive pressure is a significant factor for Big Data adoption both in organizations in the full sample and the industry specific sample. Competitive pressure measured by market structure, imports pressure of adopting Big Data so as to maintain a competitive edge. It is important to understand that stiff competition drives organizations to switch from other technologies to Big Data without investing sufficient time in infusing a holistic innovation approach that is required within the organizations (Zhu, Dong et al., 2006). In other words, the greater the competition among similar organizations, the more likely organizations adopts Big Data in order to gain a competitive edge.

Findings also indicate that adoption of Big Data is largely influenced by vendor support for both full sample and industry specific sample. It is supported by the fact that supplier support in the form of reinforcement, assistance, information sharing and problem resolution can directly impact adoption of Big Data in an organization. Thus managers for Big Data should develop strong and transparent relations with suppliers through effective communication, cooperation, coordination, and service level agreements. On the other hand, vendors should provide data and advance data analytic driven solutions to the organizations in order to maximize revenue.

Findings also support that Big Data adoption is essentially driven by data management and associated requirements. It is related to the blend of old and new best practices, skills, teams, data types, tools and technologies along with vendor built-in functionality, so that businesses at large can fully leverage Big Data availability, quality, efficiency and effectiveness. Further high availability of Big Data and their support is ensured by Big Data providers by employing multiple network providers so that even if one of them experiences difficulties or a complete failure, the provider services will not be jeopardized due to the immediate availability of another network provider. Also, they adopt high availability architecture, test platforms and applications, and maintain on-premises storage backup, or use a cloud backup, or simply not store mission-critical data on any of the Big Data platforms. Data quality can be ensured through data profiling, data normalization, semantic data management and data quality firewall. The analysis indicates a statistically significant higher magnitude of data management for Big Data adoption in the service industry as compared to the manufacturing industry. One possible explanation is that the data management techniques are less active in the manufacturing industry vis-a-vis the service industry.

Privacy concerns have been found to have a significant negative effect on Big Data adoption for both full sample and industry specific sample. Privacy concern in Big Data indicates that lesser the privacy risk in using Big Data analytics, higher the trust developed on the privacy and integrity part of Big Data. Thus in order to secure Big Data from privacy and security threats, various privacy-enhancing techniques, monitoring mechanisms, identity management standards, access control, configuration management monitoring mechanisms, and encryption schemes to ensure confidentiality, integrity, and the security are incorporated into Big Data techniques. The higher magnitude of privacy concern in service sector may be because of the lack of concern regarding security and privacy when considering a Big Data analytics as compared to manufacturing sector.

CONCLUSION

Big Data is an important evolution of information systems because of the cost-effective capture of information in a timely manner. Thus it is important to understand what contributes to BDA adoption in the enterprises. Given the TOE framework, this study created and approved an exploration model to look at the impact of nine logical variables on BDA adoption in firms.

There were four major contributions of this study:

1.   This study is an early endeavor to investigate and build up a BDA adoption model. This model is created to recognize the variables that impacts the appropriation of BDA hypothetically supported into the TOE framework:
     a.   The study identified key findings and suggestions about the determinants of BDA selection in the enterprises of India that relies on the company's technological, organizational and environmental contexts;
     b.   This study introduces an increasingly comprehensive evaluation of the components of Big Data by partitioning them in two segments – the manufacturing and service sectors;
     c.   Nine relevant factors (i.e., relative advantage, compatibility, complexity, top management support, along with firm size, competitive pressure, vendor support, data management, and privacy concerns) impact the appropriation goal of BDA; organizational readiness does not have any huge impact on selection for both full example and industry explicit example;
     d.   Among the nine determinants, complexity was the inhibitors of BDA, while remaining determinants alongside data security and data management of BDA were the facilitators of BDA adoption;
2.   This study quantitatively analyzed the applicability of the three settings (technological, organizational, and environmental) of the TOE framework and confirms that there are measurably noteworthy differences between the service and manufacturing industries;

3. This study discovered two determinants that impacted the BDA appropriation (data privacy and organizational data environment), however were rarely investigated in the earlier IT adoption research;
4. Finally, compared with prior BDA adoption research, this quantitative study used a large and representative sample that consists of numerous BDA decision makers. Thus the findings of this study are valuable and provide several important implications for BDA adoption research and practice.

IMPLICATIONS

The findings of this study are important to managers, Big Data providers and researchers in developing better strategies for Big Data adoption. It provides relevant recommendations to achieve a conducive implementation environment for Big Data adoption. The proposed model can help organizations assess the possible Big Data adoption and increase awareness about factors that influence adoption. The findings offer Big Data users with a better understanding of how technology, organizational, environmental and security challenges affect Big Data adoption. Adopters can increase their understanding for extracting maximum benefits from Big Data adoption; prospector and non-adopters can increase knowledge on challenges and prerequisite to the uptake of Big Data increasing knowledge on impediments to the uptake of new technology.

The proposed model can help Big Data providers increase their understanding of why some organizations choose to adopt Big Data, while others facing similar market conditions do not. Thus Big Data providers may need to improve their interaction with the organizations that are involved in Big Data experience, in order to create healthy environment for Big Data adoption and to remove any ambiguity surrounding the Big Data adoption. However Big Data providers need to be aware of common concerns that organizations experience when they make adoption decision, such as complexity, security etc. The proposed framework can help managers in identifying the firm's situation in terms of strength and weakness for the possible adoption of Big Data. The findings can lead managers to improve their insight in balancing decisions concerning adoption of Big Data in the future. In general, the advantage of the TOE framework is that it can include many different contextual factors, which other models may not. Therefore, the TOE model has the potential to contribute to firm managers' decision making.

CURRENT RESEARCH TRENDS

Organizations continuously investing in analytics to support digital transformations so confirming that the organization is adopting the analytics strategies are crucial to be top of the latest trends. Even though adoption of Big Data within the industry is occurring but there is gap to clearly find the pros and cons for organizations to invest in Big Data. The outcome of this study is a comprehensive model that combines technology, organization, environment and security dimension but there is need to formulate a distinct model for each industry. Thus future research could build on this study by examining big data adoption in different in sector and industries and in different countries. Also future study can test another wide range of variables that are not included in this study.

ACKNOWLEDGMENT

A prior version of this manuscript appeared in the *Information Resources Management Journal*.

REFERENCES

Abbasi, A., Sarker, S., & Chiang, R. H. L. (2016). Big data research in information systems: Toward an inclusive research agenda. *Journal of the Association for Information Systems*, *1*(2), 3. doi:10.17705/1jais.00423

Ajzen, I. (1991). The theory of planned behavior. *Organizational Behavior and Human Decision Processes*, *50*(2), 179–211. doi:10.1016/0749-5978(91)90020-T

Al Nuaimi, E., Al Neyadi, H., Mohamed, N., & Al-Jaroodi, J. (2015). Applications of big data to smart cities. *Journal of Internet Services and Applications*, *6*(1), 1–15. doi:10.118613174-015-0041-5

Alsaad, A., Mohamad, R., & Ismail, N. A. (2017). The moderating role of trust in business to business electronic commerce (B2B EC) adoption. *Computers in Human Behavior*, *68*(1), 157–169. doi:10.1016/j.chb.2016.11.040

Alshamaila, Y., Papagiannidis, S., & Li, F. (2013). Cloud computing adoption by SMEs in the north east of England: A multi-perspective framework. *Journal of Enterprise Information Management*, *26*(3), 250–275. doi:10.1108/17410391311325225

Alshawi, S., Farouk, M., & Irani, Z. (2011). Organizational, technical and data quality factors in CRM adoption – SME perspective. *Industrial Marketing Management*, *40*(3), 376–383. doi:10.1016/j.indmarman.2010.08.006

Barton, D., & Court, D. (2012). Making advanced analytics work for you. *Harvard Business Review*, *90*(1), 79–83. PMID:23074867

Bose, R., & Luo, X. (2012). Green IT adoption: A process management approach. *International Journal of Accounting & Information Management*, *20*(1), 63–77. doi:10.1108/18347641211201081

Chaudhury, A., & Bharati, P. (2008). IT outsourcing adoption by small and medium enterprises: A diffusion innovation approach. *Proceedings of the Americas Conference on Information Systems (AMCIS)*, 14-17.

Chaurasia, S., & Rosin, A. F. (2017). From big data to big impact: Analytics for teaching and learning in higher education. *Industrial and Commercial Training*, *49*(7/8), 321–328. doi:10.1108/ICT-10-2016-0069

Chen, C. P., & Zhang, C.-Y. (2014). Data-intensive applications, challenges, techniques and technologies: A survey on big data. *Information Sciences*, *275*(10), 314–347. doi:10.1016/j.ins.2014.01.015

Chen, H., Chiang, R., & Storey, V. (2012). Business intelligence and analytics: From big data to big impact. *Management Information Systems Quarterly*, *36*(4), 1165–1188. doi:10.2307/41703503

Chung, B. Y., Skibniewski, M. J., Lucas, H. C. Jr, & Kwak, Y. H. (2008). Analyzing enterprise resource planning system implementation success factors in the engineering – construction industry. *Journal of Computing in Civil Engineering*, *22*(6), 373–382. doi:10.1061/(ASCE)0887-3801(2008)22:6(373)

Cukier, K. (2010). Data, data everywhere: A special report on managing information. *The Economist, 394*, 3-5. Retrieved from https://www.economist.com/node/15557443

Davis, F. D. (1989). Perceived usefulness, perceived ease of use, and user acceptance of diffusion perspective. *Technovation*, *28*(3), 135–145.

Dubey, R., Gunasekaran, A., Childe, S. J., Wamba, S. F., & Papadopoulos, T. (2016). The impact of big data on world-class sustainable manufacturing. *International Journal of Advanced Manufacturing Technology*, *84*(1-4), 631–645. doi:10.100700170-015-7674-1

Elgendy, N., & Elragal, A. (2014). Big data analytics: A literature review paper. *Lecture Notes in Computer Science Industrial, 8557*, 214–227. 10.1007/978-3-319-08976-8_16

Fishbein, M., & Ajzen, I. (1975). *Belief, Attitude, Intention and Behavior: An introduction to theory and research*. Reading, MA: Addison-Wesley.

Gandomi, A., & Haider, M. (2015). Beyond the hype: Big data concepts, methods, and analytics. *International Journal of Information Management, 35*(2), 137–144. doi:10.1016/j.ijinfomgt.2014.10.007

Gangwar, H., & Date, H. (2016). Understanding cloud computing adoption: A model comparison approach. *Human Systems Management, 35*(2), 93–114. doi:10.3233/HSM-150857

Gangwar, H., Date, H., & Ramaswamy, R. (2015). Understanding factors of cloud computing adoption using an integrated TAM-TOE model. *Journal of Enterprise Information Management, 28*(1), 107–130. doi:10.1108/JEIM-08-2013-0065

Goes, P. (2014). Editor's comments: Big data and IS research. *Management Information Systems Quarterly, 38*(2), 3–8.

Grandon, E., & Pearson, J. M. (2004). E-commerce adoption: Perceptions of managers/owners of small and medium sized firms in Chile. *Communications of the Association for Information Systems, 13*(1), 81–102. doi:10.17705/1CAIS.01308

Gustin, C. M., Daugherty, P. J., & Stank, T. P. (1995). The effects of information availability on logistics integra. *Journal of Business Logistics, 16*(1), 1–13.

Hashem, I. A. T., Yaqoob, I., Anuar, N. B., Mokhtar, S., Gani, A., & Khan, S. U. (2015). The rise of big data on cloud computing: Review and open research issues. *Information Systems, 47*, 98–115. doi:10.1016/j.is.2014.07.006

Hazen, B. T., Boone, C. A., Ezell, J. D., & Jones-Farmer, L. A. (2014). Data quality for data science, predictive analytics, and big data in supply chain management: An introduction to the problem and suggestions for research and applications. *International Journal of Production Economics, 154*, 72–80. doi:10.1016/j.ijpe.2014.04.018

Hsu, P. F., Kraemer, K. L., & Dunkle, D. (2006). Factors of e-business use in US firms. *International Journal of Electronic Commerce, 10*(4), 9–45. doi:10.2753/JEC1086-4415100401

Hu, J., & Vasilakos, A. V. (2016). Energy big data analytics and security: Challenges and opportunities. *IEEE Transactions on Smart Grid, 7*(5), 2423–2436. doi:10.1109/TSG.2016.2563461

Huang, Z., Janz, B. D., & Frolick, M. N. (2008). A comprehensive examination of internet-EDI adoption. *Information Systems Management, 25*(3), 273–286. doi:10.1080/10580530802151228

Hung, S. Y., Hung, W. H., Tsai, C. A., & Jiang, S. C. (2010). Critical factors of hospital adoption on CRM system: Organizational and information system perspectives. *Journal of Decision Support Systems, 48*(4), 592–603. doi:10.1016/j.dss.2009.11.009

Ifinedo, P. (2011). An empirical analysis of factors influencing internet/e-business technologies adoption by SMEs in Canada. *International Journal of Information Technology & Decision Making, 10*(4), 731–766. doi:10.1142/S0219622011004543

Igbaria, M., Guimaraes, T., & Davis, G. B. (1995). Testing the determinants of microcomputer usage via a structural equation model. *Journal of Management Information Systems, 11*(4), 87–114. doi:10.1080/07421222.1995.11518061

Jagadish, H. V., Gehrke, J., Labrinidis, A., Papakonstantinou, Y., Patel, J. M., Ramakrishnan, R., & Shahabi, C. (2014). Big data and its technical challenges. *Communications of the ACM, 57*(7), 86–94. doi:10.1145/2611567

Jang, S.-H. (2010). An empirical study on the factors influencing RFID adoption and implementation. *Management Review. International Journal (Toronto, Ont.), 5*(2), 55–73.

Jeyaraj, A., Rottman, J. W., & Lacity, W. C. (2006). A review of the predictors, linkages, and biases in IT innovation adoption research. *Journal of Information Technology, 21*(1), 1–23. doi:10.1057/palgrave.jit.2000056

Koltay, T. (2015). Data literacy: In search of a name and identity. *The Journal of Documentation, 71*(2), 401–415. doi:10.1108/JD-02-2014-0026

Kuan, K. K. Y., & Chau, P. Y. K. (2001). A perception-based model for EDI adoption in small businesses using a technology-organization-environment framework. *Information & Management, 38*(8), 507–521. doi:10.1016/S0378-7206(01)00073-8

Kwon, O., Lee, N., & Shin, B. (2014). Data quality management, data usage experience and acquisition intention of big data analytics. *International Journal of Information Management, 34*(3), 387–394. doi:10.1016/j.ijinfomgt.2014.02.002

Lee, G., & Xia, W. (2006). Organizational size and IT innovation adoption: A meta-analysis. *Information & Management, 43*(8), 975–985. doi:10.1016/j.im.2006.09.003

Lee, J., Kao, H.-A., & Yang, S. (2014). Service innovation and smart analytics for Industry 4.0 and big data environment. *Procedia CIRP, 16*, 3–8. doi:10.1016/j.procir.2014.02.001

Lewis, W., Agarwal, R., & Sambamurthy, V. (2003). Sources of influence on beliefs about information technology use: An empirical study of knowledge workers. *Management Information Systems Quarterly, 27*(4), 657–678. doi:10.2307/30036552

Lian, J., Yen, D., & Wang, Y. (2014). An exploratory study to understand the critical factors affecting the decision to adopt cloud computing in Taiwan hospital. *International Journal of Information Management, 34*(1), 28–36. doi:10.1016/j.ijinfomgt.2013.09.004

Lin, A., & Chen, N.-C. (2012). Cloud computing as an innovation: Perception, attitude, and adoption. *International Journal of Information Management, 32*(6), 533–540. doi:10.1016/j.ijinfomgt.2012.04.001

Lin, H.-F., & Lin, S.-M. (2008). Factors of e-business diffusion: A test of the technology diffusion perspective. *Technovation, 28*(3), 135–145. doi:10.1016/j.technovation.2007.10.003

Lippert, S. K., & Govindarajulu, C. (2006). Technological, organizational, and environmental antecedents to web services adoption. *Antecedents to Web Services Adoption, 6*(1), 146–158.

Low, C., Chen, Y., & Wu, M. (2011). Understanding the factors of cloud computing adoption. *Industrial Management & Data Systems, 111*(7), 1006–1023. doi:10.1108/02635571111161262

Maduku, D. K., Mpinganjira, M., & Duh, H. (2016). Mobile marketing adoption intention by South African SMEs: A multi-perspective framework. *International Journal of Information Management, 36*(5), 711–723. doi:10.1016/j.ijinfomgt.2016.04.018

Manyika, J., Chui, M., Brown, B., Bughin, J., Dobbs, R., Roxburgh, C., & Byers, A. H. (2011). *Big Data: The next frontier for innovation, competition, and productivity.* Washington, DC: McKinsey Global Institute.

McAfee, A., & Brynjolfsson, E. (2012). Big data: The management revolution. *Harvard Business Review, 90*(10), 60–68. PMID:23074865

McCole, P., & Ramsey, E. (2005). A profile of adopters and non-adopters of ecommerce in SME professional service firms. *Australasian Marketing Journal, 13*(1), 36–48. doi:10.1016/S1441-3582(05)70066-5

Miller, D., & Toulouse, J.-M. (1986). Chief executive personality and corporate strategy and structure in small firms. *Management Science, 32*(11), 1389–1409. doi:10.1287/mnsc.32.11.1389

Moore, G. C., & Benbasat, I. (1991). Development of an instrument to measure the perceptions of adopting an information technology innovation. *Information Systems Research, 2*(3), 173–191. doi:10.1287/isre.2.3.192

Moura, J., & Serrão, C. (2015). Security and privacy issues of big data. In N. Zaman, M. Seliaman, M. Hassan, & F. Marquez (Eds.), *Handbook of Research on Trends and Future Directions in Big Data and Web Intelligence* (pp. 20–52). Hershey, PA: Information Science Reference. doi:10.4018/978-1-4666-8505-5.ch002

Mourtzis, D., Vlachou, E., & Milas, N. (2016). Industrial big data as a result of IoT adoption in manufacturing. *Procedia CIRP, 55*, 290–295. doi:10.1016/j.procir.2016.07.038

Murdoch, T. B., & Detsky, A. S. (2013). The inevitable application of big data to health care. *Journal of the American Medical Association, 309*(13), 1351–1352. doi:10.1001/jama.2013.393 PMID:23549579

Oliveira, S. F., Fürlinger, K., & Kranzlmüller, D. (2012). Trends in computation, communication and storage and the consequences for data intensive science. *Proceedings of the IEEE 14th International Conference on High Performance Computing and Communication & 2012 IEEE 9th International Conference on Embedded Software and Systems*, 572-579. 10.1109/HPCC.2012.83

Oliveira, T., & Martins, M. F. (2010a). Firms patterns of e-business adoption: Evidence for the European Union-27. *The Electronic Journal Information Systems Evaluation, 13*(1), 47–56.

Oliveira, T., & Martins, M. F. (2010b). Understanding e-business adoption across industries in European countries. *Industrial Management & Data Systems, 110*(9), 1337–1354. doi:10.1108/02635571011087428

Opresnk, D., & Taisch, M. (2015). The value of big data in servitization. *International Journal of Production Economics, 165*, 174–184. doi:10.1016/j.ijpe.2014.12.036

Pan, M.-J., & Jang, W.-Y. (2008). Factors of the adoption of enterprise resources planning within the technology-organization-environment framework: Taiwan's communications industry. *Journal of Computer Information Systems, 48*(3), 94–102.

Pei-Fang, H., Soumya, R., & Li-Hsieh, Y.-Y. (2014). Examining cloud computing adoption intention, pricing mechanism, and deployment model. *International Journal of Information Management*, *34*(4), 474–488. doi:10.1016/j.ijinfomgt.2014.04.006

Peng, R., Xiong, L., & Yang, Z. (2012). Exploring tourist adoption of tourism mobile payment: An empirical analysis. *Journal of Theoretical and Applied Electronic Commerce Research*, *7*(1), 21–33. doi:10.4067/S0718-18762012000100003

Premkumar, G., Ramamurthy, K., & Crum, M. (1997). Determinants of EDI adoption in the transportation industry. *European Journal of Information Systems*, *6*(2), 107–121. doi:10.1057/palgrave.ejis.3000260

Premkumar, G., & Roberts, M. (1999). Adoption of new information technologies in rural small pricing mechanism, and deployment mode. *International Journal of Information Management*, *34*, 474–488.

Ramdani, B., Kawalek, P., & Lorenzo, O. (2009). Predicting SMEs' adoption of enterprise systems. *Journal of Enterprise Information Management*, *22*(1/2), 10–24. doi:10.1108/17410390910922796

Ren, S. J., Wamba, S. F., Akter, S., Dubey, R., & Childe, S. J. (2017). Modelling quality dynamics, business value and firm performance in a big data analytics environment. *International Journal of Production Research*, *55*, 1–16.

Rogers, E. M. (1962). *Diffusion of Innovations* (1st ed.). New York: Free Press.

Rogers, E. M. (2003). *Diffusion of Innovations*. New York: Free Press.

Rui, G. (2007). *Information Systems Innovation Adoption Among Organizations: A match-based framework and empirical studies*. Singapore: National University of Singapore.

Schadt, E. E. (2012). The changing privacy landscape in the era of big data. *Molecular Systems Biology*, *8*(1), 612. doi:10.1038/msb.2012.47 PMID:22968446

Schillewaert, N., Ahearne, M. J., Frambach, R. T., & Moenaert, R. K. (2005). The adoption of information technology in the sales force. *Industrial Marketing Management*, *34*(4), 323–336. doi:10.1016/j.indmarman.2004.09.013

Sila, I. (2013). Factors affecting the adoption of B2B ecommerce technologies. *Electronic Commerce Research*, *13*(2), 199–236. doi:10.100710660-013-9110-7

Srivastava, U., & Gopalkrishnan, S. (2015). Impact of big data analytics on banking sector: Learning for Indian banks. *Procedia Computer Science*, *50*, 643–652. doi:10.1016/j.procs.2015.04.098

Sun, S., Cegielski, C. G., Jia, L., & Hall, D. J. (2016). Understanding the factors affecting the organizational adoption of big data. *Journal of Computer Information Systems*, *58*(3), 193–203. doi:10.1080/08874417.2016.1222891

Tao, F., Cheng, J., Qi, Q., Zhang, M., Zhang, H., & Sui, F. (2017). Digital twin-driven product design manufacturing and service with big data. *International Journal of Advanced Manufacturing Technology*, *94*, 1–14.

Teo, H. H., Wei, K. K., & Benbasat, I. (2003). Predicting intention to adopt interorganizational linkages: An institutional perspective. *Management Information Systems Quarterly*, *27*(1), 19–49. doi:10.2307/30036518

Teo, T. S. H., Lin, S., & Lai, K.-H. (2009). Adopters and non-adopters of e-procurement in Singapore: An empirical study. *Omega*, *37*(5), 972–987. doi:10.1016/j.omega.2008.11.001

Tornatzky, L. G., & Fleischer, M. (1990). *The Processes of Technological Innovation*. Lexington, MA: Lexington Books.

Tornatzky, L. G., & Klein, K. J. (1982). Innovation characteristics and innovation adoption-implementation: A meta-analysis of findings. *IEEE Transactions on Engineering Management*, *29*(1), 28–45. doi:10.1109/TEM.1982.6447463

Tsai, M. C., Lai, K. H., & Hsu, W. C. (2013). A study of the institutional forces influencing the adoption intention of RFID by suppliers. *Information & Management*, *50*(1), 59–65. doi:10.1016/j.im.2012.05.006

Venkatesh, V., Morris, M. G., Davis, G. B., & Davis, F. (2003). User acceptance of information technology: Toward a unified view. *Management Information Systems Quarterly*, *27*(3), 425–478. doi:10.2307/30036540

Verma, S. (2018). Mapping the intellectual structure of the big data research in the IS discipline: A citation/co-citation analysis. *Information Resources Management Journal*, *31*(1), 21–52. doi:10.4018/IRMJ.2018010102

Verma, S., & Bhattacharyya, S. S. (2017). Perceived strategic value-based adoption of big data analytics in emerging economy. *Journal of Enterprise Information Management*, *30*(3), 354–382. doi:10.1108/JEIM-10-2015-0099

Verma, S., Bhattacharyya, S. S., & Kumar, S. (2018). An extension of the technology acceptance model in the big data analytics system implementation environment. *Information Processing & Management*, *54*(5), 791–806. doi:10.1016/j.ipm.2018.01.004

Waller, M. A., & Fawcett, S. E. (2013). Data science, predictive analytics, and big data: A revolution that will transform supply chain design and management. *Journal of Business Logistics*, *34*(2), 77–84. doi:10.1111/jbl.12010

Wang, G., Gunasekaran, A., Ngai, E. W. T., & Papadopoulos, T. (2016). Big data analytics in logistics and supply chain management: Certain investigations for research and applications. *International Journal of Production Economics*, *176*, 98–110. doi:10.1016/j.ijpe.2016.03.014

Wang, Y., & Wang, Y. (2016). Factors of firms' knowledge management system implementation: An empirical study. *Computers in Human Behavior*, *64*(1), 829–842. doi:10.1016/j.chb.2016.07.055

Wang, Y., Wang, Y., & Yang, Y. (2010). Understanding the factors of RFID adoption in the manufacturing industry. *Technological Forecasting and Social Change*, *77*(5), 803–815. doi:10.1016/j.techfore.2010.03.006

Zhan, Y., Tan, K. H., Li, Y., & Tse, Y. K. (2018). Unlocking the power of big data in new product development. *Annals of Operations Research*, *270*(1/2), 577–595. doi:10.100710479-016-2379-x

Zhang, Y., Ren, S., Liu, Y., & Si, S. (2016). A big data analytics architecture for cleaner manufacturing and maintenance processes of complex product. *Journal of Cleaner Production*, *142*(2), 626–641.

Zhong, R. Y., Huang, G. Q., Lan, S., Dai, Q. Y., Chen, X., & Zhang, T. (2015). A big data approach for logistics trajectory discovery from RFID-enabled production data. *International Journal of Production Economics*, *165*, 260–272. doi:10.1016/j.ijpe.2015.02.014

Zhong, R. Y., Lan, S. L., Xu, C., Dai, Q. Y., & Huang, G. Q. (2016). Visualization of RFID enabled shop floor logistics big data in cloud manufacturing. *International Journal of Advanced Manufacturing Technology*, *84*(1), 5–16. doi:10.100700170-015-7702-1

Zhu, K., Dong, S. T., Xu, S., & Kraemer, K. L. (2006). Innovation diffusion in global contexts: Factors of post-adoption digital transformation of European companies. *European Journal of Information Systems*, *15*(9), 601–616. doi:10.1057/palgrave.ejis.3000650

Zhu, K., & Kraemer, K. L. (2005). Post-adoption variations in usage and value of e-business by organizations: Cross-country evidence from the retail industry. *Information Systems Research*, *16*(1), 61–84. doi:10.1287/isre.1050.0045

Zhu, K., Kraemer, K. L., & Xu, S. (2003). Electronic business adoption by European firms: A cross-country assessment of the facilitators and inhibitors. *European Journal of Information Systems*, *12*(4), 251–268. doi:10.1057/palgrave.ejis.3000475

Zhu, K., Kraemer, K. L., & Xu, S. (2006). The process of innovation assimilation by firms in different countries: A technology diffusion perspective on e-business. *Management Science*, *52*(10), 1557–1576. doi:10.1287/mnsc.1050.0487

KEY TERMS AND DEFINITIONS

Big Data: A dataset that is larger than a typical dataset that requires unique tools, techniques, and technologies to store, manage, and analyze data.

Big Data Analytics: Techniques, technologies, systems, methodologies, tools, and applications used to analysis for decision making.

Compatibility: The extent to which an innovation aligns with an organization's current values and/or needs.

Competitive Pressure: Amount of pressure an organization experiences from competitors that may in turn affect big data adoption.

Complexity: The extent to which an innovation is difficult to use or understand.

Data Management: Process of ensuring accuracy, availability, accessibility, and quality of large stores of data by allocating people, policies, and technologies.

Data Privacy: Protection of personal privacy during data acquisition, storage, transmission, and usage.

Environmental Context: Refers to the context in which the organization functions which may impact the decision making.

Four Vs: The four Vs refer to volume, variety, velocity, and veracity; characteristics used to describe big data.

Organizational Context: Characteristics of an organization that can facilitate or constrain adoption and implementation of an innovation.

Organizational Readiness: Term used to refer to organizational resources—technological, financial, and IT human resources/personnel—necessary for big data adoption.

Organizational Size: Refers to the number of employees in an organization.

Relative Advantage: Term used to describe whether an innovation provides an advantage to an organization over an existing technology.

Technology Organization Environment (TOE) Framework: Framework developed by Tornatzy and Fleischer (1990) to explain the process of innovation from the perspective of three organizational contexts: technological, organizational, and environmental.

Top Management Support: The extent to which top management perceives the importance of innovation and is involved in related activities.

Vendor Support: Support necessary for big data adoption – specifically for data availability, reliability, and completeness.

Related Readings

To continue IGI Global's long-standing tradition of advancing innovation through emerging research, please find below a compiled list of recommended IGI Global book chapters and journal articles in the areas of green cities, environmental management, and sustainable urban development. These related readings will provide additional information and guidance to further enrich your knowledge and assist you with your own research.

Aagaard, A. (2019). Knowledge Management Strategy Implementation Through Knowledge Ambassadors. In M. Jennex (Ed.), *Effective Knowledge Management Systems in Modern Society* (pp. 193–211). Hershey, PA: IGI Global. doi:10.4018/978-1-5225-5427-1.ch010

Ahuja, R. (2018). Hadoop Framework for Handling Big Data Needs. In R. Segall & J. Cook (Eds.), *Handbook of Research on Big Data Storage and Visualization Techniques* (pp. 101–122). Hershey, PA: IGI Global. doi:10.4018/978-1-5225-3142-5.ch004

Ahuja, R., Malik, J., Tyagi, R., & Brinda, R. (2018). Role of Open Source Software in Big Data Storage. In R. Segall & J. Cook (Eds.), *Handbook of Research on Big Data Storage and Visualization Techniques* (pp. 123–150). Hershey, PA: IGI Global. doi:10.4018/978-1-5225-3142-5.ch005

Al-Khasawneh, A., & Hijazi, H. (2019). Classifying Diabetes Disease Using Feedforward MLP Neural Networks. In N. Dey (Ed.), *Technological Innovations in Knowledge Management and Decision Support* (pp. 127–149). Hershey, PA: IGI Global. doi:10.4018/978-1-5225-6164-4.ch006

Al-Qirim, N., Rouibah, K., Serhani, M. A., Tarhini, A., Khalil, A., Maqableh, M., & Gergely, M. (2019). The Strategic Adoption of Big Data in Organizations. In Z. Sun (Ed.), *Managerial Perspectives on Intelligent Big Data Analytics* (pp. 43–54). Hershey, PA: IGI Global. doi:10.4018/978-1-5225-7277-0.ch003

Alharbi, H., & Sandhu, K. (2018). E-Learning and Information Communications Technologies (ICT) in Saudi Arabia: An Overview. In S. Swayze & V. Ford (Eds.), *Innovative Applications of Knowledge Discovery and Information Resources Management* (pp. 159–172). Hershey, PA: IGI Global. doi:10.4018/978-1-5225-5829-3.ch007

Ali, A., Nor, N. M., Ibrahim, T., Romlie, M. F., & Bingi, K. (2018). Big Data Storage for the Modeling of Historical Time Series Solar Irradiations. In R. Segall & J. Cook (Eds.), *Handbook of Research on Big Data Storage and Visualization Techniques* (pp. 433–463). Hershey, PA: IGI Global. doi:10.4018/978-1-5225-3142-5.ch016

Anderson, R., & Mansingh, G. (2019). CoMIS-KMS: An Elaborated Process Model for Transitioning MIS to KMS. In M. Jennex (Ed.), *Effective Knowledge Management Systems in Modern Society* (pp. 171–192). Hershey, PA: IGI Global. doi:10.4018/978-1-5225-5427-1.ch009

Aron, R., & Aggarwal, D. K. (2018). Resource Provisioning and Scheduling of Big Data Processing Jobs. In R. Segall & J. Cook (Eds.), *Handbook of Research on Big Data Storage and Visualization Techniques* (pp. 382–401). Hershey, PA: IGI Global. doi:10.4018/978-1-5225-3142-5.ch014

Bandera, C., Passerini, K., & Bartolacci, M. R. (2019). Knowledge Management and Entrepreneurship Research and Practice: Status, Challenges, and Opportunities. In M. Jennex (Ed.), *Effective Knowledge Management Systems in Modern Society* (pp. 45–61). Hershey, PA: IGI Global. doi:10.4018/978-1-5225-5427-1.ch003

Bansal, N., Singh, R., & Sharma, A. (2017). An Insight into State-of-the-Art Techniques for Big Data Classification. *International Journal of Information System Modeling and Design*, *8*(3), 24–42. doi:10.4018/IJISMD.2017070102

Bari, M. W., & Fanchen, M. (2017). Personal Interaction Drives Innovation: Instrumental Guanxi-Based Knowledge Café Approach. In D. Jaziri-Bouagina & G. Jamil (Eds.), *Handbook of Research on Tacit Knowledge Management for Organizational Success* (pp. 176–200). Hershey, PA: IGI Global. doi:10.4018/978-1-5225-2394-9.ch007

Bele, N., Panigrahi, P. K., & Srivastava, S. K. (2018). Knowledge Discovery From Vernacular Expressions: An Application of Social Media and Sentiment Mining. *International Journal of Knowledge Management, 14*(1), 1–18. doi:10.4018/IJKM.2018010101

Biswas, K., Vasant, P. M., Laruccia, M. B., Gámez Vintaned, J. A., & Myint, M. M. (2020). Review on Particle Swarm Optimization Approach for Optimizing Wellbore Trajectory. In J. Thomas, P. Karagoz, B. Ahamed, & P. Vasant (Eds.), *Deep Learning Techniques and Optimization Strategies in Big Data Analytics* (pp. 290–307). Hershey, PA: IGI Global. doi:10.4018/978-1-7998-1192-3.ch017

Blayney, P. J., & Sun, Z. (2019). Using Excel and Excel VBA for Preliminary Analysis in Big Data Research. In Z. Sun (Ed.), *Managerial Perspectives on Intelligent Big Data Analytics* (pp. 110–136). Hershey, PA: IGI Global. doi:10.4018/978-1-5225-7277-0.ch007

Brahimi, T., Sarirete, A., & Khalifa, S. (2018). Impact of Accreditation on Engineering Education. In M. Lytras, L. Daniela, & A. Visvizi (Eds.), *Enhancing Knowledge Discovery and Innovation in the Digital Era* (pp. 91–106). Hershey, PA: IGI Global. doi:10.4018/978-1-5225-4191-2.ch005

Brodzińska, K., Szostak, A., & Jałocha, B. (2020). Using Action Research for Improvement of Project Knowledge Management in the Public Museum. In V. Ismyrlis, T. Tarnanidis, & E. Moschidis (Eds.), *Knowledge Management Practices in the Public Sector* (pp. 123–144). Hershey, PA: IGI Global. doi:10.4018/978-1-7998-1940-0.ch006

Celestine, N. A., & Perryer, C. (2019). The Determinants of Interorganizational Knowledge Coaching Success: Looking Ahead to the Future of Knowledge Transfer. In M. Jennex (Ed.), *Effective Knowledge Management Systems in Modern Society* (pp. 146–169). Hershey, PA: IGI Global. doi:10.4018/978-1-5225-5427-1.ch008

Chedid, M., & Teixeira, L. (2017). The Knowledge Management Culture: An Exploratory Study in Academic Context. In D. Deshpande, N. Bhosale, & R. Londhe (Eds.), *Enhancing Academic Research With Knowledge Management Principles* (pp. 1–24). Hershey, PA: IGI Global. doi:10.4018/978-1-5225-2489-2.ch002

Choi, J. (2018). Roles and Impacts of Automatic Item Generation on Assessment Research, Practice, and Policy. In S. Swayze & V. Ford (Eds.), *Innovative Applications of Knowledge Discovery and Information Resources Management* (pp. 143–158). Hershey, PA: IGI Global. doi:10.4018/978-1-5225-5829-3.ch006

D., M., & S., R. (2020). Deep Learning: A Recent Computing Platform for Multimedia Information Retrieval. In J. Thomas, P. Karagoz, B. Ahamed, & P. Vasant (Eds.), *Deep Learning Techniques and Optimization Strategies in Big Data Analytics* (pp. 124-141). Hershey, PA: IGI Global. doi:10.4018/978-1-7998-1192-3.ch008

D'Avanzo, E., Lytras, M. D., Picatoste, J., Novo-Corti, I., & Adinolfi, P. (2018). Perceived Innovative Teaching Procedures in Higher Education From Students' Perspectives From a Sentiment Analysis Approach. In M. Lytras, L. Daniela, & A. Visvizi (Eds.), *Enhancing Knowledge Discovery and Innovation in the Digital Era* (pp. 126–147). Hershey, PA: IGI Global. doi:10.4018/978-1-5225-4191-2.ch007

Dalkir, K. (2017). The Role of Human Resources (HR) in Tacit Knowledge Sharing. In D. Jaziri-Bouagina & G. Jamil (Eds.), *Handbook of Research on Tacit Knowledge Management for Organizational Success* (pp. 364–386). Hershey, PA: IGI Global. doi:10.4018/978-1-5225-2394-9.ch014

Damahe, L. B., & Thakur, N. V. (2019). Review on Image Representation Compression and Retrieval Approaches. In N. Dey (Ed.), *Technological Innovations in Knowledge Management and Decision Support* (pp. 203–231). Hershey, PA: IGI Global. doi:10.4018/978-1-5225-6164-4.ch009

Dasgupta, H. (2017). Data Mining Techniques in Knowledge Management. In D. Deshpande, N. Bhosale, & R. Londhe (Eds.), *Enhancing Academic Research With Knowledge Management Principles* (pp. 200–232). Hershey, PA: IGI Global. doi:10.4018/978-1-5225-2489-2.ch008

Dekhici, L., Guerraiche, K., & Belkadi, K. (2019). Bat Algorithm With Generalized Fly for Combinatorial Production Optimization Problems: Case Studies. In N. Dey (Ed.), *Technological Innovations in Knowledge Management and Decision Support* (pp. 34–66). Hershey, PA: IGI Global. doi:10.4018/978-1-5225-6164-4.ch003

Delgado, J. C. (2018). Beyond SOA and REST for Distributed Application Integration. In S. Swayze & V. Ford (Eds.), *Innovative Applications of Knowledge Discovery and Information Resources Management* (pp. 228–257). Hershey, PA: IGI Global. doi:10.4018/978-1-5225-5829-3.ch011

Dhawale, C. A., Dhawale, K., & Dubey, R. (2020). A Review on Deep Learning Applications. In J. Thomas, P. Karagoz, B. Ahamed, & P. Vasant (Eds.), *Deep Learning Techniques and Optimization Strategies in Big Data Analytics* (pp. 21–31). Hershey, PA: IGI Global. doi:10.4018/978-1-7998-1192-3.ch002

Endres, M. L., & Chowdhury, S. (2019). Team and Individual Interactions With Reciprocity in Individual Knowledge Sharing. In M. Jennex (Ed.), *Effective Knowledge Management Systems in Modern Society* (pp. 123–145). Hershey, PA: IGI Global. doi:10.4018/978-1-5225-5427-1.ch007

Fandango, A., & Rivera, W. (2018). High Performance Storage for Big Data Analytics and Visualization. In R. Segall & J. Cook (Eds.), *Handbook of Research on Big Data Storage and Visualization Techniques* (pp. 254–275). Hershey, PA: IGI Global. doi:10.4018/978-1-5225-3142-5.ch010

Fazzin, S. (2017). Can Tacit Knowledge be Shared on Cloud?: An Opportunity for Viability From PBL. In D. Jaziri-Bouagina & G. Jamil (Eds.), *Handbook of Research on Tacit Knowledge Management for Organizational Success* (pp. 264–296). Hershey, PA: IGI Global. doi:10.4018/978-1-5225-2394-9.ch010

Ford, V., & Swayze, S. (2018). Twenty-First Century Issues Impacting Turnover of IT Professionals: From Burnout and Turnover to Workplace Wellbeing. In S. Swayze & V. Ford (Eds.), *Innovative Applications of Knowledge Discovery and Information Resources Management* (pp. 29–62). Hershey, PA: IGI Global. doi:10.4018/978-1-5225-5829-3.ch002

Gadad, V., & N., S. C. (2019). Census Data Analysis and Visualization Using R Tool: A Case Study. In Z. Sun (Ed.), *Managerial Perspectives on Intelligent Big Data Analytics* (pp. 137-161). Hershey, PA: IGI Global. doi:10.4018/978-1-5225-7277-0.ch008

Ganesan, T., Vasant, P., & Litvinchev, I. (2020). Multiobjective Optimization of a Biofuel Supply Chain Using Random Matrix Generators. In J. Thomas, P. Karagoz, B. Ahamed, & P. Vasant (Eds.), *Deep Learning Techniques and Optimization Strategies in Big Data Analytics* (pp. 206–232). Hershey, PA: IGI Global. doi:10.4018/978-1-7998-1192-3.ch013

Garretson, C. J., Lemoine, P. A., Waller, R. E., & Richardson, M. D. (2020). Knowledge Mobilization and Global Higher Education: Building Capacity for Change. In V. Ismyrlis, T. Tarnanidis, & E. Moschidis (Eds.), *Knowledge Management Practices in the Public Sector* (pp. 1–23). Hershey, PA: IGI Global. doi:10.4018/978-1-7998-1940-0.ch001

Gloet, M., & Samson, D. (2019). Knowledge and Innovation Management: Creating Value. In M. Jennex (Ed.), *Effective Knowledge Management Systems in Modern Society* (pp. 19–44). Hershey, PA: IGI Global. doi:10.4018/978-1-5225-5427-1.ch002

Goyal, M., & Bhatnagar, V. (2017). Pros and Cons of Applying Opinion Mining on Operation Management: A Big Data Perspective. In M. Kumar (Ed.), *Applied Big Data Analytics in Operations Management* (pp. 93–106). Hershey, PA: IGI Global. doi:10.4018/978-1-5225-0886-1.ch005

Gudivada, V., Apon, A., & Rao, D. L. (2018). Database Systems for Big Data Storage and Retrieval. In R. Segall & J. Cook (Eds.), *Handbook of Research on Big Data Storage and Visualization Techniques* (pp. 76–100). Hershey, PA: IGI Global. doi:10.4018/978-1-5225-3142-5.ch003

Gupta, V. (2020). Understanding the Dynamics of Knowledge Management Tools in Two Public Universities in Delhi, India. In V. Ismyrlis, T. Tarnanidis, & E. Moschidis (Eds.), *Knowledge Management Practices in the Public Sector* (pp. 145–177). Hershey, PA: IGI Global. doi:10.4018/978-1-7998-1940-0.ch007

Guster, D. C., Brown, C. G., & Rice, E. P. (2018). Scalable Data Warehouse Architecture: A Higher Education Case Study. In R. Segall & J. Cook (Eds.), *Handbook of Research on Big Data Storage and Visualization Techniques* (pp. 340–381). Hershey, PA: IGI Global. doi:10.4018/978-1-5225-3142-5.ch013

Handford, F. J. (2018). Big Data Tools for Computing on Clouds and Grids. In R. Segall & J. Cook (Eds.), *Handbook of Research on Big Data Storage and Visualization Techniques* (pp. 152–174). Hershey, PA: IGI Global. doi:10.4018/978-1-5225-3142-5.ch006

Hartmann, S., Mainka, A., & Stock, W. G. (2018). Innovation Contests: How to Engage Citizens in Solving Urban Problems? In M. Lytras, L. Daniela, & A. Visvizi (Eds.), *Enhancing Knowledge Discovery and Innovation in the Digital Era* (pp. 254–273). Hershey, PA: IGI Global. doi:10.4018/978-1-5225-4191-2.ch014

Hipólito, J. H., Ibarra, M. A., Torres-Ruiz, M., Guzmán, G., & Quintero, R. (2018). Innovation on User-Generated Content for Environmental Noise Monitoring and Analysis in the Context of Smart Cities. In M. Lytras, L. Daniela, & A. Visvizi (Eds.), *Enhancing Knowledge Discovery and Innovation in the Digital Era* (pp. 224–253). Hershey, PA: IGI Global. doi:10.4018/978-1-5225-4191-2.ch013

Horne, J. (2018). Visualizing Big Data From a Philosophical Perspective. In R. Segall & J. Cook (Eds.), *Handbook of Research on Big Data Storage and Visualization Techniques* (pp. 809–852). Hershey, PA: IGI Global. doi:10.4018/978-1-5225-3142-5.ch028

Hossain, K., Rahman, M., & Roy, S. (2019). IoT Data Compression and Optimization Techniques in Cloud Storage: Current Prospects and Future Directions. *International Journal of Cloud Applications and Computing, 9*(2), 43–59. doi:10.4018/IJCAC.2019040103

Ilvonen, I., Jussila, J., & Kärkkäinen, H. (2019). A Business-Driven Process Model for Knowledge Security Risk Management: Tackling Knowledge Risks While Realizing Business Benefits. In M. Jennex (Ed.), *Effective Knowledge Management Systems in Modern Society* (pp. 308–325). Hershey, PA: IGI Global. doi:10.4018/978-1-5225-5427-1.ch015

Iqbal, B. A. (2017). Knowledge Management Cycle. In D. Jaziri-Bouagina & G. Jamil (Eds.), *Handbook of Research on Tacit Knowledge Management for Organizational Success* (pp. 54–75). Hershey, PA: IGI Global. doi:10.4018/978-1-5225-2394-9.ch003

Islam, J., Vasant, P. M., Negash, B. M., Laruccia, M. B., & Myint, M. (2020). A Survey of Nature-Inspired Algorithms With Application to Well Placement Optimization. In J. Thomas, P. Karagoz, B. Ahamed, & P. Vasant (Eds.), *Deep Learning Techniques and Optimization Strategies in Big Data Analytics* (pp. 32–45). Hershey, PA: IGI Global. doi:10.4018/978-1-7998-1192-3.ch003

Ismyrlis, V. (2020). Practices and Challenges of Knowledge Management in the Greek Public Sector. In V. Ismyrlis, T. Tarnanidis, & E. Moschidis (Eds.), *Knowledge Management Practices in the Public Sector* (pp. 178–195). Hershey, PA: IGI Global. doi:10.4018/978-1-7998-1940-0.ch008

Jain, A., & Bhatnagar, V. (2017). Big Data in Operation Management. In M. Kumar (Ed.), *Applied Big Data Analytics in Operations Management* (pp. 1–29). Hershey, PA: IGI Global. doi:10.4018/978-1-5225-0886-1.ch001

Jain, H., Pal, A., & Kumar, M. (2017). Predictive Analytics in Operations Management. In M. Kumar (Ed.), *Applied Big Data Analytics in Operations Management* (pp. 68–92). Hershey, PA: IGI Global. doi:10.4018/978-1-5225-0886-1.ch004

Jain, S. R., & Thakur, N. V. (2019). Wireless Sensor Networks: Concepts, Analysis, Routing, and Applications. In N. Dey (Ed.), *Technological Innovations in Knowledge Management and Decision Support* (pp. 247–276). Hershey, PA: IGI Global. doi:10.4018/978-1-5225-6164-4.ch011

Jambulingam, V. K., & Santhi, V. (2017). Knowledge Discovery and Big Data Analytics: Issues, Challenges, and Opportunities. In A. Singh, N. Dey, A. Ashour, & V. Santhi (Eds.), *Web Semantics for Textual and Visual Information Retrieval* (pp. 144–164). Hershey, PA: IGI Global. doi:10.4018/978-1-5225-2483-0.ch007

Related Readings

Jamil, G. L., & Jamil, Â. D. (2017). Expliciting Tacit Knowledge: Exploring an Uncharted Path for a Questionable Trip. In D. Jaziri-Bouagina & G. Jamil (Eds.), *Handbook of Research on Tacit Knowledge Management for Organizational Success* (pp. 30–52). Hershey, PA: IGI Global. doi:10.4018/978-1-5225-2394-9.ch002

Jaziri-Bouagina, D. (2017). The Tacit Knowledge Through the Customer Experience: Conceptualization, Externalization Methods, and Use Application to Tunisian Thalassotherapy Centers. In D. Jaziri-Bouagina & G. Jamil (Eds.), *Handbook of Research on Tacit Knowledge Management for Organizational Success* (pp. 1–29). Hershey, PA: IGI Global. doi:10.4018/978-1-5225-2394-9.ch001

Jdidou, Y., & Khaldi, M. (2018). Using Recommendation Systems in MOOC: An Innovation in Education That Increases the Profitability of Students. In M. Lytras, L. Daniela, & A. Visvizi (Eds.), *Enhancing Knowledge Discovery and Innovation in the Digital Era* (pp. 176–190). Hershey, PA: IGI Global. doi:10.4018/978-1-5225-4191-2.ch010

Jennex, M. E. (2019). Using a Revised Knowledge Pyramid to Redefine Knowledge Management Strategy. In M. Jennex (Ed.), *Effective Knowledge Management Systems in Modern Society* (pp. 1–18). Hershey, PA: IGI Global. doi:10.4018/978-1-5225-5427-1.ch001

Jennex, M. E., & Durcikova, A. (2019). Integrating IS Security With Knowledge Management: What Can Knowledge Management Learn From IS Security Vice Versa? In M. Jennex (Ed.), *Effective Knowledge Management Systems in Modern Society* (pp. 267–283). Hershey, PA: IGI Global. doi:10.4018/978-1-5225-5427-1.ch013

K., J., & R., A. (2018). Big Data Technologies and Management. In S. Swayze, & V. Ford (Eds.), *Innovative Applications of Knowledge Discovery and Information Resources Management* (pp. 196-210). Hershey, PA: IGI Global. doi:10.4018/978-1-5225-5829-3.ch009

Kadan, A. B., & Subbian, P. S. V., J., N., H., V., R. T., & Nath, S. S. (2020). Classification of Fundus Images Using Neural Network Approach. In J. Thomas, P. Karagoz, B. Ahamed, & P. Vasant (Eds.), Deep Learning Techniques and Optimization Strategies in Big Data Analytics (pp. 91-106). Hershey, PA: IGI Global. doi:10.4018/978-1-7998-1192-3.ch006

Kamel, S. H., Megahed, I., & Atteya, H. (2019). The Impact of Creating a Business Intelligence Platform on Higher Education: The Case of the American University in Cairo. In Z. Sun (Ed.), *Managerial Perspectives on Intelligent Big Data Analytics* (pp. 232–259). Hershey, PA: IGI Global. doi:10.4018/978-1-5225-7277-0.ch013

Kasemsap, K. (2017). Knowledge Discovery and Data Visualization: Theories and Perspectives. *International Journal of Organizational and Collective Intelligence*, 7(3), 56–69. doi:10.4018/IJOCI.2017070105

Katsanika, E., & Gotzamani, K. (2020). Communication Barriers and Social Capital: Improving Information and Knowledge Flows in Public Services. In V. Ismyrlis, T. Tarnanidis, & E. Moschidis (Eds.), *Knowledge Management Practices in the Public Sector* (pp. 76–104). Hershey, PA: IGI Global. doi:10.4018/978-1-7998-1940-0.ch004

Khamparia, A., & Pandey, B. (2017). Impact of Interactive Multimedia in E-Learning Technologies: Role of Multimedia in E-Learning. In D. Deshpande, N. Bhosale, & R. Londhe (Eds.), *Enhancing Academic Research With Knowledge Management Principles* (pp. 171–199). Hershey, PA: IGI Global. doi:10.4018/978-1-5225-2489-2.ch007

Kirilov, L., Guliashki, V., & Staykov, B. (2019). Web-Based Decision Support System for Solving Multiple-Objective Decision-Making Problems. In N. Dey (Ed.), *Technological Innovations in Knowledge Management and Decision Support* (pp. 150–175). Hershey, PA: IGI Global. doi:10.4018/978-1-5225-6164-4.ch007

Koitzsch, K. E. (2018). The Image as Big Data Toolkit: An Application Case Study in Image Analysis, Feature Recognition, and Data Visualization. In R. Segall & J. Cook (Eds.), *Handbook of Research on Big Data Storage and Visualization Techniques* (pp. 497–548). Hershey, PA: IGI Global. doi:10.4018/978-1-5225-3142-5.ch018

Konagala, V., & Bano, S. (2020). Fake News Detection Using Deep Learning: Supervised Fake News Detection Analysis in Social Media With Semantic Similarity Method. In J. Thomas, P. Karagoz, B. Ahamed, & P. Vasant (Eds.), *Deep Learning Techniques and Optimization Strategies in Big Data Analytics* (pp. 166–177). Hershey, PA: IGI Global. doi:10.4018/978-1-7998-1192-3.ch011

Krishnamoorthy, M., Ahamed, B. B., Suresh, S., & Alagappan, S. (2020). Deep Learning Techniques and Optimization Strategies in Big Data Analytics: Automated Transfer Learning of Convolutional Neural Networks Using Enas Algorithm. In J. Thomas, P. Karagoz, B. Ahamed, & P. Vasant (Eds.), *Deep Learning Techniques and Optimization Strategies in Big Data Analytics* (pp. 142–153). Hershey, PA: IGI Global. doi:10.4018/978-1-7998-1192-3.ch009

Krishnamurthy, S., & Akila, V. (2017). Information Retrieval Models: Trends and Techniques. In A. Singh, N. Dey, A. Ashour, & V. Santhi (Eds.), *Web Semantics for Textual and Visual Information Retrieval* (pp. 17–42). Hershey, PA: IGI Global. doi:10.4018/978-1-5225-2483-0.ch002

Related Readings

Krishnan, S., & Jayavel, K. (2018). Distributed Streaming Big Data Analytics for Internet of Things (IoT). In R. Segall & J. Cook (Eds.), *Handbook of Research on Big Data Storage and Visualization Techniques* (pp. 303–338). Hershey, PA: IGI Global. doi:10.4018/978-1-5225-3142-5.ch012

Kumar, R., Pattnaik, P. K., & Pandey, P. (2017). Conversion of Higher into Lower Language Using Machine Translation. In A. Singh, N. Dey, A. Ashour, & V. Santhi (Eds.), *Web Semantics for Textual and Visual Information Retrieval* (pp. 92–107). Hershey, PA: IGI Global. doi:10.4018/978-1-5225-2483-0.ch005

Lal, S. B., Sharma, A., Chaturvedi, K. K., Farooqi, M. S., Kumar, S., Mishra, D. C., & Jha, M. (2017). State-of-the-Art Information Retrieval Tools for Biological Resources. In A. Singh, N. Dey, A. Ashour, & V. Santhi (Eds.), *Web Semantics for Textual and Visual Information Retrieval* (pp. 203–226). Hershey, PA: IGI Global. doi:10.4018/978-1-5225-2483-0.ch010

Larry, L., & Von Canon, W. A. Jr. (2018). Information Technology Pre-Risk Governance. In S. Swayze & V. Ford (Eds.), *Innovative Applications of Knowledge Discovery and Information Resources Management* (pp. 63–85). Hershey, PA: IGI Global. doi:10.4018/978-1-5225-5829-3.ch003

Levy, M., & Salem, R. (2020). Implementing a Knowledge Management-Based Model for Lessons Learned. In V. Ismyrlis, T. Tarnanidis, & E. Moschidis (Eds.), *Knowledge Management Practices in the Public Sector* (pp. 196–219). Hershey, PA: IGI Global. doi:10.4018/978-1-7998-1940-0.ch009

Lofaro, R. J. (2019). Knowledge Engineering, Cognitive Ergonomics, and Knowledge Management in 2017: A New Delphi Paradigm With Applications. In M. Jennex (Ed.), *Effective Knowledge Management Systems in Modern Society* (pp. 78–97). Hershey, PA: IGI Global. doi:10.4018/978-1-5225-5427-1.ch005

Luna-Soto, V., Quintero, R., Torres-Ruiz, M., Moreno-Ibarra, M., & Escamilla, I. (2018). Innovation on Geo-Enrichment of Texts Using Gazetteers for Massive Open On-Line Courses. In M. Lytras, L. Daniela, & A. Visvizi (Eds.), *Enhancing Knowledge Discovery and Innovation in the Digital Era* (pp. 274–286). Hershey, PA: IGI Global. doi:10.4018/978-1-5225-4191-2.ch015

Mahyoub, F. H., & Abdullah, R. (2020). Protein Secondary Structure Prediction Approaches: A Review With Focus on Deep Learning Methods. In J. Thomas, P. Karagoz, B. Ahamed, & P. Vasant (Eds.), *Deep Learning Techniques and Optimization Strategies in Big Data Analytics* (pp. 251–273). Hershey, PA: IGI Global. doi:10.4018/978-1-7998-1192-3.ch015

Malhotra, M., & Singh, A. (2017). A Study on Models and Methods of Information Retrieval System. In A. Singh, N. Dey, A. Ashour, & V. Santhi (Eds.), *Web Semantics for Textual and Visual Information Retrieval* (pp. 43–68). Hershey, PA: IGI Global. doi:10.4018/978-1-5225-2483-0.ch003

Malik, K. R., & Ahmad, T. (2017). Technique for Transformation of Data From RDB to XML Then to RDF. In A. Singh, N. Dey, A. Ashour, & V. Santhi (Eds.), *Web Semantics for Textual and Visual Information Retrieval* (pp. 70–91). Hershey, PA: IGI Global. doi:10.4018/978-1-5225-2483-0.ch004

Man-Im, A., Ongsakul, W., & Madhu, M. N. (2020). Heuristic Optimization Algorithms for Power System Scheduling Applications: Multi-Objective Generation Scheduling With PSO. In J. Thomas, P. Karagoz, B. Ahamed, & P. Vasant (Eds.), *Deep Learning Techniques and Optimization Strategies in Big Data Analytics* (pp. 178–205). Hershey, PA: IGI Global. doi:10.4018/978-1-7998-1192-3.ch012

Manaf, H. A., & Harvey, W. S. (2017). Sharing Managerial Tacit Knowledge: A Case Study of Managers Working in Malaysia's Local Government. In D. Jaziri-Bouagina & G. Jamil (Eds.), *Handbook of Research on Tacit Knowledge Management for Organizational Success* (pp. 335–363). Hershey, PA: IGI Global. doi:10.4018/978-1-5225-2394-9.ch013

Maravilhas, S., & Martins, J. S. (2017). Tacit Knowledge in Maker Spaces and Fab Labs: From Do It Yourself (DIY) to Do It With Others (DIWO). In D. Jaziri-Bouagina & G. Jamil (Eds.), *Handbook of Research on Tacit Knowledge Management for Organizational Success* (pp. 297–316). Hershey, PA: IGI Global. doi:10.4018/978-1-5225-2394-9.ch011

Masud, M. (2018). Knowledge Innovation Through Update Propagation in Collaborative Data Sharing Systems. In M. Lytras, L. Daniela, & A. Visvizi (Eds.), *Enhancing Knowledge Discovery and Innovation in the Digital Era* (pp. 191–203). Hershey, PA: IGI Global. doi:10.4018/978-1-5225-4191-2.ch011

Matiatou, M. (2018). Internal Branding as Innovation Tenet: A Transformational Paradigm Shift. In M. Lytras, L. Daniela, & A. Visvizi (Eds.), *Enhancing Knowledge Discovery and Innovation in the Digital Era* (pp. 287–312). Hershey, PA: IGI Global. doi:10.4018/978-1-5225-4191-2.ch016

Mbale, J. (2017). ZAMREN Big Data Management (ZAMBiDM) Envisaging Efficiency and Analytically Manage IT Resources. In M. Kumar (Ed.), *Applied Big Data Analytics in Operations Management* (pp. 55–67). Hershey, PA: IGI Global. doi:10.4018/978-1-5225-0886-1.ch003

McCloskey, D. W. (2018). Exploring the Impact of Flexible and Permeable Work-Life Boundaries in a Mobile World. In S. Swayze & V. Ford (Eds.), *Innovative Applications of Knowledge Discovery and Information Resources Management* (pp. 1–28). Hershey, PA: IGI Global. doi:10.4018/978-1-5225-5829-3.ch001

McKay, D. S., & Ellis, T. J. (2019). Measuring the Relationship Among Learning Enablers and IT Project Success. In M. Jennex (Ed.), *Effective Knowledge Management Systems in Modern Society* (pp. 212–235). Hershey, PA: IGI Global. doi:10.4018/978-1-5225-5427-1.ch011

Mendes, L. (2017). TQM and Knowledge Management: An Integrated Approach Towards Tacit Knowledge Management. In D. Jaziri-Bouagina & G. Jamil (Eds.), *Handbook of Research on Tacit Knowledge Management for Organizational Success* (pp. 236–263). Hershey, PA: IGI Global. doi:10.4018/978-1-5225-2394-9.ch009

Mesbahi, N., Kazar, O., Benharzallah, S., Zoubeidi, M., & Rezki, D. (2019). A Clustering Approach Based on Cooperative Agents to Improve Decision Support in ERP. In N. Dey (Ed.), *Technological Innovations in Knowledge Management and Decision Support* (pp. 1–18). Hershey, PA: IGI Global. doi:10.4018/978-1-5225-6164-4.ch001

Mishra, I., Bandyopadhyay, R., Ghosh, S., & Swetapadma, A. (2019). Analysis of Cutting-Edge Regression Algorithms Used for Data Analysis. In Z. Sun (Ed.), *Managerial Perspectives on Intelligent Big Data Analytics* (pp. 199–213). Hershey, PA: IGI Global. doi:10.4018/978-1-5225-7277-0.ch011

Mkrttchian, V., Gamidullaeva, L. A., & Panasenko, S. (2019). Optimizing and Enhancing Digital Marketing Techniques in Intellectual Big Data Analytics. In Z. Sun (Ed.), *Managerial Perspectives on Intelligent Big Data Analytics* (pp. 98–109). Hershey, PA: IGI Global. doi:10.4018/978-1-5225-7277-0.ch006

Moridpour, S., Mazloumi, E., & Hesami, R. (2017). Application of Artificial Neural Networks in Predicting the Degradation of Tram Tracks Using Maintenance Data. In M. Kumar (Ed.), *Applied Big Data Analytics in Operations Management* (pp. 30–54). Hershey, PA: IGI Global. doi:10.4018/978-1-5225-0886-1.ch002

Mortier, T., & Anderson, D. (2017). Understanding Tacit Knowledge in Decision Making. In D. Jaziri-Bouagina & G. Jamil (Eds.), *Handbook of Research on Tacit Knowledge Management for Organizational Success* (pp. 418–435). Hershey, PA: IGI Global. doi:10.4018/978-1-5225-2394-9.ch016

Moshonsky, M., Serenko, A., & Bontis, N. (2019). Practical Relevance of Management Research: The Role of Doctoral Program Graduates. In M. Jennex (Ed.), *Effective Knowledge Management Systems in Modern Society* (pp. 236–265). Hershey, PA: IGI Global. doi:10.4018/978-1-5225-5427-1.ch012

Mulay, P., & Ahire, P. (2017). Knowledge Management Academic Research: "NUMPATIBILITY" – Numeral Era of Compatibility. In D. Deshpande, N. Bhosale, & R. Londhe (Eds.), *Enhancing Academic Research With Knowledge Management Principles* (pp. 45–91). Hershey, PA: IGI Global. doi:10.4018/978-1-5225-2489-2.ch004

N., R. (2020). Arrhythmia Detection Based on Hybrid Features of T-Wave in Electrocardiogram. In J. Thomas, P. Karagoz, B. Ahamed, & P. Vasant (Eds.), *Deep Learning Techniques and Optimization Strategies in Big Data Analytics* (pp. 1-20). Hershey, PA: IGI Global. doi:10.4018/978-1-7998-1192-3.ch001

Narang, S. K., Kumar, S., & Verma, V. (2017). Knowledge Discovery From Massive Data Streams. In A. Singh, N. Dey, A. Ashour, & V. Santhi (Eds.), *Web Semantics for Textual and Visual Information Retrieval* (pp. 109–143). Hershey, PA: IGI Global. doi:10.4018/978-1-5225-2483-0.ch006

Nikishova, M. I., & Kuznetsov, M. E. (2019). Is Artificial Intelligence a New Dawn or Challenge for Corporate Decision Making? In Z. Sun (Ed.), *Managerial Perspectives on Intelligent Big Data Analytics* (pp. 20–42). Hershey, PA: IGI Global. doi:10.4018/978-1-5225-7277-0.ch002

Okechukwu, O. C. (2018). Big Data Visualization Tools and Techniques. In R. Segall & J. Cook (Eds.), *Handbook of Research on Big Data Storage and Visualization Techniques* (pp. 465–496). Hershey, PA: IGI Global. doi:10.4018/978-1-5225-3142-5.ch017

Olinsky, A., Quinn, J. T., & Schumacher, P. A. (2018). Visualization of Predictive Modeling for Big Data Using Various Approaches When There Are Rare Events at Differing Levels. In R. Segall & J. Cook (Eds.), *Handbook of Research on Big Data Storage and Visualization Techniques* (pp. 604–631). Hershey, PA: IGI Global. doi:10.4018/978-1-5225-3142-5.ch021

Oncioiu, I., Petrescu, A. G., Mândricel, D. A., & Ifrim, A. M. (2019). Proactive Information Security Strategy for a Secure Business Environment. In Z. Sun (Ed.), *Managerial Perspectives on Intelligent Big Data Analytics* (pp. 214–231). Hershey, PA: IGI Global. doi:10.4018/978-1-5225-7277-0.ch012

Ooms, R., Spruit, M. R., & Overbeek, S. (2019). 3PM Revisited: Dissecting the Three Phases Method for Outsourcing Knowledge Discovery. *International Journal of Business Intelligence Research, 10*(1), 80–93. doi:10.4018/IJBIR.2019010105

Ophir, D. (2018). Visualization and Storage of Big Data for Linguistic Applications. In R. Segall & J. Cook (Eds.), *Handbook of Research on Big Data Storage and Visualization Techniques* (pp. 723–748). Hershey, PA: IGI Global. doi:10.4018/978-1-5225-3142-5.ch025

Ozlen, K., & Handzic, M. (2019). A Contingency Perspective for Knowledge Management Solutions in Different Decision-Making Contexts. In M. Jennex (Ed.), *Effective Knowledge Management Systems in Modern Society* (pp. 62–77). Hershey, PA: IGI Global. doi:10.4018/978-1-5225-5427-1.ch004

Pandey, A., & Banerjee, S. (2017). Test Suite Optimization Using Chaotic Firefly Algorithm in Software Testing. *International Journal of Applied Metaheuristic Computing, 8*(4), 41–57. doi:10.4018/IJAMC.2017100103

Papanikou, M. (2020). Risk Assessment: Knowledge Management Paradigms, Big Data, and Aviation Policy Making. In V. Ismyrlis, T. Tarnanidis, & E. Moschidis (Eds.), *Knowledge Management Practices in the Public Sector* (pp. 47–75). Hershey, PA: IGI Global. doi:10.4018/978-1-7998-1940-0.ch003

Piaggesi, D. (2018). An Innovation-Based and Sustainable Knowledge Society: The Triple Helix Approach. In M. Lytras, L. Daniela, & A. Visvizi (Eds.), *Enhancing Knowledge Discovery and Innovation in the Digital Era* (pp. 13–35). Hershey, PA: IGI Global. doi:10.4018/978-1-5225-4191-2.ch002

Puri, K., & Mulay, P. (2017). Knowledge Management in Academic Community: Code and Content-Based Plagiarism Prevention MARG. In D. Deshpande, N. Bhosale, & R. Londhe (Eds.), *Enhancing Academic Research With Knowledge Management Principles* (pp. 115–170). Hershey, PA: IGI Global. doi:10.4018/978-1-5225-2489-2.ch006

Quinn, C. J., Quinn, M. J., Olinsky, A., & Quinn, J. T. (2018). Issues and Methods for Access, Storage, and Analysis of Data From Online Social Communities. In R. Segall & J. Cook (Eds.), *Handbook of Research on Big Data Storage and Visualization Techniques* (pp. 402–432). Hershey, PA: IGI Global. doi:10.4018/978-1-5225-3142-5.ch015

Quintana, M. G., & Aránguiz, M. S. (2018). Use of ICT to Innovate in Teaching and Learning Processes in Higher Education: Case Examples of Universities in Chile. In M. Lytras, L. Daniela, & A. Visvizi (Eds.), *Enhancing Knowledge Discovery and Innovation in the Digital Era* (pp. 36–55). Hershey, PA: IGI Global. doi:10.4018/978-1-5225-4191-2.ch003

R., R., Tiwari, H., Patel, J., R., R., & R., K. (2020). Bidirectional GRU-Based Attention Model for Kid-Specific URL Classification. In J. Thomas, P. Karagoz, B. Ahamed, & P. Vasant (Eds.), *Deep Learning Techniques and Optimization Strategies in Big Data Analytics* (pp. 78-90). Hershey, PA: IGI Global. doi:10.4018/978-1-7998-1192-3.ch005

Radhakrishnan, S., & Vijayarajan, V. (2020). Optimized Deep Learning System for Crop Health Classification Strategically Using Spatial and Temporal Data. In J. Thomas, P. Karagoz, B. Ahamed, & P. Vasant (Eds.), *Deep Learning Techniques and Optimization Strategies in Big Data Analytics* (pp. 233–250). Hershey, PA: IGI Global. doi:10.4018/978-1-7998-1192-3.ch014

Rahaman, M. S., & Vasant, P. (2020). Artificial Intelligence Approach for Predicting TOC From Well Logs in Shale Reservoirs: A Review. In J. Thomas, P. Karagoz, B. Ahamed, & P. Vasant (Eds.), *Deep Learning Techniques and Optimization Strategies in Big Data Analytics* (pp. 46–77). Hershey, PA: IGI Global. doi:10.4018/978-1-7998-1192-3.ch004

Rahman, H. U., Khan, R. U., & Ali, A. (2018). Programming and Pre-Processing Systems for Big Data Storage and Visualization. In R. Segall & J. Cook (Eds.), *Handbook of Research on Big Data Storage and Visualization Techniques* (pp. 228–253). Hershey, PA: IGI Global. doi:10.4018/978-1-5225-3142-5.ch009

Raman, L. (2017). Application of Knowledge Management in University Research and Higher Education: An Experiment With Communities of Practice (COP). In D. Deshpande, N. Bhosale, & R. Londhe (Eds.), *Enhancing Academic Research With Knowledge Management Principles* (pp. 92–114). Hershey, PA: IGI Global. doi:10.4018/978-1-5225-2489-2.ch005

Rascão, J. P. (2017). The Marketing of Information and Knowledge Management. In D. Jaziri-Bouagina & G. Jamil (Eds.), *Handbook of Research on Tacit Knowledge Management for Organizational Success* (pp. 127–155). Hershey, PA: IGI Global. doi:10.4018/978-1-5225-2394-9.ch005

Ravasan, A. Z., Zare, A., & Bamakan, S. M. (2018). ERP Post-Implementation Success Assessment: An Extended Framework. In S. Swayze & V. Ford (Eds.), *Innovative Applications of Knowledge Discovery and Information Resources Management* (pp. 86–116). Hershey, PA: IGI Global. doi:10.4018/978-1-5225-5829-3.ch004

Rehioui, F. (2019). Approach of Modelization and Management on Software Components. In N. Dey (Ed.), *Technological Innovations in Knowledge Management and Decision Support* (pp. 98–126). Hershey, PA: IGI Global. doi:10.4018/978-1-5225-6164-4.ch005

Rezende, D. A. (2018). Strategic Digital City Projects: Innovative Information and Public Services Offered by Chicago (USA) and Curitiba (Brazil). In M. Lytras, L. Daniela, & A. Visvizi (Eds.), *Enhancing Knowledge Discovery and Innovation in the Digital Era* (pp. 204–223). Hershey, PA: IGI Global. doi:10.4018/978-1-5225-4191-2.ch012

Rodrigue, T. K. (2018). Information Technology Security as Scored by Management Budget. In S. Swayze & V. Ford (Eds.), *Innovative Applications of Knowledge Discovery and Information Resources Management* (pp. 258–280). Hershey, PA: IGI Global. doi:10.4018/978-1-5225-5829-3.ch012

Rodriguez, E., & Edwards, J. S. (2019). Knowledge Management in Support of Enterprise Risk Management. In M. Jennex (Ed.), *Effective Knowledge Management Systems in Modern Society* (pp. 284–307). Hershey, PA: IGI Global. doi:10.4018/978-1-5225-5427-1.ch014

Roy, S., & Berry, M. W. (2018). Mining Multimodal Big Data: Tensor Methods and Applications. In R. Segall & J. Cook (Eds.), *Handbook of Research on Big Data Storage and Visualization Techniques* (pp. 674–702). Hershey, PA: IGI Global. doi:10.4018/978-1-5225-3142-5.ch023

Sahu, A. K., Sahu, N. K., & Sahu, A. K. (2019). Agile Supplier Assessment Using Generalized Interval-Valued Trapezoidal Fuzzy Numbers. In N. Dey (Ed.), *Technological Innovations in Knowledge Management and Decision Support* (pp. 67–97). Hershey, PA: IGI Global. doi:10.4018/978-1-5225-6164-4.ch004

Saravanan, V., Alagan, A., & Woungang, I. (2018). Big Data in Massive Parallel Processing: A Multi-Core Processors Perspective. In R. Segall & J. Cook (Eds.), *Handbook of Research on Big Data Storage and Visualization Techniques* (pp. 276–302). Hershey, PA: IGI Global. doi:10.4018/978-1-5225-3142-5.ch011

Sedkaoui, S., & Khelfaoui, M. (2019). Building an Analytics Culture to Boost a Data-Driven Entrepreneur's Business Model. In Z. Sun (Ed.), *Managerial Perspectives on Intelligent Big Data Analytics* (pp. 260–291). Hershey, PA: IGI Global. doi:10.4018/978-1-5225-7277-0.ch014

Segall, R. S., & Cook, J. S. (2018). Overview of Big-Data-Intensive Storage and Its Technologies. In R. Segall & J. Cook (Eds.), *Handbook of Research on Big Data Storage and Visualization Techniques* (pp. 33–74). Hershey, PA: IGI Global. doi:10.4018/978-1-5225-3142-5.ch002

Segall, R. S., & Niu, G. (2018). Overview of Big Data and Its Visualization. In R. Segall & J. Cook (Eds.), *Handbook of Research on Big Data Storage and Visualization Techniques* (pp. 1–32). Hershey, PA: IGI Global. doi:10.4018/978-1-5225-3142-5. ch001

Semlali, B. B., El Amrani, C., & Ortiz, G. (2020). Hadoop Paradigm for Satellite Environmental Big Data Processing. *International Journal of Agricultural and Environmental Information Systems*, *11*(1), 23–47. doi:10.4018/IJAEIS.2020010102

Shidaganti, G. I., & Prakash, S. (2017). A Conceptual Framework for Educational System Operation Management Synchronous with Big Data Approach. In M. Kumar (Ed.), *Applied Big Data Analytics in Operations Management* (pp. 107–132). Hershey, PA: IGI Global. doi:10.4018/978-1-5225-0886-1.ch006

Simard, A. J. (2017). Organizational Social Context: The Foundation of Tacit Knowledge Management. In D. Jaziri-Bouagina & G. Jamil (Eds.), *Handbook of Research on Tacit Knowledge Management for Organizational Success* (pp. 76–126). Hershey, PA: IGI Global. doi:10.4018/978-1-5225-2394-9.ch004

Singh, A., Dey, N., & Ashour, A. S. (2017). Scope of Automation in Semantics-Driven Multimedia Information Retrieval From Web. In A. Singh, N. Dey, A. Ashour, & V. Santhi (Eds.), *Web Semantics for Textual and Visual Information Retrieval* (pp. 1–16). Hershey, PA: IGI Global. doi:10.4018/978-1-5225-2483-0.ch001

Singh, A., & Sharma, A. (2017). Web Semantics for Personalized Information Retrieval. In A. Singh, N. Dey, A. Ashour, & V. Santhi (Eds.), *Web Semantics for Textual and Visual Information Retrieval* (pp. 166–186). Hershey, PA: IGI Global. doi:10.4018/978-1-5225-2483-0.ch008

Singh, J., Gimekar, A. M., & Venkatesan, S. (2017). An Overview of Big Data Security with Hadoop Framework. In M. Kumar (Ed.), *Applied Big Data Analytics in Operations Management* (pp. 165–181). Hershey, PA: IGI Global. doi:10.4018/978-1-5225-0886-1.ch008

Singh, S., & Singh, J. (2017). Management of SME's Semi Structured Data Using Semantic Technique. In M. Kumar (Ed.), *Applied Big Data Analytics in Operations Management* (pp. 133–164). Hershey, PA: IGI Global. doi:10.4018/978-1-5225-0886-1.ch007

Sousa, M. J. (2017). Tacit Knowledge as a Driver for Competitiveness. In D. Jaziri-Bouagina & G. Jamil (Eds.), *Handbook of Research on Tacit Knowledge Management for Organizational Success* (pp. 318–334). Hershey, PA: IGI Global. doi:10.4018/978-1-5225-2394-9.ch012

Spruit, M., & Adriana, T. (2018). Business Intelligence in Secondary Education: Data-Driven Innovation by Quality Measurement. In M. Lytras, L. Daniela, & A. Visvizi (Eds.), *Enhancing Knowledge Discovery and Innovation in the Digital Era* (pp. 56–90). Hershey, PA: IGI Global. doi:10.4018/978-1-5225-4191-2.ch004

Stefanou, V., & Kotsovoulou, M. (2018). Use of Presentations in the Classroom: How Innovative Can It Be? In M. Lytras, L. Daniela, & A. Visvizi (Eds.), *Enhancing Knowledge Discovery and Innovation in the Digital Era* (pp. 162–175). Hershey, PA: IGI Global. doi:10.4018/978-1-5225-4191-2.ch009

Strang, K. D., & Sun, Z. (2019). Managerial Controversies in Artificial Intelligence and Big Data Analytics. In Z. Sun (Ed.), *Managerial Perspectives on Intelligent Big Data Analytics* (pp. 55–74). Hershey, PA: IGI Global. doi:10.4018/978-1-5225-7277-0.ch004

Stranieri, A., & Balasubramanian, V. (2019). Remote Patient Monitoring for Healthcare: A Big Challenge for Big Data. In Z. Sun (Ed.), *Managerial Perspectives on Intelligent Big Data Analytics* (pp. 163–179). Hershey, PA: IGI Global. doi:10.4018/978-1-5225-7277-0.ch009

Sun, Z. (2019). Intelligent Big Data Analytics: A Managerial Perspective. In Z. Sun (Ed.), *Managerial Perspectives on Intelligent Big Data Analytics* (pp. 1–19). Hershey, PA: IGI Global. doi:10.4018/978-1-5225-7277-0.ch001

Swayze, S., Gronow, T. M., & Sweet, J. (2018). Using Social Media for Healthcare Recruiting. In S. Swayze & V. Ford (Eds.), *Innovative Applications of Knowledge Discovery and Information Resources Management* (pp. 211–227). Hershey, PA: IGI Global. doi:10.4018/978-1-5225-5829-3.ch010

Thomas, J. J., Tran, T. H., Lechuga, G. P., & Belaton, B. (2020). Convolutional Graph Neural Networks: A Review and Applications of Graph Autoencoder in Chemoinformatics. In J. Thomas, P. Karagoz, B. Ahamed, & P. Vasant (Eds.), *Deep Learning Techniques and Optimization Strategies in Big Data Analytics* (pp. 107–123). Hershey, PA: IGI Global. doi:10.4018/978-1-7998-1192-3.ch007

Thota, C., Manogaran, G., Lopez, D., & Sundarasekar, R. (2018). Architecture for Big Data Storage in Different Cloud Deployment Models. In R. Segall & J. Cook (Eds.), *Handbook of Research on Big Data Storage and Visualization Techniques* (pp. 196–226). Hershey, PA: IGI Global. doi:10.4018/978-1-5225-3142-5.ch008

Tsironis, L. K., & Ismyrlis, V. (2020). The Role of Middle Managers in Knowledge Creation and Diffusion: An Examination in Greek Organizations. In V. Ismyrlis, T. Tarnanidis, & E. Moschidis (Eds.), *Knowledge Management Practices in the Public Sector* (pp. 105–122). Hershey, PA: IGI Global. doi:10.4018/978-1-7998-1940-0.ch005

Tsironis, L. K., & Tarnanidis, T. (2020). A Mapping of Knowledge Management Techniques and Tools for Sustainable Growth in the Public Sector. In V. Ismyrlis, T. Tarnanidis, & E. Moschidis (Eds.), *Knowledge Management Practices in the Public Sector* (pp. 24–46). Hershey, PA: IGI Global. doi:10.4018/978-1-7998-1940-0.ch002

Ursyn, A., & L'Astorina, E. (2018). Visualization of Big Data Sets Using Computer Graphics. In R. Segall & J. Cook (Eds.), *Handbook of Research on Big Data Storage and Visualization Techniques* (pp. 578–603). Hershey, PA: IGI Global. doi:10.4018/978-1-5225-3142-5.ch020

Usman, M., & Usman, M. (2018). Conceptual Model for Predictive Analysis on Large Data. In *Predictive Analysis on Large Data for Actionable Knowledge: Emerging Research and Opportunities* (pp. 59–90). Hershey, PA: IGI Global. doi:10.4018/978-1-5225-5029-7.ch003

Usman, M., & Usman, M. (2018). Experimental Study I: Automobile Dataset. In *Predictive Analysis on Large Data for Actionable Knowledge: Emerging Research and Opportunities* (pp. 91–110). Hershey, PA: IGI Global. doi:10.4018/978-1-5225-5029-7.ch004

Usman, M., & Usman, M. (2018). Experimental Study II: Adult Dataset. In *Predictive Analysis on Large Data for Actionable Knowledge: Emerging Research and Opportunities* (pp. 111–132). Hershey, PA: IGI Global. doi:10.4018/978-1-5225-5029-7.ch005

Usman, M., & Usman, M. (2018). Experimental Study III: Forest Cover Type Dataset. In *Predictive Analysis on Large Data for Actionable Knowledge: Emerging Research and Opportunities* (pp. 133–150). Hershey, PA: IGI Global. doi:10.4018/978-1-5225-5029-7.ch006

Related Readings

Usmani, S., Rehman, F., Umair, S., & Khan, S. A. (2018). A Review of Security Challenges in Cloud Storage of Big Data. In R. Segall & J. Cook (Eds.), *Handbook of Research on Big Data Storage and Visualization Techniques* (pp. 175–195). Hershey, PA: IGI Global. doi:10.4018/978-1-5225-3142-5.ch007

V., P., & R., P. (2020). Dimensionality Reduction With Multi-Fold Deep Denoising Autoencoder. In J. Thomas, P. Karagoz, B. Ahamed, & P. Vasant (Eds.), *Deep Learning Techniques and Optimization Strategies in Big Data Analytics* (pp. 154-165). Hershey, PA: IGI Global. doi:10.4018/978-1-7998-1192-3.ch010

Valentina, F. N. (2017). The Tacit Knowledge and the Knowledge Management Processes: Developing a Relationship-Based Knowledge Matrix Using Simulation to Improve Performance. In D. Jaziri-Bouagina & G. Jamil (Eds.), *Handbook of Research on Tacit Knowledge Management for Organizational Success* (pp. 201–235). Hershey, PA: IGI Global. doi:10.4018/978-1-5225-2394-9.ch008

Vanani, I. R., & Kheiri, M. S. (2018). Big Data and Its Role in Facilitating the Visualization of Financial Analytics. In R. Segall & J. Cook (Eds.), *Handbook of Research on Big Data Storage and Visualization Techniques* (pp. 704–722). Hershey, PA: IGI Global. doi:10.4018/978-1-5225-3142-5.ch024

Vargas-Vera, M. (2018). An Analysis of Student Performance in a Digital Electronics Design Course. In M. Lytras, L. Daniela, & A. Visvizi (Eds.), *Enhancing Knowledge Discovery and Innovation in the Digital Era* (pp. 107–125). Hershey, PA: IGI Global. doi:10.4018/978-1-5225-4191-2.ch006

Vargas-Vera, M. (2018). The Development of a Virtual University Campus Using Second Life. In M. Lytras, L. Daniela, & A. Visvizi (Eds.), *Enhancing Knowledge Discovery and Innovation in the Digital Era* (pp. 148–161). Hershey, PA: IGI Global. doi:10.4018/978-1-5225-4191-2.ch008

Verma, C., & Pandey, R. (2018). Statistical Visualization of Big Data Through Hadoop Streaming in RStudio. In R. Segall & J. Cook (Eds.), *Handbook of Research on Big Data Storage and Visualization Techniques* (pp. 549–577). Hershey, PA: IGI Global. doi:10.4018/978-1-5225-3142-5.ch019

Vijayakumar, S., Dasari, N., Bhushan, B., & Reddy, R. (2017). Semantic Web-Based Framework for Scientific Workflows in E-Science. In A. Singh, N. Dey, A. Ashour, & V. Santhi (Eds.), *Web Semantics for Textual and Visual Information Retrieval* (pp. 187–202). Hershey, PA: IGI Global. doi:10.4018/978-1-5225-2483-0.ch009

Vijayakumar, S., Thakare, V. R. J. A., Bhushan, S. B., & Santhi, V. (2017). Role of Social Networking Sites in Enhancing Teaching Environment. In A. Singh, N. Dey, A. Ashour, & V. Santhi (Eds.), Web Semantics for Textual and Visual Information Retrieval (pp. 227-243). Hershey, PA: IGI Global. doi:10.4018/978-1-5225-2483-0.ch011

Visvizi, A., Lytras, M. D., & Daniela, L. (2018). (Re)Defining Smart Education: Towards Dynamic Education and Information Systems for Innovation Networks. In M. Lytras, L. Daniela, & A. Visvizi (Eds.), *Enhancing Knowledge Discovery and Innovation in the Digital Era* (pp. 1–12). Hershey, PA: IGI Global. doi:10.4018/978-1-5225-4191-2.ch001

Wallis, M., Kumar, K., & Gepp, A. (2019). Credit Rating Forecasting Using Machine Learning Techniques. In Z. Sun (Ed.), *Managerial Perspectives on Intelligent Big Data Analytics* (pp. 180–198). Hershey, PA: IGI Global. doi:10.4018/978-1-5225-7277-0.ch010

Welekar, R., & Thakur, N. V. (2019). Possible Approaches for Character Recognition With Existing Methodologies and State-of-the-Art Techniques. In N. Dey (Ed.), *Technological Innovations in Knowledge Management and Decision Support* (pp. 232–246). Hershey, PA: IGI Global. doi:10.4018/978-1-5225-6164-4.ch010

Yeomans, J. S. (2019). Simultaneous Modelling-to-Generate-Alternatives Procedure Employing the Firefly Algorithm. In N. Dey (Ed.), *Technological Innovations in Knowledge Management and Decision Support* (pp. 19–33). Hershey, PA: IGI Global. doi:10.4018/978-1-5225-6164-4.ch002

Yeşil, S., & Hırlak, B. (2019). Exploring Knowledge-Sharing Barriers and Their Implications. In M. Jennex (Ed.), *Effective Knowledge Management Systems in Modern Society* (pp. 99–122). Hershey, PA: IGI Global. doi:10.4018/978-1-5225-5427-1.ch006

You, J. (2017). Institutionalization of Informal Learning Behaviors for Effective Tacit Knowledge Management. In D. Jaziri-Bouagina & G. Jamil (Eds.), *Handbook of Research on Tacit Knowledge Management for Organizational Success* (pp. 157–175). Hershey, PA: IGI Global. doi:10.4018/978-1-5225-2394-9.ch006

Young, D., & Choi, J. (2018). Information and Computer Technologies for Improving International Assessment. In S. Swayze & V. Ford (Eds.), *Innovative Applications of Knowledge Discovery and Information Resources Management* (pp. 173–194). Hershey, PA: IGI Global. doi:10.4018/978-1-5225-5829-3.ch008

Younsi, F., Hamdadou, D., & Chakhar, S. (2019). A Multicriteria Spatiotemporal System for Influenza Epidemic Surveillance. In N. Dey (Ed.), *Technological Innovations in Knowledge Management and Decision Support* (pp. 176–202). Hershey, PA: IGI Global. doi:10.4018/978-1-5225-6164-4.ch008

Zacarias, M., & Martins, P. V. (2018). Agile Business Process and Practice Alignment Methodology: A Case-Study-Based Analysis. In S. Swayze & V. Ford (Eds.), *Innovative Applications of Knowledge Discovery and Information Resources Management* (pp. 118–142). Hershey, PA: IGI Global. doi:10.4018/978-1-5225-5829-3.ch005

Zaharia, M. H. (2019). Using Intelligent Agents Paradigm in Big Data Security Risks Mitigation. In Z. Sun (Ed.), *Managerial Perspectives on Intelligent Big Data Analytics* (pp. 76–97). Hershey, PA: IGI Global. doi:10.4018/978-1-5225-7277-0.ch005

About the Contributors

Susan Swayze holds a Ph.D. in Education from the University of California Los Angeles and an M.B.A. from the Duke University Fuqua School of Business. She is an accomplished scholar who leverages her qualitative and quantitative research expertise to develop courses, teach adult students, and advise dissertation research. Dr. Swayze's research interests include psychological capital, diversity and inclusion, adult learning in online environments, and data-driven decision-making. She also provides interview and survey-based consulting services in the areas of program evaluation and organizational development. During the past 10 years, Dr. Swayze has produced over 100 scholarly works—including edited books, journal articles, book chapters, conference presentations, and workshops.

* * *

James R. Calvin, PhD (With Distinction), New York University joined the Johns Hopkins Carey Business School in April 1996. He is Professor of Management and Organization with expertise in the areas of leadership development, organizational life, community economic development and nonprofit organizations. James is currently Interim Director of the Center for Africana Studies at Johns Hopkins. James is member of the International Board of PYXERA Global an organization that works globally with business, governments and communities in 90 countries. Dr. Calvin has broad global experience in the areas of community development, organization development, leadership development, executive coaching, diversity and Inclusion, and negotiation. He is a keynoter to associations, business, government, education and NGO groups across the United States and internationally in Australia, Cameroon, Shanghai, China, Canada, Colombia, Ghana, Hong Kong, Kuwait, Mexico, New Zealand, Peru, Portugal, St. Lucia, Scotland, Thailand, and the United Kingdom.

Michael Dreyfuss is a tenured faculty member in the Department of Industrial Engineering and Management in the Jerusalem College of Technology. He holds a Ph.D. and an M.Sc. in Industrial Engineering from the Ben Gurion University of the

Negev, as well as a B.Sc. in Computer Sciences and B.Sc. in Industrial Engineering and Management from the Jerusalem College of Technology.

Hemlata Gangwar is working as an Assistant Professor of Information System at Pune Institute of Business Management, India. She is a Fellow Programme in Management (FPM) on Technology Management from National Institute of Industrial Engineering (NITIE), Mumbai, India. She has done Masters in Computer Applications. Her current research interests are in the areas of technology adoption, cloud computing, big data analytics. Her work has been published in Information Resources Management Journal, Journal of Enterprise Information Management, Human System Management, and Global Business Review.

Yahel Giat is a tenured faculty member in the Department of Industrial Engineering and Management in the Jerusalem College of Technology. He holds a Ph.D. and an M.Sc. in Industrial Engineering from the Georgia Institute of Technology, as well as an M.Sc. in Economics, a B.Sc. in Electrical Engineering, and B.A. in Computer Sciences from the Israel Institute of Technology.

Letitia Larry is an executive-level Information Technology consultant with 20 plus years of experience, specializing in epic solutions, systems and human capital transformations across federal agencies and commercial enterprises. Dr. Larry earned an Ed.D. in Human and Organizational Learning from the George Washington University and also possesses an M.S. in Computer Information Systems and a B.S. in Applied Mathematics. Dr. Larry continues to expand her experience and expertise as a scholar and practitioner.

Donna Weaver McCloskey is an Associate Professor in Management/Information Systems at Widener University in Chester, Pennsylvania. She holds a Ph.D. in Decision Sciences from Drexel University, an M.B.A. from Widener University, and a B.S. in Finance and Management Information Systems from the University of Delaware. Her research interests are the adoption of new technologies and the changing work-life boundary. Dr. McCloskey's work has been published in over 14 academic journal articles, 9 book chapters, and presented at numerous regional, national and international conferences.

Adesola Ogundimu is an Instructional Designer at the Johns Hopkins Carey Business School. She holds a PhD in Instructional Technology from Ohio University, a Master's degree in Information and Telecommunication Systems also from Ohio University, and a Bachelor's degree in Library and Information Studies from the University of Ibadan. Her research and design work focuses on information literacy and digital literacy for meaningful digital age learning, digital accessibility in online learning environments and learner engagement in synchronous online learning. As technology and digital media continue to change knowledge structures and the nature of learning, Adesola believes that it is important for educators to be mindful of the impact of learning technologies on the learning environment, learning outcomes, learner identities and the overall quality of the educational experience they are trying to create.

Jing Quan is a Professor in the Department of Information and Decision Sciences in Perdue School of Business at Salisbury University. He holds a Ph.D. from the University of Florida. His research interests include the organizational impact of information technology (IT), IS security, and IT professional and personnel issues. His work has appeared in such journals as Journal of Management Information Systems, Communications of the ACM, Communications of the AIS, Information Resources Management Journal, International Journal of Information Management, Journal of Global Information Management, Journal of Computer Information Systems, and Journal of Organization and End User Computing. He serves on the editorial review boards of Information Resources Management Journal and Journal of Global Information Management.

Index

Ensure Quality Research is Introduced to the Academic Community

Become an IGI Global Reviewer for Authored Book Projects

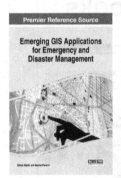
Premier Reference Source

Emerging GIS Applications for Emergency and Disaster Management

Premier Reference Source

Managerial Strategies and Green Solutions for Project Sustainability

Premier Reference Source

Comparative Approaches to Using R and Python for Statistical Data Analysis

Premier Reference Source

Solutions for High-Touch Communications in a High-Tech World

The overall success of an authored book project is dependent on quality and timely reviews.

In this competitive age of scholarly publishing, constructive and timely feedback significantly expedites the turnaround time of manuscripts from submission to acceptance, allowing the publication and discovery of forward-thinking research at a much more expeditious rate. Several IGI Global authored book projects are currently seeking highly-qualified experts in the field to fill vacancies on their respective editorial review boards:

Applications and Inquiries may be sent to:
development@igi-global.com

Applicants must have a doctorate (or an equivalent degree) as well as publishing and reviewing experience. Reviewers are asked to complete the open-ended evaluation questions with as much detail as possible in a timely, collegial, and constructive manner. All reviewers' tenures run for one-year terms on the editorial review boards and are expected to complete at least three reviews per term. Upon successful completion of this term, reviewers can be considered for an additional term.

If you have a colleague that may be interested in this opportunity, we encourage you to share this information with them.

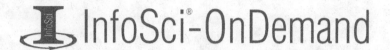
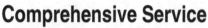

Printed in the United States
By Bookmasters